C. A. ARTHUR
1881-1885

G. CLEVELAND
1885-89-93-97

BENJ. HARRISON
1889-1893

T. ROOSEVELT
1901

WM. McKINLEY
1898-1901

PRESIDENTS OF THE UNITED STATES.

FAMOUS AMERICAN STATESMEN & ORATORS

PAST AND PRESENT

WITH

BIOGRAPHICAL SKETCHES

— AND —

THEIR FAMOUS ORATIONS

IN SIX VOLUMES

VOLUME VI

ALEXANDER K. McCLURE, LL.D.

EDITOR

Author of "Lincoln and Men of War Times," "Our Presidents and How We Make Them," etc.

BYRON ANDREWS

of the "National Tribune," Washington, D. C.

ASSOCIATE EDITOR

Author of "The Eastern Question," "The Life of Logan," "One of the People" (McKinley), "Monroe and His Doctrine," etc.

NEW YORK

F. F. LOVELL PUBLISHING COMPANY

8 25.

McClure

v. 6

COPYRIGHT, 1902,
F. F. LOVELL PUBLISHING CO.

—BECKTOLD—
PRINTING AND BOOK MFG. CO.
ST. LOUIS, MO.

Beveridge, Albert J., an American politician and orator, born in Highland Co., Ohio, October 6, 1862. His parents removed to Indiana soon after his birth, and his boyhood was one of hard work. Securing an education with difficulty he presently became a law clerk in Indianapolis, and subsequently established a practice of his own. He entered politics in 1884 by speaking in behalf of Blaine and was prominent in later campaigns, particularly in that of 1896, when his speeches attracted general attention. In 1899, he was chosen to the United States Senate as a Republican. He is intensely partisan in his sympathies, devoting more time to party, it has been said, than any other man in his State. He is an able debater and a fluent, ready, political speaker.

FOR THE GREATER REPUBLIC, NOT FOR IMPERIALISM

ADDRESS DELIVERED AT THE UNION LEAGUE OF PHILADELPHIA, FEBRUARY 15, 1899.

GENTLEMEN OF THE UNION LEAGUE,—The Republic never retreats. Why should it retreat? The Republic is the highest form of civilization, and civilization must advance. The Republic's young men are the most virile and unwasted of the world, and they pant for enterprise worthy of their power. The Republic's preparation has been the self-discipline of a century, and that preparedness has found its task. The Republic's opportunity is as noble as its strength, and that opportunity is here. The Republic's duty is as sacred as its opportunity is real, and Americans never desert their duty.

1—6

The Republic could not retreat if it would; whatever its destiny, it must proceed. For the American Republic is a part of the movement of a race,—the most masterful race of history,—and race movements are not to be stayed by the hand of man. They are mighty answers to Divine commands. Their leaders are not only statesmen of peoples—they are prophets of God. The inherent tendencies of a race are its highest law. They precede and survive all statutes, all constitutions. The first question real statesmanship asks is: What are the abiding characteristics of my people? From that basis all reasoning may be natural and true. From any other basis all reasoning must be artificial and false.

The sovereign tendencies of our race are organization and government. We govern so well that we govern ourselves. We organize by instinct. Under the flag of England our race builds an empire out of the ends of earth. In Australia it is to-day erecting a nation out of fragments. In America it wove out of segregated settlements that complex and wonderful organization called the American Republic. Everywhere it builds. Everywhere it governs. Everywhere it administers order and law. Everywhere it is the spirit of regulated liberty. Everywhere it obeys that Voice not to be denied which bids us strive and rest not, makes of us our brothers' keeper, and appoints us steward under God of the civilization of the world.

Organization means growth. Government means administration. When Washington pleaded with the States to organize into a consolidated people, he was the advocate of perpetual growth. When Abraham Lincoln argued for the indivisibility of the Republic, he became the prophet of the Greater Republic. And when they did both, they were but the interpreters of the tendencies of the race. That is what made them Washington and Lincoln. Had they been separatists and contractionists they would not have been Washington and Lincoln—they would have been Davis and Calhoun. They are the great Americans because they were the supreme constructors and conservers of organized government among the American people, and to-day William McKinley, as divinely guided as they, is carrying to its conclusion the tremendous syllogism of which the works of Washington and Lincoln are the premises.

God did not make the American people the mightiest human force of all time simply to feed and die. He did not give our race the brain of organization and heart of domination to no purpose and no end. No; he has given us a task equal to our talents. He has appointed for us a destiny equal to our endowments. He has made us the lords of civilization that we may administer civilization. Such administration is needed in Cuba. Such administration is needed in the Philippines. And Cuba and the Philippines are in our hands.

If it be said that, at home, tasks as large as our strength await us,—that politics are to be purified, want relieved, municipal government perfected, the relations of capital and labor better adjusted,—I answer: Has England's discharge of her duty to the world corrupted her politics? Are not her cities, like

Birmingham, the municipal models upon which we build our reforms? Is her labor problem more perplexed than ours? Considering the newness of our country, is it as bad as ours? And is not the like true of Holland—even of Germany.

And what of England? England's immortal glory is not Agincourt or Waterloo. It is not her merchandise or commerce. It is Australia, New Zealand, and Africa reclaimed. It is India redeemed. It is Egypt, mummy of the nations, touched into modern life. England's imperishable renown is in English science throttling the plague in Calcutta, English law administering order in Bombay, English energy planting an industrial civilization from Cairo to the Cape, and English discipline creating soldiers, men, and finally citizens, perhaps, even out of the fellaheen of the dead land of the Pharaohs. And yet the liberties of Englishmen were never so secure as now. And that which is England's undying fame has also been her infinite profit, so sure is duty golden in the end.

And what of America? With the twentieth century the real task and true life of the Republic begins. And we are prepared. We have learned restraint from a hundred years of self-control. We are instructed by the experience of others. We are advised and inspired by present example. And our work awaits us.

The dominant notes in American history have thus far been self-government and internal improvement. But these were not ends only; they were means also. They were modes of preparation. The dominant notes in American life heretofore have been self-government and internal development. The dominant notes in American life henceforth will be not only self-government and internal development, but also administration and world improvement. It is the arduous but splendid mission of our race. It is ours to govern in the name of civilized liberty. It is ours to administer order and law in the name of human progress. It is ours to chasten, that we may be kind. It is ours to cleanse, that we may save. It is ours to build, that free institutions may finally enter and abide. It is ours to bear the torch of Christianity where midnight has reigned a thousand years. It is ours to reinforce that thin red line which constitutes the outposts of civilization all around the world.

If it be said that this is vague talk of an indefinite future, we answer that it is the specific program of the present hour. Civil government is to be perfected in Porto Rico. The future of Cuba is to be worked out by the wisdom of events. Ultimately, annexation is as certain as the island's existence. Even if Cubans are capable of self-government, every interest points to union. We and they may blunder forward and timidly try the devices of doubt; but in the end Jefferson's desire will be fulfilled and Cuba will be a part of the great Republic. And, whatever befalls, definite and immediate work awaits us. Harbors are to be dredged, sanitation established, highways built, railroads constructed, postal service organized, common schools opened—all by or under the government of the American Republic.

The Philippines are ours forever. Let faint hearts anoint their fears with the thought that some day

American administration and American duty there
may end. But they never will end. England's occupation of Egypt was to be temporary; but events,
which are the commands of God, are making it permanent. And now God has given us this Pacific empire
for civilized administration. The first office of administration is order. Orders must be established
throughout the archipelago. The spoiled child, Aguinaldo, may not stay the march of civilization. Rebellion against the authority of the flag must be crushed
without delay, for hesitation encourages revolt; and
without anger, for the turbulent children know not
what they do. And then civilization must be organized, administered, and maintained. Law and justice
must rule where savagery, tyranny, and caprice have
rioted. The people must be taught the art of orderly
and continuous industry. A hundred wildernesses
are to be subdued. Unpenetrated regions must be ex-
plored. Unviolated valleys must be tilled. Unmas-
tered forests must be felled. Unriven mountains must
be torn asunder, and their riches of iron and gold and
ores of price must be delivered to the world. We are
to do in the Philippines what Holland does in Java, or
England in New Zealand or the Cape, or else work
out new methods and new results of our own nobler
than any the world has seen. All this is not indefinite;
it is the very specification of duty.

The frail of faith declare that these peoples are not
fitted for citizenship. It is not proposed to make them
citizens. Those who see disaster in every forward
step of the Republic prophesy that Philippine labor will
overrun our country and starve our workingmen.

But the Javanese have not so overrun Holland; New Zealand's Malays, Australia's bushmen, Africa's Kaffirs, Zulus, and Hottentots, and India's millions of surplus labor have not so overrun England. Whips of scorpions could not lash the Filipinos to this land of fervid enterprise, sleepless industry, and rigid order.

Those who measure duty by dollars cry out at the expense. When did America ever count the cost of righteousness? And, besides, this Republic must have a mighty navy in any event. And new markets secured, new enterprises opened, new resources in timber, mines, and products of the tropics acquired, and the vitalization of all our industries which will follow will pay back a thousandfold all the Government spends in discharging the highest duty to which the Republic can be called.

Those who mutter words and call it wisdom deny the constitutional power of the Republic to govern Porto Rico, Cuba, the Philippines; for if we have the power in Porto Rico, we have the power in the Philippines. The Constitution is not interpreted by degrees of latitude or longitude. It is a hoary objection. There have always been those who have proclaimed the unconstitutionality of progress. The first to deny the power of the Republic's government were those who opposed the adoption of the Constitution itself, and they and their successors have denied its vitality and intelligence to this day. They denied the Republic's government the power to create a national bank; to make internal improvements; to issue greenbacks; to make gold the standard of value; to preserve property and life in States where treasonable Governors refused to call for aid.

Let them read Hamilton, and understand the meaning of implied powers. Let them read Marshall, and learn that the Constitution is the people's ordinance of national life, capable of growth as great as the people's growth. Let them learn the golden rule of constitutional interpretation. The Constitution was made for the American people; not the American people for the Constitution. Let them study the history, purposes, and instincts of our race, and then read again the Constitution, which is but an expression of the development of that race. Power to govern territory acquired! What else does the Constitution mean when it says, "Congress shall have power to dispose of and make all needful rules and regulations respecting the territory or other property of the United States?"

But aside from these express words of the American Constitution, the Republic has power to govern in the Pacific, the Caribbean, or in any other portion of the globe where Providence commands. Aside from the example of Alaska, all our territories, and the experience of a century, the Republic has the power to administer civilization wherever interest and duty call. It is the power which inheres in and is a part of the Government itself. And the Constitution does not deny the Government this inherent power residing in the very nature of all government. Who, then, can deny it? Those who do, write a new Constitution of their own, and interpret that. Those who do, dispute history. Those who do, are alien to the instincts of our race.

All protests against the Greater Republic are tolerable except this constitutional objection. But they who resist the Republic's career in the name of the Constitution are not to be endured. They are jugglers of words. Their counsel is the wisdom of verbiage. They deal not with realities, neither give heed to vital things. The most magnificent fact in history is the mighty movement and mission of our race, and the most splendid phase of that world-redeeming movement is the entrance of the American people as the greatest force in all the earth to do their part in administering civilization among mankind, and they are not to be halted by a ruck of words called constitutional arguments. Pretenders to legal learning have always denounced all virile interpretations of the Constitution. The so-called constitutional lawyers in Marshall's day said that he did not understand the Constitution, because he looked, not at its syllables, but surveyed the whole instrument, and behold in its profound meaning and infinite scope the sublime human processes of which it is an expression. The Constitution is not a prohibition of our progress. It is not an interdict to our destiny. It is not a treatise on geography. Let the flag advance; the word " retreat " is not in the Constitution. Let the Republic govern as conditions demand; the Constitution does not benumb its brain nor palsy its hand.

The Declaration of Independence applies only to peoples capable of self-government. Otherwise, how dared we administer the affairs of the Indians? How dare we continue to govern them to-day? Precedent does not impair natural and inalienable rights. And how is the world to be prepared for self-government? Savagery can not prepare itself. Barbarism must be assisted toward the light. Assuming that these people can be made capable of self-government, shall we have no part in this sacred and glorious cause?

And if self-government is not possible for them, shall we leave them to themselves? Shall tribal wars scourge them, disease waste them, savagery brutalize then more and more? Shall their fields lie fallow, their forests rot, their mines remain sealed, and all the purposes and possibilities of nature be nullified? If not, who shall govern them rather than the kindest and most merciful of the world's great race of administrators, the people of the American Republic? Who lifted from us the judgment which makes men of our blood our brothers' keepers?

We do not deny them liberty. The administration of orderly government is not denial of liberty. The administration of equal justice is not denial of liberty. Teaching the habits of industry is not denial of liberty. Development of the wealth of the land is not denial of liberty. If they are, then civilization itself is denial of liberty. Denial of liberty to whom? There are 12,000,000 of people in the Philippines, divided into thirty tribes. Aguinaldo is of the Tagal tribe of 2,000,000 souls, and he has an intermittent authority over less than 50,000 of these.

To deliver these islands to him and his crew would be to establish an autocracy of barbarism. It would be to license spoliation. It would be to plant the republic of piracy, for such a government could not prevent that crime in piracy's natural home. It would be to make war certain among the powers of earth, who would dispute with arms each other's possession of a Pacific empire from which that ocean can be ruled. The blood already shed is but a drop to that which would flow if America should desert its post in the Pacific. And the blood already spilled was poured out upon the altar of the world's regeneration. Manila is as noble as Omdurman, and both are holier than Jericho.

Retreat from the Philippines on any pretext would be the master cowardice of history. It would be the betrayal of a trust as sacred as humanity. It would be a crime against Christian civilization, and would mark the beginning of the decadence of our race. And so, thank God, the Republic never retreats.

The fervent moral resolve throughout the Republic is not "a fever of expansion." It is a tremendous awakening of the people, like that of Elizabethan England. It is no fever, but the hot blood of the most magnificent young manhood of all time; a manhood begotten while yet the splendid moral passion of the war for national life filled the thought of all the land with ideals worth dying for, and charged its very atmosphere with noble purposes and a courage which dared put destiny to the touch—a manhood which contains a million Roosevelts, Woods, Hobsons, and Duboces, who grieve that they, too, may not so conspicuously serve their country, civilization, and mankind.

Indeed, these heroes are great because they are typical. American manhood to-day contains the master administrators of the world, and they go forth for the healing of the nations. They go forth in the cause of civilization. They go forth for the betterment of man; they go forth, and the word on their lips is Christ and his peace—not conquest and its pillage. They go forth to prepare the peoples, through decades, and may be centuries, of patient effort, for the great gift of American institutions. They go forth, not for imperialism, but for the Greater Republic.

Imperialism is not the word for our vast work. Imperialism, as used by the opposers of national greatness, means oppression, and we oppress not. Imperialism, as used by the opposers of national destiny, means monarchy, and the days of monarchy are spent. Imperialism, as used by the opposers of national progress, is a word to frighten the faint of heart, and so is powerless with the fearless American people.

Who honestly believes that the liberties of 80,000,-000 Americans will be destroyed because the Republic administers civilization in the Philippines? Who honestly believes that free institutions are stricken unto death because the Republic, under God, takes its place as the first power of the world? Who honestly believes that we plunge to our doom when we march forward in a path of duty prepared by a higher wisdom than our own? Those who so believe have lost their faith in the immortality of liberty. Those who so believe deny the vitality of the American people. Those who so believe are infidels to the providence of God. Those who so believe have lost the reckoning of events, and think it sunset when it is, in truth, only the breaking of another day—the day of the Greater Republic, dawning as dawns the twentieth century.

The Republic never retreats. Its flag is the only

flag that has never known defeat. Where the flag leads we follow, for we know that the hand that bears it onward is the unseen hand of God. We follow the flag and independence is ours. We follow the flag and nationality is ours. We follow the flag and oceans are ruled. We follow the flag and, in Occident and Orient, tyranny falls and barbarism is subdued. We follow the flag at Trenton and Valley Forge; at Saratoga and upon the crimson seas; at Buena Vista and Chapultepec; at Gettysburg and Missionary Ridge; at Santiago and Manila; and everywhere and always it means larger liberty, nobler opportunity, and greater human happiness, for everywhere and always it means the blessings of the Greater Republic. And so God leads, we follow the flag, and the Republic never retreats.

Porter, Horace, an American soldier and diplomat, born at Huntingdon, Pa., April 15, 1837. He was educated at the United States Military Academy, and during the Civil War was an officer on the staffs of McClellan, Rosecrans and Grant. He has since filled important posts and from 1897 has been ambassador to France. He is an able speaker, and has published, "Campaigning with Grant." Among notable addresses by him are the speech, "Our Guests," "The Triumph of American Invention," and a speech commemorating General Sherman.

THE TRIUMPH OF AMERICAN INVENTION.

ADDRESS BEFORE THE NEW ENGLAND SOCIETY,
DECEMBER 22, 1877.

MR. PRESIDENT,—I suppose it was a matter of necessity, calling on some of us from other States to speak for you to-night, for we have learned from the history of Priscilla and John Alden that a New-Englander may be too modest to speak for himself. But this modesty, like some of the greater blessings of the war, has been more or less disguised to-night.

We have heard from the eloquent gentleman on my left all about the good-fellowship and the still better fellowships in the rival universities of Harvard and Yale. We have heard from my sculptor friend upon the extreme right all about Hawthorne's tales, and all the great *Storys* that have emanated from Salem; but I am not a little surprised that in this age, when speeches are made principally by those running for office, you should call upon one engaged only in running cars, and more particularly upon one brought up in the military service, where the practice of running is not regarded as strictly professional. It occurred to me some years ago that the occupation of moving cars would be fully as congenial as that of stopping bullets—as a steady business, so when I left Washington I changed my profession.

I know how hard it is to believe that persons from Washington ever change their professions. In this regal age, when every man is his own sovereign, somebody had to provide palaces, and, as royalty is not supposed to have any permanent abiding-place in a country like this, it was thought best to put these palaces on wheels; and, since we have been told by reliable authority that "uneasy lies the head that wears a crown," we thought it necessary to introduce every device to enable those crowned heads to rest as easily as possible.

Of course we cannot be expected to do as much for the travelling public as the railway companies. They at times put their passengers to death. We only put them to sleep. We don't pretend that all the devices, patents, and inventions upon these cars are due to the genius of the management. Many of the best suggestions have come from the travellers themselves, especially New-England travellers.

Some years ago, when the bedding was not supposed to be as fat as it ought to be, and the pillows were accused of being constructed upon the homœopathic principle, a New-Englander got on a car one night. Now, it is a remarkable fact that a New-Englander never goes to sleep in one of these cars. He lies awake all night, thinking how he can improve upon every device and patent in sight. He poked his head out of the upper berth at midnight, hailed the porter and said, " Say, have you got such a thing as a corkscrew about you?"

" We don't 'low no drinkin' sperits aboa'd these yer cars, sah," was the reply.

"Tain't that," said the Yankee, " but I want to get hold onto one of your pillows that kind of worked its way into my ear."

The pillows have since been enlarged.

I notice that in the general comprehensiveness of the sentiment which follows this toast you allude to that large and liberal class of patrons, active though defunct, known as " deadheads." It is said to be a quotation from Shakespeare. That is a revelation. It proves conclusively that Shakespeare must at one time have resided in the State of Missouri. It is well known that the term was derived from a practice upon a Missouri railroad, where, by a decision of the courts, the railroad company had been held liable in heavy damages in case of accidents where a passenger lost an arm or a leg, but when he was killed outright his friends seldom sued, and he never did; and the company never lost any money in such cases.

In fact, a grateful mother-in-law would occasionally pay the company a bonus.

The conductors on that railroad were all armed with hatchets, and in case of an accident they were instructed to go around and knock every wounded passenger in the head, thus saving the company large amounts of money; and these were reported to the general office as " deadheads," and in railway circles the term has ever since been applied to passengers where no money consideration is involved.

One might suppose, from the manifestations around these tables for the first three hours to-night, that the toast " Internal Improvements " referred more especially to the benefiting of the true inwardness of the New-England men; but I see that the sentiment which follows contains much more than human stomachs, and covers much more ground than cars. It soars into the realms of invention.

Unfortunately the genius of invention is always accompanied by the demon of unrest. A New-England Yankee can never let well enough alone. I have always supposed him to be the person specially alluded to in Scripture as the man who has found out many inventions. If he were a Chinese pagan, he would invent a new kind of Joss to worship every week. You get married and settle down in your home. You are delighted with everything about you. You rest in blissful ignorance of the terrible discomforts that surround you, until a Yankee friend comes to visit you. He at once tells you you mustn't build a fire in that chimney-place; that he knows the chimney will smoke; that if he had been there when it was built he could have shown you how to give a different sort of flare to the flue.

You go to read a chapter in the family Bible. He tells you to drop that; that he has just written an enlarged and improved version, that can just put that old book to bed.

You think you are at least raising your children in

general uprightness; but he tells you if you don't go out at once and buy the latest patent article in the way of steel leg-braces and put on the baby, that the baby will grow up bow-legged.

He intimates, before he leaves, that if he had been around to advise you before you were married, he could have got you a much better wife.

These are some of the things that reconcile a man to sudden death.

Such occurrences as these, and the fact of so many New-Englanders being residents of this city and elsewhere, show that New-England must be a good place —to come from.

At the beginning of the war we thought we could shoot people rapidly enough to satisfy our consciences, with single-loading rifles; but along came the inventive Yankee and produced revolvers and repeaters, and Gatling guns, and magazine guns—guns that carried a dozen shots at a time.

I didn't wonder at the curiosity exhibited in this direction by a backwoods Virginian we captured one night. The first remark he made was, " I would like to see one of them thar new-fangled weepons of yourn. They tell me, sah, it's a most remarkable eenstrument. They say, sah, it's a kind o' repeatable, which you can load it up enough on Sunday to fiah it off all the rest of the week."

Then there was every sort of new invention in the way of bayonets. Our distinguished Secretary of State has expressed an opinion to-night that bayonets are bad things to sit down on. Well, they are equally bad things to be tossed up on. If he continues to hold up such terrors to the army, there will have to be important modifications in the uniform. A soldier won't know where to wear his breastplate.

But there have not only been inventions in the way of guns but important inventions in the way of firing them. In these days a man drops on his back, coils himself up, sticks up one foot, and fires off his gun over the top of his great toe.

It changes the whole stage business of battle. It used to be the man who was shot, but now it is the man who shoots that falls on his back and turns up his toes. The consequence is that the whole world wants American arms, and as soon as they get them they go to war to test them. Russia and Turkey had no sooner bought a supply than they went to fighting. Greece got a schooner-load, and although she has not yet taken a part in the struggle, yet ever since the digging up of the lost limbs of the Venus of Milo it has been feared that this may indicate a disposition on the part of Greece generally to take up arms.

But there was one inveterate old inventor that you had to get rid of, and you put him on to us Pennsylvanians—Benjamin Franklin.

Instead of stopping in New York, in Wall Street, as such men usually do, he continued on into Pennsylvania to pursue his *kiting* operations. He never could let well enough alone. Instead of allowing the lightning to occupy the heavens as the sole theater for its pyrotechnic displays, he showed it how to get down on to the earth, and then he invented the lightning-rod to catch it. Houses that had got along perfectly well for years without any lightning at all now thought they must have a rod to catch a portion of it every time it came around. Nearly every house in the country was equipped with a lightning-rod through Franklin's direct agency.

You, with your superior New-England intelligence, succeeded in ridding yourselves of him; but in Pennsylvania, though we have made a great many laudable efforts in a similar direction, somehow or other we have never once succeeded in getting rid of a lightning-rod agent.

Then the lightning was introduced on the telegraph wires, and now we have the duplex and quadruplex instruments, by which any number of messages can be sent from opposite ends of the same wire at the same time, and they all appear to arrive at the front in good order.

Electricians have not yet told us which message lies down and which one steps over it, but they all seem to bring up in the right camp without confusion. I shouldn't wonder if this principle were introduced before long in the operating of railroads. We may then see trains running in opposite directions pass each other on a single-track road.

There was a New-England quartermaster in charge of railroads in Tennessee, who tried to introduce this principle during the war. The result was discouraging. He succeeded in telescoping two or three trains every day. He seemed to think that the easiest way to shorten up a long train and get it on a short siding was to telescope it. I have always thought that if that man's attention had been turned in an astronomical direction he would have been the first man to telescope the satellites of Mars.

The latest invention in the application of electricity is the telephone. By means of it we may be able soon to sit in our houses and hear all the speeches without going to the New-England dinner. The telephone enables an orchestra to keep at a distance of miles away when it plays. If the instrument can be made to keep hand-organs at a distance, its popularity will be inde-scribable. The worst form I have ever known an in-vention to take was one that was introduced in a coun-try town, when I was a boy, by a Yankee of musical turn of mind, who came along and taught every branch of education by singing. He taught geography by singing, and to combine accuracy of memory with patriotism, he taught the multiplication-table to the tune of Yankee Doodle.

This worked very well as an aid to the memory in school, but when the boys went into business it often led to inconvenience. When a boy got a situation in a grocery store and customers were waiting for their change, he never could tell the product of two numbers without commencing at the beginning of the table and singing up till he had reached those numbers. In case the customer's ears had not received a proper musical training this practice often injured the busi-ness of the store.

It is said that the Yankee has always manifested a disposition for making money, but he never struck a proper field for the display of his genius until we got to making paper money. Then every man who owned a printing-press wanted to try his hand at it. I remember that in Washington ten cents' worth of rags picked up in the street would be converted the next day into thousands of dollars.

An old mule and cart used to haul up the currency from the Printing Bureau to the door of the Treasury Department. Every morning, as regularly as the morning came, that old mule would back up and dump a cart-load of the sinews of war at the Treasury.

A patriotic son of Columbia, who lived opposite, was sitting on the doorstep of his house one morning, looking mournfully in the direction of the mule. A friend came along, and seeing that the man did not look as pleasant as usual, said to him, " What is the matter? It seems to me you look kind of disconsolate this morning."

" I was just thinking," he replied, " what would become of this government if that old mule was to break down."

Now they propose to give us a currency which is brighter and heavier, but not worth quite as much as the rags. Our financial horizon has been dimmed by it for some time, but there is a lining of silver to every cloud. We are supposed to take it with 412½ grains of silver—a great many more grains of allowance. Congress seems disposed to pay us in the " dollar of our daddies "—in the currency which we were familiar with in our childhood. Congress seems determined to pay us off in something that is " childlike and Bland."

But I have detained you too long already; the excellent President of your Society has for the last five minutes been looking at me like a man who might be

expected, at any moment, to break out in the disconsolate language of Bildad the Shuhite to the patriarch
Job, "How long will it be ere ye make an end of
words?"

Let me say then, in conclusion, that, coming as I
do from the unassuming State of Pennsylvania, and
standing in the presence of the dazzling genius of
New-England, I wish to express the same degree of
humility that was expressed by a Dutch Pennsylvania
farmer in a railroad car at the breaking out of the
war. A New-Englander came in who had just heard
of the fall of Fort Sumter, and he was describing it to
the farmer and his fellow passengers. He said that
in the fort they had an engineer from New-England,
who had constructed the traverses, and the embrasures,
and the parapets in such a manner as to make everybody within the fort as safe as if he had been at home;
and on the other side the Southerners had an engineer
who had been educated in New-England, and he had
with his scientific attainments, succeeded in making
the batteries of the bombarders as safe as any harvest
field, and the bombardment had raged for two whole
days, and the fort had been captured, and the garrison
had surrendered, and not a man was hurt on either
side. A great triumph for science, and a proud day
for New-England education. Said the farmer, " I
suppose dat ish all right, but it vouldn't do to send
any of us Pennsylvany fellers down dare to fight mit
dose pattles. Like as not ve vould shoost pe fools
enough to kill somepody."

White, Andrew D., an eminent American scholar and diplomat, born at Homer, N. Y., November 7, 1832. He was professor of history in the University of Michigan, 1857–64, and sat in the New York Senate, 1863–67. In the last named year he was appointed the first president of Cornell University, holding office till 1885. He was minister to Germany, 1879–81, and in 1897 was appointed ambassador to Germany, which position he still (1902) holds. He is an able public speaker, and is held in high esteem as a writer, " The Warfare of Science " being his most important work.

" THE APOSTLE OF PEACE AMONG THE NATIONS."

SPEECH DELIVERED AT THE PEACE CONFERENCE AT THE HAGUE.

YOUR EXCELLENCIES, Mr. Burgomaster, Gentlemen of the University Faculties, My Honored Colleagues of the Peace Conference, Ladies and Gentlemen,—The Commission of the United States comes here this day to discharge a special duty. We are instructed to acknowledge, on behalf of our country, one of its many great debts to the Netherlands.

This debt is that which, in common with the whole world, we owe to one of whom all civilized lands are justly proud,—the poet, the scholar, the historian, the statesman, the diplomatist, the jurist, the author of the treatise " De Jure Belli ac Pacis."

Of all works not claiming divine inspiration, that book, written by a man proscribed and hated both for his politics and his religion, has proved the greatest blessing to humanity. More than any other it has prevented unmerited suffering, misery, and sorrow; more than any other it has ennobled the military profession; more than any other it has promoted the blessings of peace and diminished the horrors of war.

On this tomb, then, before which we now stand, the delegates of the United States are instructed to lay a simple tribute to him whose mortal remains rest beneath it—Hugo de Groot, revered and regarded with gratitude by thinking men throughout the world as "Grotius."

Naturally we have asked you to join us in this simple ceremony. For his name has become too great to be celebrated by his native country alone; too great to be celebrated by Europe alone; it can be fitly celebrated only in the presence of representatives from the whole world.

For the first time in human history there are now assembled delegates with a common purpose from all the nations, and they are fully represented here. I feel empowered to speak words of gratitude, not only from my own country, but from each of these. I feel that my own country, though one of the youngest in the great sisterhood of nations, utters at this shrine to-day, not only her own gratitude, but that of every part of Europe, of all the great Powers of Asia, and of the sister republics of North and South America.

From nations now civilized, but which Grotius knew only as barbarous; from nations which in his time were yet unborn; from every land where there are men who admire genius, who reverence virtue, who respect patriotism, who are grateful to those who have given their lives to toil, hardship, disappointment, and sacrifice, for humanity,—from all these come thanks and greetings heartily mingled with our own.

The time and place are well suited to the acknowledgment of such a debt. As to time, as far as the world at large is concerned, I remind you, not only that this is the first conference of the entire world, but that it has, as its sole purpose, a further evolution of the principles which Grotius first, of all men, developed thoroughly and stated effectively. So far as the United States is concerned, it is the time of our most sacred national festival—the anniversary of our national independence. What more fitting period, then, in the history of the world and of our own country, for a tribute to one who has done so much, not only for our sister nations, but for ourselves.

And as to the place. This is the ancient and honored city of Delft. From its Haven, not distant, sailed the "Mayflower"—bearing the Pilgrim Fathers, who, in a time of obstinate and bitter persecution, brought to the American continent the germs of that toleration which had been especially developed among them during their stay in the Netherlands, and of which Grotius was an apostle. In this town Grotius was born; in this temple he worshipped; this pavement he trod when a child; often were these scenes revisited by him in his boyhood; at his death his mortal body was placed in this hallowed ground. Time and place, then, would both seem to make this tribute fitting.

In the vast debt which all nations owe to Grotius, the United States acknowledges its part gladly. Perhaps in no other country has his thought penetrated more deeply and influenced more strongly the great mass of the people. It was the remark of Alexis de Tocqueville, the most philosophic among all students of American institutions, that one of the most striking and salutary things in American life is the widespread study of law. De Tocqueville was undoubtedly right. In all parts of our country the law of nations is especially studied by large bodies of young men in colleges and universities; studied, not professionally merely, but from the point of view of men eager to understand the fundamental principles of international rights and duties.

The works of our compatriots, Wheaton, Kent, Field, Woolsey, Dana, Lawrence, and others, in developing more and more the ideas to which Grotius first gave life and strength, show that our country has not cultivated in vain this great field which Grotius opened.

As to the bloom and fruitage evolved by these writers out of the germ ideas of Grotius I might give many examples, but I will mention merely three:

The first example shall be the act of Abraham Lincoln. Amid all the fury of civil war he recognized the necessity of a more humane code for the conduct of our armies in the field; and he entrusted its preparation to Francis Lieber, honorably known to jurists throughout the world, and at that time Grotius's leading American disciple.

My second example shall be the act of General Ulysses Grant. When called to receive the surrender of his great opponent, General Lee, after a long and bitter contest, he declined to take from the vanquished general the sword which he had so long and so bravely worn; imposed no terms upon the conquered armies save that they should return to their homes; allowed no reprisals; but simply said, " Let us have peace."

My third example shall be the act of the whole people of the United States. At the close of that most bitter contest, which desolated thousands of homes, and which cost nearly a million of lives, no revenge was taken by the triumphant Union on any of the separatist statesmen who had brought on the great struggle, or on any of the soldiers who had conducted it; and, from that day to this, north and south, once every year, on Decoration Day, the graves of those who fell wearing the blue of the North and the gray of the South are alike strewn with flowers. Surely I may claim for my countrymen that, whatever other shortcomings and faults may be imputed to them, they have shown themselves influenced by those feelings of mercy and humanity which Grotius, more than any other, brought into the modern world.

In the presence of this great body of eminent jurists from the courts, the cabinets, and the universities of all nations, I will not presume to attempt any full development of the principles of Grotius or to estimate his work; but I will briefly present a few considerations regarding his life and work which occur to one who has contemplated them from another and distant country.

There are, of course, vast advantages in the study of so great a man from the nearest point of view; from his own land, and by those who from their actual experience must best know his environment. But a more distant point of view is not without its uses. Those who cultivate the slopes of some vast mountain know it best; yet those who view it from a distance may sometimes see it brought into new relations and invested with new glories.

Separated thus from the native land of Grotius by the Atlantic, and perhaps by a yet broader ocean of customary thinking; unbiassed by any of that patriotism so excusable and indeed so laudable in the land where he was born; an American jurist naturally sees, first, the relations of Grotius to the writers who preceded him. He sees other and lesser mountain peaks of thought emerging from the clouds of earlier history, and he acknowledges a debt to such men as Isidore of Seville, Suarez, Ayala, and Gentilis. But when all this is acknowledged he clearly sees Grotius, while standing among these men, grandly towering above them. He sees in Grotius the first man who brought the main principles of those earlier thinkers to bear upon modern times,—increasing them from his own creative mind, strengthening them from the vast stores of his knowledge, enriching them from his imagination, glorifying them with his genius.

His great mind brooded over that earlier chaos of opinion, and from his heart and brain, more than from those of any other, came a revelation to the modern world of new and better paths toward mercy and peace. But his agency was more than that. His coming was like the rising of the sun out of the primeval abyss; his work was both creative and illuminative. We may reverently insist that in the domain of in-

ternational law, Grotius said " Let there be light," and
there was light.

The light he thus gave has blessed the earth for
these three centuries past, and it will go on through
many centuries to come, illuminating them ever more
and more.

I need hardly remind you that it was mainly un-
heeded at first. Catholics and Protestants alike failed
to recognize it. " The light shone in the darkness, and
the darkness comprehended it not."

By Calvinists in Holland and France, and by Luth-
erans in Germany, his great work was disregarded if
not opposed; and at Rome it was placed on the Index
of books forbidden to be read by Christians.

The book, as you know, was published amid the
horrors of the Thirty Years' War; the great Gustavus
is said to have carried it with him always, and he evi-
dently at all times bore its principles in his heart. But
he alone, among all the great commanders of his time,
stood for mercy. All the cogent arguments of Grotius could not prevent the fearful destruction of Magde-
burg, or diminish, so far as we can now see, any of
the atrocities of that fearful period.

Grotius himself may well have been discouraged; he
may well have repeated the words attributed to the
great Swedish chancellor whose ambassador he afterward became, " Go forth, my son, and see with how
little wisdom the world is governed." He may well
have despaired as he reflected that throughout his
whole life he had never known his native land save in
perpetual, heartrending war; nay, he may well have
been excused for thinking that all his work for hu-

manity had been in vain when there came to his death-bed no sign of any ending of the terrible war of thirty years.

For not until three years after he was laid in this tomb did the plenipotentiaries sign the Treaty of Münster All this disappointment and sorrow and life-long martyrdom invests him, in the minds of Americans, as doubtless in your minds, with an atmosphere of sympathy, veneration, and love.

Yet we see that the great light streaming from his heart and mind continued to shine; that it developed and fructified human thought; that it warmed into life new and glorious growths of right reason as to international relations; and we recognize the fact that, from his day to ours, the progress of reason in theory and of mercy in practice has been constant on both sides of the Atlantic.

It may be objected that this good growth, so far as theory was concerned, was sometimes anarchic, and that many of its developments were very different from any that Grotius intended or would have welcomed. For if Puffendorff swerved much from the teachings of his great master in one direction, others swerved even more in other directions, and all created systems more or less antagonistic. Yet we can now see that all these contributed to a most beneficent result,—to the growth of a practice ever improving, ever deepening, ever widening, ever diminishing bad faith in time of peace and cruelty in time of war.

It has also been urged that the system which Grotius gave to the world has been utterly left behind as the world has gone on; that the great writers on international law in the present day do not accept it; that Grotius developed everything out of an idea of natural law which was merely the creation of his own mind, and based everything on an origin of jural rights and duties which never had any real being; that he deduced his principles from a divinely planted instinct which many thinkers are now persuaded never existed, acting in a way contrary to everything revealed by modern discoveries in the realm of history.

It is at the same time insisted against Grotius that he did not give sufficient recognition to the main basis of the work of modern international jurists; to positive law, slowly built on the principles and practice of various nations in accordance with their definite agreements and adjustments.

In these charges there is certainly truth; but I trust that you will allow one from a distant country to venture an opinion that, so far from being to the discredit of Grotius, this fact is to his eternal honor.

For there was not, and there could not be at that period, anything like a body of positive international law adequate to the new time. The spirit which most thoroughly permeated the whole world, whether in war or peace, when Grotius wrote was the spirit of Machiavelli,—unmoral, immoral. It has been dominant for more than a hundred years. To measure the service rendered by the theory of Grotius, we have only to compare Machiavelli's " Prince " with Grotius's " De Jure Belli ac Pacis." Grant that Grotius's basis of international law was, in the main, a theory of natural law which is no longer held: grant that he made no sufficient recognition of positive law; we must nevertheless acknowledge that his system, at the time he presented it, was the only one which could ennoble men's theories or reform their practice.

From his own conception of the attitude of the Divine Mind toward all the falsities of his time grew a theory of international morals which supplanted the principles of Machiavelli: from his conception of the attitude of the Divine Mind toward all the cruelties which he had himself known in the Seventy Years' War of the Netherlands, and toward all those of which tidings were constantly coming from the German Thirty Years' War, came inspiration to promote a better practice in war.

To one, then, looking at Grotius from afar, as doubtless to many among yourselves, the theory which Grotius adopted seems the only one which, in his time, could bring any results for good to mankind.

I am also aware that one of the most deservedly eminent historians and publicists of the Netherlands during our own time has censured Grotius as the main source of the doctrine which founds human rights upon an early social compact, and, therefore, as one who proposed the doctrines which have borne fruit in the writings of Rousseau and in various modern revolutions.

I might take issue with this statement; or I might fall back upon the claim that Grotius's theory has proved, at least, a serviceable provisional hypothesis; but this is neither the time nor the place to go fully into so great a question. Yet I may at least say that it would ill become me, as a representative of the United States, to impute to Grotius, as a fault, a theory out of which sprang the nationality of my country: a doctrine embodied in that Declaration of Independence which is this day read to thousands on thousands of assemblies in all parts of the United States, from the Atlantic to the Pacific, and from the Great Lakes to the Gulf of Mexico.

But, however the Old World may differ from the New on this subject, may we not all agree that, whatever Grotius's responsibility for this doctrine may be, its evils would have been infinitely reduced could the men who developed it have caught his spirit,—his spirit of broad toleration, of wide sympathy, of wise moderation, of contempt for " the folly of extremes," of search for the great principles which unite men rather than for the petty differences which separate them?

It has also been urged against Grotius that his interpretation of the words *jus gentium** was a mistake, and that other mistakes have flowed from this. Grant it; yet we, at a distance, believe that we see in it one of the happiest mistakes ever made; a mistake comparable in its fortunate results to that made by Columbus when he interpreted a statement in our sacred books, regarding the extent of the sea as compared with the land, to indicate that the western continent could not be far from Spain,—a mistake which probably more than anything else encouraged him to sail for the New World.

It is also not infrequently urged by eminent European writers that Grotius dwelt too little on what international law really was, and too much on what, in his opinion, it ought to be. This is but another form

* The right of nations, in other words, international law.

oi an argument against him already stated. But is it certain, after all, that Grotius was so far wrong in this as some excellent jurists have thought him? May it not be that, in the not distant future, international law, while mainly basing its doctrines upon what nations have slowly developed in practice may also draw inspiration more and more from " that Power in the Universe, not ourselves, which makes for righteousness."

An American, recalling that greatest of all arbitrations yet known, the German Arbitration of 1872, naturally attributes force to the reasoning of Grotius. The heavy damages which the United States asked at that time, and which Great Britain honorably paid, were justified mainly, if not wholly, not on the practice of nations then existing, but upon what it was claimed ought to be the practice; not upon positive law, but upon natural justice: and that decision forms one of the happiest landmarks in modern times; it ended all quarrel between the two nations concerned, and bound them together more firmly than ever.

But while there may be things in the life and work of Grotius which reveal themselves differently to those who study him from a near point of view and to those who behold him from afar, there are thoughts on which we may all unite, lessons which we may learn alike, and encouragements which may strengthen us all for the duties of this present hour.

For, as we now stand before these monuments, there come to us, not only glimpses of the irony of history, but a full view of the rewards of history. Resounding under these arches and echoing among these col-

umns, prayer and praise have been heard for five hundred years. Hither came, in hours of defeat and hours
of victory, that mighty hero whose remains rest in
yonder shrine and whose fame is part of the world's
fairest heritage. But when, just after William the
Silent had been laid in the vaults beneath our feet,
Hugo de Groot, as a child, gazed with wonder on this
grave of the father of his country, and when, in his
boyhood, he here joined in prayer and praise and caught
inspiration from the mighty dead, no man knew that
in this beautiful boy, opening his eyes upon these
scenes which we now behold, not only the Netherlands,
but the whole human race, had cause for the greatest
of thanksgivings.

And when, in perhaps the darkest hour of modern
Europe, in 1625, his great book was born, yonder organ might well have pealed forth a most triumphant
Te Deum; but no man recognized the blessing which
in that hour had been vouchsafed to mankind; no voice
of thanksgiving was heard.

But if the dead, as we fondly hope, live beyond the
grave; if, undisturbed by earthly distractions, they
are all the more observant of human affairs; if, freed
from earthly trammels, their view of life in our lower
world is illumined by that infinite light which streams
from the source of all that is true and beautiful and
good,—may we not piously believe that the mighty
and beneficent shade of William of Orange recognized
with joy the birth-hour of Grotius as that of a compa-
triot who was to give the Netherlands a lasting glory?
May not that great and glorious spirit have also looked
lovingly upon Grotius as a boy lingering on this spot

where we now stand, and recognized him as one whose work was to go on adding in every age new glory to the nation which the mighty Prince of the House of Orange had, by the blessing of God, founded and saved; may not, indeed, that great mind have foreseen in that divine light, another glory not then known to mortal ken? Who shall say that in the effluence of divine knowledge he may not have beheld Grotius, in his full manhood, penning the pregnant words of the "De Jure Belli ac Pacis," and that he may not have foreseen—as largely resulting from it—what we behold to-day, as an honor of the august Monarch who convoked it, to the Netherlands who have given it splendid hospitality, and to all modern states here represented,—the first conference of the entire world ever held, and that conference assembled to increase the securities for peace and to diminish the horrors of war.

For, my honored colleagues of the Peace Conference, the germ of this work in which we are all so earnestly engaged lies in a single sentence of Grotius's great book. Others, indeed, had proposed plans for the peaceful settlement of differences between nations, and the world remembers them with honor: to all of them, from Henry IV, and Kant, and St. Pierre, and Penn, and Bentham, down to the humblest writer in favor of peace, we may well feel grateful; but the germ of arbitration was planted in modern thought when Grotius, urging arbitration and mediation as preventing war, wrote these solemn words in the "De Jure Belli ac Pacis"; "Maxime autem christiani reges et civitates tenentur hanc inire viam ad arma vitanda." *

* "But above all, Christian kings and states are bound to take his way of avoiding recourse to arms."

My honored colleagues and friends, more than once
I have come as a pilgrim to this sacred shrine. In my
young manhood, more than thirty years ago, and at
various times since, I have sat here and reflected upon
what these mighty men here entombed have done for
the world, and what, though dead, they yet speak to
mankind. I seem to hear them still.

From this tomb of William the Silent comes, in this
hour, a voice bidding the Peace Conference be brave,
and true, and trustful in that Power in the Universe
which works for righteousness.

From this tomb of Grotius I seem to hear a voice
which says to us, as the delegates of the nations: " Go
on with your mighty work: avoid, as you would avoid
the germs of pestilence, those exhalations of international hatred which take shape in monstrous falla-
cies and morbid fictions regarding alleged antagonistic
interests. Guard well the treasures of civilization with
which each of you is entrusted; but bear in mind that
you hold a mandate from humanity. Go on with your
work. Pseudo-philosophers will prophesy malignantly
against you; pessimists will laugh you to scorn; cynics
will sneer at you; zealots will abuse you for what you
have not done; sublimely unpractical thinkers will re-
vile you for what you have done; ephemeral critics
will ridicule you as dupes; enthusiasts, blind to the
difficulties in your path and to everything outside their
little circumscribed fields, will denounce you as traitors
to humanity. Heed them not,—go on with your work.
Heed not the clamor of zealots, or cynics, or pessimists, or pseudo-philosophers, or enthusiasts or fault-
finders. Go on with the work of strengthening peace

and humanizing war; give greater scope and strength to provisions which will make war less cruel; perfect those laws of war which diminish the unmerited sufferings of populations; and, above all, give to the world at least a beginning of an effective, practicable scheme of arbitration."

These are the words which an American seems to hear issuing from this shrine to-day; and I seem also to hear from it a prophecy. I seem to hear Grotius saying to us: "Fear neither opposition nor detraction. As my own book, which grew out of the horrors of the Wars of Seventy and the Thirty Years' War, contained the germ from which your great Conference has grown, so your work, which is demanded by a world bent almost to breaking under the weight of ever-increasing armaments, shall be a germ from which future Conferences shall evolve plans ever fuller, better, and nobler."

And I also seem to hear a message from him to the jurists of the great universities who honor us with their presence to-day, including especially that renowned University of Leyden which gave to Grotius his first knowledge of the law; and that eminent University of Konigsberg, which gave him his most philosophical disciple: to all of these I seem to hear him say: "Go on in your labor to search out the facts and to develop the principles which shall enable future Conferences to build more and more broadly, more and more loftily for peace."

And now, your excellencies, Mr. Burgomaster, and honored deans of the various universities of the Netherlands, a simple duty remains to me. In accordance

with instructions from the President and on behalf of
the people of the United States of America, the American Commission at the Peace Conference, by my hand,
lays on the tomb of Grotius this simple tribute. It
combines the oak, symbolical of civic virtue, with the
laurel, symbolical of victory. It bears the following
inscription :

"TO THE MEMORY OF HUGO GROTIUS
IN REVERENCE AND GRATITUDE
FROM THE UNITED STATES OF AMERICA
ON THE OCCASION OF THE INTERNATIONAL PEACE
CONFERENCE AT THE HAGUE
JULY 4, 1899."

—and it encloses two shields, one bearing the arms of
the House of Orange and of the Netherlands, the other
bearing the arms of the United States of America; and
both these shields are bound firmly together. They
represent the gratitude of our country, one of the
youngest among the nations of the earth, to this old
and honored Commonwealth,—gratitude for great services in days gone by, gratitude for recent courtesies and
kindnesses; and above all they represent to all time a
union of hearts and minds in both lands for peace between the nations.

Corwin, Thomas, an American orator and politician, born in Bourbon county, Ky., July 29, 1794; died in Washington, D. C., December 18, 1865. His early opportunities were limited, but after studying law he was admitted to the Ohio bar in 1818, and in 1822 he entered the Ohio Legislature, where he made a spirited speech against the introduction of the whipping post into Ohio. In 1829 he was sent to Congress as Representative, and was very prominent there as a Whig leader. In 1840 Corwin was the successful candidate for the governorship of Ohio, speaking several times a day during a three months' campaign, but was defeated in a similar campaign in 1842. He entered the National Senate in 1844, and there distinguished himself as a determined opponent of the war with Mexico. He was Secretary of the Treasury under Fillmore, member of Congress, 1861–64, and subsequently minister to Mexico. He was a brilliant orator, both in the court-room and in Congress. His speech in the Senate on the Mexican War in 1847, is one of his most important addresses.

FROM SPEECH ON THE MEXICAN WAR.

DELIVERED IN THE UNITED STATES SENATE, FEBRUARY 11, 1847.

THE President has said he does not expect to hold Mexican territory by conquest. Why then conquer it? Why waste thousands of lives and millions of money fortifying towns and creating governments, if, at the end of the war, you retire from the graves of your soldiers and the desolated country of your foes, only to get money from Mexico for the expense of all your toil and sacrifice? Who ever heard, since Christianity was propagated among men, of a nation taxing its people, enlisting its young men, and marching off two thousand miles to fight a people merely to be paid for it in money? What is this but hunting a market for blood, selling the lives of your young men, marching them in regiments to be slaughtered and paid for like oxen and brute beasts?

Sir, this is, when stripped naked, that atrocious idea first promulgated in the President's message, and now advocated here, of fighting on till we can get our indemnity for the past as well as the present slaughter. We have chastised Mexico, and if it were worth while to do so, we have, I dare say, satisfied the world that we can fight. What now? Why the mothers of America are asked to send another of their sons to blow out the brains of Mexicans because they refuse to pay the price of the first who fell there fighting for glory! And what if the second fall, too? The Executive, the parental reply is, " We shall have him paid for; we shall get full indemnity!"

Sir, I have no patience with this flagitious notion of fighting for indemnity, and this under the equally absurd and hypocritical pretence of securing an honorable peace. An honorable peace! If you have accomplished the objects of the war—if indeed you had an object which you dare to avow—cease to fight and you will have peace. Conquer your insane love of false glory, and you will " conquer a peace."

Sir, if your commander-in-chief will not do this, I will endeavor to compel him, and as I find no other means I shall refuse supplies—without money of the people he cannot go further. He asks me for that money; I wish him to bring your armies home, to cease shedding blood for money; if he refuses, I will refuse supplies, and then I know he must, he will cease his further sale of the lives of my countrymen.

May we not, ought we not now to do this? I can hear no reason why we should not, except this: It is said that we are in war, wrongfully it may be, but, being in, the President is responsible, and we must give him the means he requires! He responsible! Sir, we, we are responsible, if, having the power to stay this plague, we refuse to do so. When it shall be so —when the American Senate and the American House of Representatives can stoop from their high position and yield a dumb compliance with the behests of a President who is, for the time being, commander of your army; when they will open the treasury with one hand, and the veins of all the soldiers in the land with the other, merely because the President commands, then, sir, it matters little how soon some Cromwell shall come into this hall and say, " The Lord hath no further need of you here."

When we fail to do the work " whereunto we were sent," we shall be, we ought to be, removed, and give place to others who will. The fate of the barren fig-tree will be ours—Christ cursed it and it withered.

Mr. President, I dismiss this branch of the subject, and beg the indulgence of the Senate to some reflections on the particular bill now under consideration. I voted for a bill somewhat like the present at the last session—our army was then in the neighborhood of our line. I then hoped that the President did sincerely desire a peace. Our army had not then penetrated far into Mexico and I did hope that with the two millions then proposed we might get peace and avoid the slaughter, the shame, the crime, of an aggressive, unprovoked war. But now you have overrun half of Mexico, you have exasperated and irritated her people, you claim indemnity for all expenses incurred in doing this mischief and boldly ask her to give up New Mexico and California; and, as a bribe to her patriotism, seizing on her property, you offer three millions to pay the soldiers she has called out to repel your invasion on condition that she will give up to you at least one third of her whole territory. This is the modest—I should say, the monstrous—proposition now before us as explained by the chairman of the committee on foreign relations [Mr. Sevier], who reported the bill. I cannot now give my consent to this.

But, sir, I do not believe you will succeed. I am not informed of your prospects of success with this measure of peace. The chairman of the committee on foreign relations tells us that he has every reason to believe that peace can be obtained if we grant this appropriation. What reason have you, Mr. Chairman, for that opinion? "Facts which I cannot disclose to you—correspondence which it would be improper to name here—facts which I know, but which you are not permitted to know, have satisfied the committee that peace may be purchased if you will but grant these three millions of dollars."

Now, Mr. President, I wish to know if I am required to act upon such opinions of the chairman of the committee on foreign relations, formed upon facts which he refuses to disclose to me? No! I must know the facts before I can form my judgment. But I am to take it for granted that there must be some prospect of an end to this dreadful war—for it is a dreadful war, being, as I believe in my conscience it is, an unjust war. Is it possible that for three millions you can purchase a peace with Mexico? How? By the purchase of California? Mr. President, I know not what facts the chairman of the committee on foreign affairs may have had access to. I know not what secret agents have been whispering into the ears of the authorities of Mexico; but of one thing I am certain, that by a cession of California and New Mexico you never can purchase a peace with her.

You may wrest provinces from Mexico by war— you may hold them by the right of the strongest—you may rob her; but a treaty of peace to that effect with the people of Mexico, legitimately and freely made, you never will have! I thank God that it is so, as well for the sake of the Mexican people as ourselves; for, unlike the senator from Alabama [Mr. Bagby], I do not value the life of a citizen of the United States above the lives of a hundred thousand Mexican women and children—a rather cold sort of philanthropy, in my judgment. For the sake of Mexico, then, as well as our own country, I rejoice that it is an impossibility that you can obtain by treaty from her those territories under the existing state of things.

I am somewhat at a loss to know on what plan of operations gentlemen having charge of this war intend to proceed. We hear much said of the terror of your arms. The affrighted Mexican, it is said, when you shall have drenched his country in blood, will sue for peace, and thus you will indeed " conquer peace."

This is the heroic and savage tone in which we have heretofore been lectured by our friends on the other side of the chamber, especially by the senator from Michigan [General Cass].

But suddenly the chairman of the committee on foreign relations comes to us with a smooth phrase of diplomacy made potent by the gentle suasion of gold. The chairman of the committee on military affairs calls for thirty millions of money and ten thousand regular troops; these, we are assured, shall " conquer peace," if the obstinate Celt refuses to treat till we shall whip him in another field of blood. What a delightful scene in the nineteenth century of the Christian era!

What an interesting sight to see these two representatives of war and peace moving in grand procession through the halls of the Montezumas! The senator from Michigan [General Cass], red with the blood of recent slaughter, the gory spear of Achilles in his hand and the hoarse clarion of war in his mouth, blowing a blast " so loud and deep " that sleeping echoes of the lofty Cordilleras start from their caverns and return the sound, till every ear from Panama to Santa Fé is deafened with the roar. By his side, with " modest mien and downcast look," comes the senator from Arkansas [Mr. Sevier], covered from head to foot with a gorgeous robe, glittering and embossed with three millions of shining gold, putting to shame " the wealth of Ormus or of Ind." The olive of Minerva graces his brow; in his right hand is the delicate rebec. from which are breathed, in Lydian measure, notes " that tell of naught but love and peace."

I fear very much you will scarcely be able to explain

to the simple, savage mind of the half-civilized Mexicans the puzzling dualism of this scene, at once gorgeous and grotesque. Sir, I scarcely understand the meaning of all this myself. If we are to vindicate our rights by battles—in bloody fields of war—let us do it. If that is not the plan, why then let us call back our armies into our own territory, and propose a treaty with Mexico, based upon the proposition that money is better for her and land is better for us. Thus we can treat Mexico like an equal and do honor to ourselves.

But what is it you ask? You have taken from Mexico one fourth of her territory, and you now propose to run a line comprehending about another third, and for what? I ask, Mr. President, for what? What has Mexico got from you for parting with two thirds of her domain? She has given you ample redress for every injury of which you have complained. She has submitted to the award of your commissioners, and up to the time of the rupture with Texas faithfully paid it. And for all that she has lost (not through or by you, but which loss has been your gain), what requital do we, her strong, rich, robust neighbor, make? Do we send our missionaries there " to point the way to heaven? " Or do we send the schoolmasters to pour daylight into her dark places, to aid her infant strength to conquer freedom and reap the fruit of the independence herself alone had won?

No, no, none of this do we! But we send regiments, storm towns, and our colonels prate of liberty in the midst of the solitudes their ravages have made. They proclaim the empty forms of social compact to a people bleeding and maimed with wounds received in defending their hearthstones against the invasion of these very men who shoot them down and then exhort them to be free. Your chaplains of the navy throw aside the New Testament and seize a bill of rights. The Rev. Don Walter Colton, I see, abandons the Sermon on the Mount, and betakes himself to Blackstone and Kent, and is elected a justice of the peace! He takes military possession of some town in California, and instead of teaching the plan of the atonement and the way of salvation to the poor, ignorant Celt, he presents Colt's pistol to his ear, and calls on him to take "trial by jury and habeas corpus," or nine bullets in his head. Oh! Mr. President, are you not the lights of the earth, if not its salt? You, you are indeed opening the eyes of the blind in Mexico, with a most emphatic and exoteric power. Sir, if all this were not a sad, mournful truth, it would be the very *ne plus ultra* of the ridiculous.

But, sir, let us see what, as the chairman of the committee on foreign relations explains it, we are to get by the combined processes of conquest and treaty.

What is the territory, Mr. President, which you propose to wrest from Mexico? It is consecrated to the heart of the Mexican by many a well-fought battle with his old Castilian master. His Bunker Hills, and Saratogas, and Yorktowns are there. The Mexican can say, "There I bled for liberty! and shall I surrender that consecrated home of my affections to the Anglo-Saxon invaders? What do they want with it? They have Texas already. They have possessed themselves of the territory between the Nueces and the Rio

Grande. What else do they want? To what shall I point my children as memorials of that independence which I bequeath to them when those battlefields shall have passed from my possession?"

Sir, had one come and demanded Bunker Hill of the people of Massachusetts, had England's lion ever showed himself there, is there a man over thirteen and under ninety who would not have been ready to meet him; is there a river on this continent that would not have run red with blood; is there a field but would have been piled high with the unburied bones of slaughtered Americans before these consecrated battlefields of liberty should have been wrested from us? But this same American goes into a sister republic and says to poor, weak Mexico, "Give up your territory—you are unworthy to possess it—I have got one half already—all I ask of you is to give up the other!"

England might as well, in the circumstances I have described, have come and demanded of us, "Give up the Atlantic slope—give up this trifling territory from the Alleghany mountains to the sea; it is only from Maine to St. Mary's—only about one third of your republic, and the least interesting portion of it." What would be the response? They would say we must give this up to John Bull. Why? "He wants room." The senator from Michigan says he must have this. Why, my worthy Christian brother, on what principle of justice? "I want room!"

Sir, look at this pretence of want of room! With twenty millions of people you have about one thousand million of acres of land, inviting settlement by every conceivable argument—bringing them down to a quar-

3—6

ter of a dollar an acre, and allowing every man to squat where he pleases. But the senator from Michigan says we will be two hundred millions in a few years, and we want room. If I were a Mexican I would tell you, " Have you not room in your own country to bury your dead men? If you come into mine we will greet you with bloody hands and welcome you to hospitable graves."

Why, says the chairman of this committee on foreign relations, it is the most reasonable thing in the world! We ought to have the Bay of San Francisco. Why? Because it is the best harbor on the Pacific! It has been my fortune, Mr. President, to have practised a good deal in criminal courts in the course of my life, but I never yet heard a thief arraigned for stealing a horse plead that it was the best horse that he could find in the country! We want California. What for? Why, says the senator from Michigan, we will have it; and the senator from South Carolina, with a very mistaken view, I think, of policy, says you can't keep our people from going there. Let them go and seek their happiness in whatever country or clime it pleases them.

All I ask of them is, not to require this government to protect them with that banner consecrated to war waged for principles eternal, enduring truth. Sir, it is not meet that our old flag should throw its protecting folds over expeditions for lucre or for land. But you still say you want room for your people. This has been the plea of every robber-chief from Nimrod to the present hour. I dare say, when Tamerlane descended from his throne built of seventy thousand human skulls, and marched his ferocious battalions to further slaughter, I dare say he said, " I want room."

Bajazet was another gentleman of kindred tastes and wants with us Anglo-Saxons—he " wanted room." Alexander, too, the mighty " Macedonian madman," when he wandered with his Greeks to the plains of India and fought a bloody battle on the very ground where recently England and the Sikhs engaged in strife for " room," was no doubt in quest of some California there. Many a Monterey had he to storm to get " room."

Sir, he made quite as much of that sort of history as you ever will. Mr. President, do you remember the last chapter in that history? It is soon read. Oh! I wish we could but understand its moral. Ammon's son (so was Alexander named), after all his victories, died drunk in Babylon! The vast empire he conquered to " get room," became the prey of the generals he had trained; it was disparted, torn to pieces, and so ended. Sir, there is a very significant appendix; it is this: The descendants of the Greeks—of Alexander's Greeks—are now governed by a descendant of Attila!

Mr. President, while we are fighting for room let us ponder deeply this appendix. I was somewhat amazed the other day to hear the senator from Michigan declare that Europe had quite forgotten us till these battles waked them up. I suppose the senator feels grateful to the President for " waking up " Europe. Does the President, who is, I hope, read in civic as well as military lore, remember the saying of one who had pored upon history long—long, too, upon man, his nature and true destiny? Montesquieu did not think highly of this way of " waking up." "Happy," says he, " is that nation whose annals are tiresome."

The senator from Michigan has a different view of this. He thinks that a nation is not distinguished until it is distinguished in war; he fears that the slumbering faculties of Europe have not been able to ascertain that there are twenty millions of Anglo-Saxons here making railroads and canals, and speeding all the arts of peace to the utmost accomplishment of the most refined civilization. They do not know it! And what is the wonderful expedient which this democratic method of making history would adopt in order to make us known? Storming cities, desolating peaceful, happy homes, shooting men—aye, sir, such is war —and shooting women, too!

Sir, I have read in some account of your battle of Monterey, of a lovely Mexican girl, who, with the benevolence of an angel in her bosom and the robust courage of a hero in her heart, was busily engaged during the bloody conflict, amid the crash of falling houses, the groans of the dying, and the wild shriek of battle, in carrying water to slake the burning thirst of the wounded of either host. While bending over a wounded American soldier a cannon-ball struck her and blew her to atoms. Sir, I do not charge my brave, generous-hearted countrymen who fought that fight with this. No, no! We who send them—we who know that scenes like this, which might send tears of sorrow " down Pluto's iron cheek," are the invariable, inevitable attendants on war—we are accountable for this. And this—this is the way we are to be made

known to Europe. This—this is to be the undying renown of free, republican America! "She has stormed
a city—killed many of its inhabitants of both sexes—
she has room!" So it will read. Sir, if this were our
only history, then may God of his mercy grant that
its volume may speedily come to a close.

Why is it, sir, that we, the United States, a people
of yesterday compared with the older nations of the
world, should be waging war for territory—for
"room?" Look at your country, extending from the
Alleghany Mountains to the Pacific Ocean, capable
itself of sustaining in comfort a larger population than
will be in the whole Union for one hundred years to
come. Over this vast expanse of territory your population is now so sparse that I believe we provided, at
the last session, a regiment of mounted men to guard
the mail from the frontier of Missouri to the mouth of
the Columbia; and yet you persist in the ridiculous assertion, "I want room." One would imagine, from
the frequent reiteration of the complaint, that you had
a bursting, teeming population, whose energy was
paralyzed, whose enterprise was crushed, for want of
space. Why should we be so weak or wicked as to offer
this idle apology for ravaging a neighboring republic?
It will impose on no one at home or abroad.

Do we not know, Mr. President, that it is a law never
to be repealed that falsehood shall be short-lived? Was
it not ordained of old that truth only shall abide forever? Whatever we may say to-day, or whatever we
may write in our books, the stern tribunal of history
will review it all, detect falsehood, and bring us to
judgment before that posterity which shall bless or

curse us, as we may act now, wisely or otherwise. We may hide in the grave (which awaits us all) in vain: we may hope there, like the foolish bird that hides its head in the sand, in the vain belief that its body is not seen; yet even there this preposterous excuse of want of " room " shall be laid bare and the quick-coming future will decide that it was a hypocritical pretence under which we sought to conceal the avarice which prompted us to covet and to seize by force that which was not ours.

Mr. President, this uneasy desire to augment our territory has depraved the moral sense and blunted the otherwise keen sagacity of our people. What has been the fate of all nations who have acted upon the idea that they must advance! Our young orators cherish this notion with a fervid but fatally mistaken zeal. They call it by the mysterious name of " destiny." " Our destiny," they say, is " onward," and hence they argue, with ready sophistry, the propriety of seizing upon any territory and any people that may lie in the way of our " fated " advance. Recently these progressives have grown classical; some assiduous student of antiquities has helped them to a patron saint. They have wandered back into the desolated Pantheon, and there, among the polytheistic relics of that " pale mother of dead empires," they have found a god whom these Romans, centuries gone by, baptized " Terminus."

Sir, I have heard much and read somewhat of this gentleman Terminus. Alexander, of whom I have spoken, was a devotee of this divinity. We have seen the end of him and his empire. It was said to be an attribute of this god that he must always advance and never recede. So both republican and imperial Rome believed. It was, as they said, their destiny. And for a while it did seem to be even so. Roman Terminus did advance. Under the eagles of Rome he was carried from his home on the Tiber to the farthest East on the one hand, and to the far West, among the then barbarous tribes of western Europe, on the other.

But at length the time came when retributive justice had become " a destiny." The despised Gaul calls out the contemned Goth, and Attila with his Huns answers back the battle-shout to both. The " blue-eyed nations of the North," in succession or united, pour forth their countless hosts of warriors upon Rome and Rome's always-advancing god Terminus. And now the battle-axe of the barbarian strikes down the conquering eagle of Rome. Terminus at last recedes, slowly at first, but finally he is driven to Rome, and from Rome to Byzantium. Whoever would know the further fate of this Roman deity, so recently taken under the patronage of American democracy, may find ample gratification of his curiosity in the luminous pages of Gibbon's " Decline and Fall."

Such will find that Rome thought as you now think, that it was her destiny to conquer provinces and nations, and no doubt she sometimes said, as you say, " I will conquer a peace," and where now is she, the mistress of the world? The spider weaves his web in her palaces, the owl sings his watch-song in her towers. Teutonic power now lords it over the servile remnant, the miserable memento of old and once omnipotent Rome. Sad, very sad, are the lessons which time has written for us. Through and in them all I see nothing but the inflexible execution of that old law which ordains as eternal that cardinal rule, "Thou shalt not covet thy neighbor's goods, nor anything which is his." Since I have lately heard so much about the dismemberment of Mexico I have looked back to see how, in the course of events, which some call "Providence," it has fared with other nations who engaged in this work of dismemberment. I see that in the latter half of the eighteenth century three powerful nations, Russia, Austria and Prussia, united in the dismemberment of Poland. They said, too, as you say, "It is our destiny." They "wanted room." Doubtless each of these thought, with his share of Poland, his power was too strong ever to fear invasion, or even insult. One had his California, another his New Mexico, and the third his Vera Cruz. Did they remain untouched and incapable of harm? Alas! no—far, very far, from it. Retributive justice must fulfil its destiny, too.

A very few years pass off, and we hear of a new man, a Corsican lieutenant, the self-named "armed soldier of democracy," Napoleon. He ravages Austria, covers her land with blood, drives the Northern Cæsar from his capital, and sleeps in his palace. Austria may now remember how her power trampled upon Poland. Did she not pay dear, very dear, for her California?

But has Prussia no atonement to make? You see this same Napoleon, the blind instrument of Providence at work there. The thunders of his cannon at Jena proclaim the work of retribution for Poland's wrongs; and the successors of the Great Frederick, the drill-sergeant of Europe, are seen flying across the sandy plain that surrounds their capital, right glad if they may escape captivity or death. But how fares it with the Autocrat of Russia? Is he secure in his share of the spoils of Poland? No. Suddenly we see, sir, six hundred thousand armed men marching to Moscow. Does his Vera Cruz protect him now? Far from it. Blood, slaughter, desolation spread abroad over the land, and finally the conflagration of the old commercial metropolis of Russia closes the retribution she must pay for her share in the dismemberment of her weak and impotent neighbor.

Mr. President, a mind more prone to look for the judgments of heaven in the doings of men than mine cannot fail in this to see the providence of God. When Moscow burned, it seemed as if the earth was lighted up that the nations might behold the scene. As that mighty sea of fire gathered and heaved and rolled upward and yet higher till its flames licked the stars and fired the whole heavens, it did seem as though the God of the nations was writing in characters of flame on the front of his throne that doom that shall fall upon the strong nation which tramples in scorn upon the weak. And what fortune awaits him, the appointed executor of this work, when it was all done? He too, conceived the notion that his destiny was pointed onward to universal dominion. France was too small—Europe, he thought, should bow down before him.

But as soon as this idea took possession of his soul, he, too, becomes powerless. His Terminus must recede, too. Right there, while he witnessed the humiliation and doubtless meditated the subjugation of Russia, He who holds the winds in his fist gathered the snows of the north and blew them upon his six hundred thousand men; they fled—they froze—they perished. And now the mighty Napoleon, who had resolved on universal dominion, he, too, is summoned to answer for the violation of that ancient law, "Thou shalt not covet anything which is thy neighbor's." How is the mighty fallen! He, beneath whose proud footstep Europe trembled, he is now an exile at Elba, and now finally a prisoner on the rock of St. Helena, and there, on a barren island, in an unfrequented sea, in the crater of an extinguished volcano, there is the death-bed of the mighty conqueror. All his annexations have come to that! His last hour is now come, and he, the man of destiny, he who had rocked the world as with the throes of an earthquake, is now powerless, still—even as a beggar, so he died. On the wings of a tempest that raged with unwonted fury, up to the throne of the only Power that controlled him, while he lived, went the fiery soul of that wonderful warrior, another witness to the existence of that eternal decree that they who do not rule in righteousness shall perish from the earth. He has found "room" at last.

And France,—she, too, has found "room." Her "eagles" now no longer scream along the banks of the Danube, the Po, and the Borysthenes. They have returned home, to their old eyrie, between the Alps, the Rhine, and the Pyrenees. So shall it be with yours. You may carry them to the loftiest peaks of the Cordilleras, they may wave with insolent triumph in the halls of the Montezumas, the armed men of Mexico may quail before them, but the weakest hand in Mexico, uplifted in prayer to the God of Justice, may call down against you a Power in the presence of which the iron hearts of your warriors shall be turned into ashes.

Bryant, William Cullen, an American poet, journalist and orator, born at Cummington, Mass., November 23, 1794; died in New York City, June 12, 1878. He took an early interest in public affairs, and wrote political poems when still a boy. In 1828 he became assistant editor of the "Evening Post" of New York City, and four years later its chief editor, in which position he remained for a half century. His poetry is of a thoughtful, meditative character, and makes but slight appeal to the mass of readers. During the later years of Bryant's life he was a favorite orator on civic occasions, his speeches being always happily worded and in excellent taste. His latest appearance in public was on the occasion of his address at the unveiling of the Mazzini bust in Central Park on May 29, 1878. His address of welcome to Kossuth is one of his happiest efforts.

WELCOME TO LOUIS KOSSUTH.

DELIVERED AT A BANQUET GIVEN BY THE PRESS OF NEW YORK, DECEMBER 15, 1851.

LET me ask you to imagine the contest, in which the United States asserted their independence of Great Britain, had been unsuccessful, that our armies, through treason or a league of tyrants against us, had been broken and scattered, that the great men who led them, and who swayed our councils, our Washington, our Franklin, and the venerable President of the American Congress, had been driven forth as exiles. If there had existed at that day, in any part of the civilized world, a powerful republic, with institutions resting on the same foundations of liberty, which our own countrymen sought to establish, would there have been

in that republic any hospitality too cordial, any sympathy too deep, any zeal for their glorious but unfortunate cause, too fervent or too active to be shown toward
these illustrious fugitives? Gentlemen, the case I have
supposed is before you. The Washingtons, the Frank-
lins, the Hancocks of Hungary, driven out by a far
worse tyranny than was ever endured here, are wan-
derers in foreign lands. Some of them have sought
a refuge in our country—one sits with his company our
guest to-night, and we must measure the duty we owe
them by the same standard which we would have had
history apply, if our ancestors had met with a fate like
theirs.

I have compared the exiled Hungarians to the great
men of our own history. Difficulty, my brethren, is
the nurse of greatness; a harsh nurse, who roughly
rocks her foster-children into strength and athletic
proportion. The mind grappling with great aims and
wrestling with mighty ingredients, grows, by a certain
necessity, to their stature. Scarce anything so con-
vinces me of the capacity of the human intellect for indefinite expansion in the different stages of its being,
as this power of enlarging itself to the compass of surrounding emergencies. These men have been trained
to greatness by a quicker and surer method than a
peaceful country and a tranquil period can know.

But it is not merely or principally for their personal
qualities that we honor them; we honor them for the
cause in which they failed so gloriously. Great issues
hang upon that cause, and great interests of mankind
are crushed by its downfall. I was on the continent
of Europe when the treason of Görgey laid Hungary

bound at the feet of the Tsar. Europe was at that
time in the midst of the reaction; the ebb tide was rush-
ing violently back, sweeping all that the friends of freedom had planned into the black bosom of the deep. In
France the liberty of the press was extinct—Paris in
a state of siege—the soldiery of that republic had just
quenched in blood the freedom of Rome—Austria had
suppressed liberty in northern Italy—absolutism was
restored in Russia, along the Rhine, and in the towns
and villages of Würtemburg and Bavaria, troops withdrawn from the barracks, and garrisons filled the
streets and kept the inhabitants quiet with the bayonet
at their breast. Hungary at that moment alone upheld, and upheld with a firm hand and dauntless heart,
the blazing torch of liberty. To Hungary were turned
the eyes, to Hungary clung the hopes of all who did
not despair of the freedom of Europe.

I recollect that while the armies of Russia were moving like a tempest from the North upon the Hungarian
host, the progress of events was watched with the deepest solicitude by the people of Germany. I was at that
time in Munich, the splendid capital of Bavaria. The
Germans seemed for the time to have put off their
usual character, and scrambled for the daily prints, wet
from the press, with such eagerness that I almost
thought myself in America. The news of the catastrophe at last arrived; Görgey had betrayed the cause
of Hungary, and yielded to the demands of the Rus-
sians. Immediately a funeral gloom settled like a noon-
day darkness upon the city. I heard the muttered ex-
clamations of the people, "It is all over—the last hope
of European liberty is gone."

Russia did not misjudge. If she had allowed Hungary to become independent, or free, the reaction in favor of absolutism had been incomplete; there would have been one perilous example of successful resistance to despotism—in one corner of Europe a flame would have been kept alive, at which the other nations might have rekindled, among themselves, the light of liberty. Hungary was subdued; but does any one who hears me believe that the present state of things in Europe will last? The despots themselves fear that it will not; and made cruel by their fears, are heaping chain on chain around the limbs of their subjects.

They are hastening the event they dread. Every added shackle galls, into a more fiery impotence, those who wear them. I look with mingling hope and horror to the day—a day bloodier, perhaps, than we have yet seen—when the exasperated nations shall snap their chains and start to their feet. It may well be that Hungary, made less patient of the yoke by the remembrance of her own many and glorious struggles for independence, and better fitted than other nations, by the peculiar structure of her institutions, for founding the liberty of her citizens on a rational basis, will take the lead. In that glorious and hazardous enterprise, in that hour of care, need, and peril, I hope she will be cheered and strengthened with aid from this side of the Atlantic; aid given not with the stinted hand, not with a cowardly and selfish apprehension, lest we should not err on the safe side—wisely if you please. I care not with how broad a regard to the future, but in large, generous, effectual measure.

And you, our guest, fearless, eloquent, large of heart

and of mind, whose one thought is the salvation of oppressed Hungary, unfortunate but undiscouraged, struck down in the battle of liberty, but great in defeat, and gathering strength for future triumphs, receive this action at our hands, that in this great attempt of man to repossess himself of the rights which God gave him, though the strife be waged under a distant belt of longitude, and with the mightiest despotism of the world, the Press of America takes part with you and your countrymen. I give you—" LOUIS KOSSUTH."

ADDRESS AT THE FOUNDING OF THE METROPOLITAN ART MUSEUM.

DELIVERED AT THE UNION CLUB HOUSE, NOVEMBER 23, 1869.

WE are assembled, my friends, to consider the subject of founding in this city a museum of art, a repository of the productions of artists of every class, which shall be in some measure worthy of this great metropolis and of the wide empire of which New York is the commercial centre. I understand that no rivalry with any other project is contemplated, no competition save with similar institutions in other countries, and then only such modest competition as a museum in its infancy may aspire to hold with those which were founded centuries ago, and are enriched with the additions made by the munificence of successive generations. No precise method of reaching this result has been determined on, but the object of the present meeting is to awaken the public, so far as our proceedings can influence the general mind to the importance of taking early and effectual measures for founding such a museum as I have described.

Our city is the third great city of the civilized world. Our republic has already taken its place among the great powers of the earth; it is great in extent, great in population, great in the activity and enterprise of her people. It is the richest nation in the world if paying off an enormous national debt with a rapidity unexampled in history be any proof of riches; the richest in the world if contented submission to heavy taxation be a sign of wealth; the richest in the world if quietly to allow itself to be annually plundered of immense sums by men who seek public stations for their individual profit be a token of public prosperity.

My friends, if a tenth part of what is every year stolen from us in this way, in the city where we live, under pretence of the public service, and poured profusely into the coffers of political rogues, were expended on a museum of art, we might have, deposited in spacious and stately buildings, collections formed of works left by the world's greatest artists, which would be the pride of our country. We might have an annual revenue which would bring to the museum every stray statue and picture of merit for which there should be no ready sale to individuals, every smaller collection in the country which its owner could no longer conveniently keep, every noble work by the artists of former ages which by any casualty, after long remaining on the walls of some ancient building, should be again thrown upon the world.

But what have we done—numerous as our people are, and so rich as to be contentedly cheated and

plundered, what have we done toward founding such
a repository? We have hardly made a step toward it.
Yet, beyond the sea there is the little kingdom of Sax-
ony, with an area even less than that of Massachusetts,
and a population but little larger, possessing a museum
of the fine arts, marvellously rich, which no man who
visits the continent of Europe is willing to own that
he has not seen.

There is Spain, a third-rate power of Europe, and
poor besides, with a museum of fine arts at her capital
the opulence and extent of which absolutely bewilder
the visitor. I will not speak of France or of England,
conquering nations, which have gathered their treasures of art in part from regions over-run by their
armies; nor yet of Italy, the fortunate inheritor of
so many glorious productions of her own artists. But
there are Holland and Belgium, kingdoms almost too
small to be heeded by the greater powers of Europe in
the consultations which decide the destinies of nations,
and these little kingdoms have their public collections
of art, the resort of admiring visitors from all parts of
the civilized world.

But in our country, when the owner of a private
gallery of art desires to leave his treasures where they
can be seen by the public, he looks in vain for any
institution to which he can send them. A public-
spirited citizen desires to employ a favorite artist upon
some great historical picture; there are no walls on
which it can hang in public sight. A large collection
of works of art, made at great cost, and with great
pains, gathered perhaps during a lifetime, is for sale
in Europe. We may find here men willing to con-

tribute to purchase it, but if it should be brought to our country there is no edifice here to give it hospitality.

In 1857, during a visit to Spain, I found in Madrid a rich private collection of pictures, made by Medraza, an aged painter, during a long life, and at a period when frequent social and political changes in that country dismantled many palaces of the old nobility of the works of art which adorned them. In that collection were many pictures by the illustrious elder artists of Italy, Spain, and Holland. The whole might have been bought for half its value, but if it had been brought over to our country we had no gallery to hold it.

The same year I stood before the famous Campana collection of marbles, at Rome, which was then waiting for a purchaser—a noble collection, busts and statues of the ancient philosophers, orators, and poets, the majestic forms of Roman senators, the deities of ancient mythology,

" The fair humanities of old religion."

but if they had been purchased by our countrymen and landed here, we should have been obliged to leave them in boxes, just as they were packed.

Moreover, we require an extensive public gallery to contain the greater works of our own painters and sculptors. The American soil is prolific of artists. The fine arts blossom not only in the populous regions of our country, but even in its solitary places. Go where you will, into whatever museum of art in the Old World, you find there artists from the new, contemplating or copying the masterpieces of art which they contain. Our artists swarm in Italy. When I was last at Rome, two years since, I found the number of American artists residing there as two to one compared with those from the British isles. But there are beginners among us who have not the means of resorting to distant countries for that instruction in art which is derived from carefully studying works of acknowledged excellence. For these a gallery is needed at home which shall vie with those abroad, if not in the multitude, yet in the merit of the works it contains.

Yet further, it is unfortunate for our artists, our painters especially, that they too often find their genius cramped by the narrow space in which it is constrained to exert itself. It is like a bird in a cage which can only take short flights from one perch to another and longs to stretch its wings in an ampler atmosphere. Producing works for private dwellings, our painters are for the most part obliged to confine themselves to cabinet pictures, and have little opportunity for that larger treatment of important subjects which a greater breadth of canvas would allow them, and by which the higher and nobler triumphs of their art have been achieved.

There is yet another view of the subject, and a most important one. When I consider, my friends, the prospect which opens before this great mart of the western world I am moved by feelings which I feel it somewhat difficult clearly to define. The growth of our city is already wonderfully rapid; it is every day spreading itself into the surrounding region, and overwhelming it like an inundation. Now that our great railway has been laid from the Atlantic to the Pacific, Eastern Asia and Western Europe will shake hands over our republic. New York will be the mart from which Europe will receive a large proportion of the products of China, and will become not only a centre of commerce for the New World, but for that region which is to Europe the most remote part of the Old. A new impulse will be given to the growth of our city, which I cannot contemplate without an emotion akin to dismay. Men will flock in greater numbers than ever before to plant themselves on a spot so favorable to the exchange of commodities between distant regions; and here will be an aggregation of human life, a concentration of all that ennobles and all that degrades humanity, on a scale which the imagination cannot venture to measure. To great cities resort not only all that is eminent in talent, all that is splendid in genius, and all that is active in philanthropy; but also all that is most dexterous in villainy, and all that is most foul in guilt. It is in the labyrinths of such mighty and crowded populations that crime finds its safest lurking-places; it is there that vice spreads its most seductive and fatal snares, and sin is pampered and festers and spreads its contagion in the greatest security.

My friends, it is important that we should encounter the temptations to vice in this great and too rapidly growing capital by attractive entertainments of an innocent and improving character. We have libraries and reading-rooms, and this is well; we have also spacious halls for musical entertainments, and that also is well; but there are times when we do not care to read and are satiate with the listening to sweet sounds, and when we more willingly contemplate works of art. It is the business of the true philanthropist to find means of gratifying this preference. We must be beforehand with vice in our arrangements for all that gives grace and cheerfulness to society. The influence of works of art is wholesome, ennobling, instructive. Besides the cultivation of the sense of beauty—in other words, the perception of order, symmetry, proportion of parts, which is of near kindred to the moral sentiments—the intelligent contemplation of a great gallery of works of art is a lesson in history, a lesson in biography, a lesson in the antiquities of different countries. Half our knowledge of the customs and modes of life among the ancient Greeks and Romans is derived from the remains of ancient art.

Let it be remembered to the honor of art that if it has ever been perverted to the purposes of vice, it has only been at the bidding of some corrupt court or at the desire of some opulent and powerful voluptuary whose word was law. When intended for the general eye no such stain rests on the works of art. Let me close with an anecdote of the influence of a well-known work. I was once speaking to the poet Rogers in commendation of the painting of Ary Scheffer entitled " Christ the Consoler." " I have an engraving of it," he answered, " hanging at my bedside, where it meets my eye every morning." The aged poet, over whom already impended the shadow that shrouds the entrance to the next world, found his morning meditations guided by that work to the founder of our religion.

Potter, Henry C., a distinguished American clergyman, born at Schenectady, N. Y., May 25, 1835. He is the son of Alonzo Potter, a former bishop of Pennsylvania, and entered the Episcopal ministry in 1857. After ministering to parishes at Greensburg, Pa., and Troy, N. Y., he was rector of Grace church, New York City, 1868–83. He was elected assistant bishop of New York in the last named year, becoming sole bishop of that diocese in 1887. He has taken a deep interest in civic and national problems, upon which he has written much and also spoken frequently in public. He is an eloquent speaker, and his sermons and political and social addresses are characterized by earnestness and sound judgment. Several collections of his sermons and other addresses have been made.

MEMORIAL DISCOURSE ON PHILLIPS BROOKS.

"It is the Spirit that quickeneth, the flesh profiteth nothing: the words that I speak unto you, they are spirit, and they are life."—John vi, 63.

THE discourse from which I take these words finds both its occasion and its key in the miracle which preceded it. In a day when some people are fond of saying that the most powerful motives that attract people to the religion of Christ are what Bishop Butler called " secondary motives," it is interesting to note that of some, at any rate, this has been true from the beginning. Christ takes the five loaves and two fishes, blesses them, divides them, and distributes them; and lo, the hunger of a mighty throng is satisfied. His boundless compassion finds no limit to its expression,

and the twelve baskets full of fragments tell of resources which no emergency could exhaust.

There must, indeed, have been some in that vast con-
course who understood what the wonder meant.
There must have been some aching hearts, as well as
hungry mouths, that pierced through the shell of the
sign to the innermost meaning of that for which it
stood.   But there were others, it would seem, who did
not.   There were others to whom, then as now, another's affluence of gifts was only one more reason for
demands, and they the lowest, that could know no limit.
These people were there, over against Jesus then, as
there are people now who stand over any gifted nature
just to reveal how sensuous are their hungers and how
much they must have to satisfy them.

And so it is that Jesus follows the miracle with the
sermon.   It is, in one aspect of it, a counterpart of all
his preaching.   A large proportion of those to whom
he spoke could see in his mighty works only their
coarser side and be moved by his miracle of enlarge-
ment only to ask that it may be wrought again and
again to satisfy a bodily hunger.   And so he sets to
work to lift it all,—the miracle, the bread with which
he wrought it, the hunger wich it satisfied—up into
that higher realm where, bathed in the light of heaven,
it shone a revelation of the aim of God to meet and
feed the hungers of the soul.

This is the thought that echoes and re-echoes, like
some great refrain, from first to last through all that
he says: " Labor not for the meat that perisheth, but
for that which endureth unto everlasting life."   " My
Father giveth you the true bread from heaven."   And

then, as if he would bring out into clearer relief the great thought that he is seeking to communicate, " I am the bread of life: he that cometh to me shall never hunger; and he that believeth in me shall never thirst." " The bread that I will give is my flesh, which I will give for the life of the world." " Verily, verily, I say unto you, except ye eat the flesh of the Son of Man and drink his blood, ye have no life in you. For my flesh is meat indeed, and my blood is drink indeed. He that eateth my flesh and drinketh my blood dwelleth in me and I in him."

One can readily enough understand the enormous shock of language such as this to a sensuous and sense-loving people. To say, indeed, that it had no meaning to them, would be as wide of the mark as to say that it had no other meaning than that which they put upon it. But it is, plainly, to show that other, inner meaning, which from the beginning to the end of the discourse they seem so incapable of discerning, that the whole discussion gathers itself up and opens itself out in the words with which I began: " It is the Spirit that quickeneth; the flesh profiteth nothing: the words that I speak unto you, they are spirit, and they are life."

How the thunders of old disputes, like the rumbling of heavy artillery through distant and long-deserted valleys, come with these words, echoing down to us from all the past! It is a reflection of equal solemnity and sadness that no ordinarily well-instructed Christian disciple can hear the sixth chapter of St. John's Gospel read as one of the Church's Lessons without having called up before his mind's eye one of the bitterest and most vehement controversies which for a thousand years has rent the Church of God.

On the one side stand the mystics, and on the other the literalists; and behind them both is that divinely-instituted Sacrament which, as in turn the one or the other has contended, is here, or is not here, referred to. Happy are we if we have come to learn that here, as so often in the realm of theological controversy, both are right and both are wrong.

For on the one hand it is impossible to deal candidly with these words of Christ's and not discern that they are works of general rather than of specific import; that they were spoken to state a truth rather than to foreshadow a rite. On the other hand it is no less impossible to read them and not perceive that there is in them a distinct if not specific foreshadowing of that holy ordinance which we know as the Eucharistic Feast. It is indeed incredible that " just a year before the Eucharist was instituted the Founder of this, the most distinctive element of Christian worship, had no thought of it in his mind. Surely, for long beforehand, that institution was in his thoughts; and, if so, the coincidences are too exact to be fortuitous." * This is the other aspect of the discourse.

But, as the great Bishop Durham has said, " the discourse cannot refer primarily to the Holy Communion, nor, again, can it be simply prophetic of that Sacrament. The teaching has a full and consistent meaning in connection with the actual circumstances, and it treats essentially of spiritual realities with which no external act, as such, can be [co-] extensive."

* Plummer, St. John's Gospel, p. 146.

Calm words and wise, which touch unerringly the core and substance of the whole matter and bring us face to face with that larger truth which most of all concerns us who are here to-day.

For, first of all, it belongs to you and me to remember why we are here and in what supreme relation. This is a Council of the Church; and, whatever conception some of us may have of that word in other and wider aspects of its meaning, there can be no question of its meaning here. The Church, with us and for the present occasion, at any rate, is this Church whose sons we are, whose Orders we bear, in whose Convention we sit, whose Bishop we mourn, and whose Bishop you are soon to elect.

In other words, that is an organized, visible, tangible, audible body, situate here in the Commonwealth of Massachusetts, of which now at any rate I am talking, and with which you are to be concerned. It is an institution having an earthly as well as a heavenly pedigree and history, and having earthly as well as heavenly means to employ and tasks to perform.

There can be, there ought to be, no indefiniteness, no uncertainty about this. Whatever of such indefiniteness there may have been in the life and work of the Church in other days, we have all, or almost all of us, come to the conclusion that the time for it is ended now. If the Church is to do her work in the world she must have an organized life, and a duly commissioned ministry, and duly administered sacraments, and a vast variety of means and agencies, instruments and mechanisms, with which to accomplish that work. And when we come to Convention we must talk about these things, and add up long rows of figures, and take account of the lists of priests and deacons, and the rest, and make mention of vestries, and guilds, and parish houses, and sisterhoods, and all the various arms and tools with which the Church is fighting the battle of the Lord.

Yes, we must; and he who despises these things, or the least of them, is just as foolish and unreasonable as he who despises his eye or his hand when either are set over against that motive-power of eye or hand which we call an idea. One often hears, when ecclesiastical bodies such as this have adjourned, a wail of dissatisfaction that so much time and thought should have been expended in things that were, after all, only matters of secondary importance; and the fine scorn for such things which is at such times expressed is often itself as excessive and as disproportionate to greater and graver things as that of which it speaks.

But, having said this, is it not my plain duty to tell you, brethren of the diocese of Massachusetts, that he who stops over-long in the mere mechanism of religion is verily missing that for which religion stands? Here, indeed, it must be owned is, if not our greatest danger, one of the greatest. All life is full of that strange want of intellectual and moral perspective which fails to see how secondary, after all, are means to ends; and how he only has truly apprehended the office of religion who has learned, when undertaking in any wise to present it or represent it, to hold fast to that which is the one central thought and fact of all: " It is the Spirit that quickeneth; the flesh profiteth nothing: the words that I speak unto you, they are spirit, and they are life."

And this brings me—in how real and vivid a way I am sure you must feel as keenly as I—face to face with him of whom I am set to speak to-day. In one aspect of it my task—from which at the first view any one might well shrink—is made comparatively easy by words which have been spoken already.

Never before in the history, not only of our own communion, but of any or all communions, has the departure of a religious teacher been more widely noted and deplored than in the case of him of whom this Commonwealth and this diocese have been bereaved. Never before, surely, in the case of any man whom we can recall, has the sense of loss and bereavement been more distinctly a personal one,—extending to multitudes in two hemispheres who did not know him, who had never seen or heard him, and yet to whom he had revealed himself in such real and helpful ways.

It has followed, inevitably, from this, that that strong tide of profound feeling has found expression in many and most unusual forms, and it will be among the most interesting tasks of the future biographer of the late Bishop of Massachusetts to take note of these various memorials and to trace in them the secret of his unique power and influence.

But just because they have, so many of them, in such remarkable variety and from sources so diverse, been written or spoken, and no less because a Memoir of Phillips Brooks is already undertaken by hands pre-eminently designated for that purpose, I may wisely here confine myself to another and very different task.

I shall not attempt, therefore, even the merest outline of a biographical review. I shall not undertake to analyze, nor, save incidentally, even to refer to, the influences and inheritances that wrought in the mind and upon the life of your late friend and teacher. I shall still less attempt to discover the open secret of his rare and unique charm and attractiveness as a man; and I shall least of all endeavor to forecast the place which history will give to him among the leaders and builders of our age. Brief as was his ministry in his higher office, and to our view all too soon ended, I shall be content to speak of him as a bishop,—of his divine right, as I profoundly believe, to a place in the Episcopate, and of the pre-eminent value of his distinctive and incomparable witness to the highest aim and purpose of that office.

And first of all let me say a word in regard to the way in which he came to it. When chosen to the Episcopate of this diocese, your late bishop had already at least once, as we all know, declined that office. It was well known to those who knew him best that, as he had viewed it for a large part of his ministry, it was a work for which he had no especial sympathy either as to its tasks, or, as he had understood them, its opportunities.

But the time undoubtedly came when, as to this, he modified his earlier opinions; and the time came too, as I am most glad to think, when he was led to feel that if he were called to such an office he might find in it an opportunity for widening his own sympathies and for estimating more justly those with whom previously he had believed himself to have little in common.

It was the inevitable condition of his strong and deep convictions that he should not always or easily understand or make due allowance for men of different opinions. It was—God and you will bear me witness that this is true!—one of the noblest characteristics of his fifteen months' episcopate that, as a bishop, men's rightful liberty of opinion found in him not only a large and generous tolerance, but a most beautiful and gracious acceptance. He seized, instantly and easily, that which will be forever the highest conception of the episcopate in its relations whether to the clergy or the laity, its paternal and fraternal character; and his "sweet reasonableness," both as a father and as a brother, shone through all that he was and did.

For one I greatly love to remember this,—that when the time came that he himself, with the simple naturalness which marked all that he did, was brought to reconsider his earlier attitude toward the episcopal office, and to express with characteristic candor his readiness to take up its work if he should be chosen to it, he turned to his new, and to him most strange task with a supreme desire to do it in a loving and whole hearted way, and to make it helpful to every man, woman, and child with whom he came in contact. What could have been more like him than that, in that last address which he delivered to the choir-boys at Newton, he should have said to them, "When you meet me let me know that you know me." Another might easily have been misunderstood in asking those whom he might by chance encounter to salute him; but he knew, and the boys knew, what he had in mind,—how he and they were all striving to serve one Master, and how each—he most surely as much as they—was to gain strength and cheer from mutual recognition in the spirit of a common brotherhood.

And thus it was always; and this it was that allied itself so naturally to that which was his never-ceasing endeavor—to lift all men everywhere to that which was, with him, the highest conception of his office, whether as a preacher or as a bishop,—the conception of God as a Father, and of the brotherhood of all men as mutually related in him.

In an address which he delivered during the last General Convention in Baltimore to the students of Johns Hopkins University, he spoke substantially these words:

"In trying to win a man to a better life, show him not the evil but the nobleness of his nature. Lead him to enthusiastic contemplations of humanity in its perfection, and when he asks, Why, if this is so, do not I have this life?—then project on the background of his enthusiasm his own life; say to him, ' Because you are a liar, because you blind your soul with licentiousness, shame is born,—but not a shame of despair. It is soon changed to joy. Christianity becomes an opportunity, a high privilege, the means of attaining to the most exalted ideal—and the only means.'

"Herein must lie all real power; herein lay Christ's power, that he appreciated the beauty and richness of humanity, that it is very near the Infinite, very near to God. These two facts—we are the children of God, and God is our Father—make us look very differently at ourselves, very differently at our neighbors, very

differently at God. We should be surprised, not at
our good deeds, but at our bad ones. We should expect good as more likely to occur than evil; we should
believe that our best moments are our truest. I was
once talking with an acquaintance about whose religious position I knew nothing, and he expressed a very
hopeful opinion in regard to a matter about which I
was myself very doubtful.

"'Why,' I said to him, 'You are an optimist.'

"'Of course I am an optimist,' he replied, 'because
I am a Christian.'

"I felt that as a reproof. The Christian must be
an optimist."

Men and brethren, I set these words over against
those of his Master with which I began, and the two
in essence are one. "The words that I speak unto
you, they are spirit, and they are life." There is a
life nobler and diviner than any that we have dreamed
of. To the poorest and meanest of us, as to the best
and most richly-dowered, it is alike open. To turn
toward it, to reach up after it, to believe in its ever-
recurring nearness, and to glorify God in attaining to
it, this is the calling of a human soul.

Now then, what, I ask you, is all the rest of religion
worth in comparison with this?—not what is it worth
in itself, but what is its place relatively to this? This,
I maintain, is the supreme question for the Episcopate,
as it ought to be the supreme question with the Ministry of any and every order. And therefore it is, I
affirm, that, in bringing into the Episcopate with such
unique vividness and power this conception of his office,

4 – 6

your bishop rendered to his order and to the Church of God everywhere a service so transcendent. A most gifted and sympathetic observer of our departed brother's character and influence has said of him, contrasting him with the power of institutions, " His life will always suggest the importance of the influence of the individual man as compared with institutional Christianity."

In one sense, undoubtedly, this is true; but I should prefer to say that his life-work will always show the large and helpful influence of a great soul upon institutional Christianity. It is a superficial and unphilosophical temperament that disparages institutions; for institutions are only another name for that organized force and life by which God rules the world. But it is undoubtedly and profoundly true that you no sooner have an institution, whether in society, in politics, or in religion, than you are threatened with the danger that the institution may first exaggerate itself and then harden and stiffen into a machine; and that in the realm of religion, pre-eminently, those whose office it should be to quicken and infuse it with new life should themselves come at last to " worship the net and the drag." And just here you find in the history of religion in all ages the place of the prophet and the seer. He is to pierce through the fabric of the visible structure to that soul of things for which it stands. When, in Isaiah, the Holy Ghost commands the prophet, " Lift up thy voice with strength; lift it up, be not afraid: say unto the cities of Judah, Behold your God!" it is not alone, you see, his voice that he is to lift up. No, no! It is the vision of the unseen and divine. "Say unto the cities of Judah, Behold your God!"

Over and over again that voice breaks in upon the slumbrous torpor of Israel and smites the dead souls of priests and people alike. Now it is a Balaam, now it is an Elijah, a David, an Isaiah, a John the Baptist, a Paul the Apostle, a Peter the Hermit, a Savonarola, a Huss, a Whitefield, a Wesley, a Frederick Maurice, a Frederick Robertson, a John Keble (with his clear spiritual insight, and his fine spiritual sensibility), a Phillips Brooks.

Do not mistake me. I do not say that there were not many others. But these names are typical, and that for which they stand cannot easily be mistaken. I affirm without qualification that, in that gift of vision and of exaltation for which they stand, they stand for the highest and the best,—that one thing for which the Church of God most of all stands, and of which so long as it is the Church Militant it will most of all stand in need: to know that the end of all its mechanisms and ministries is to impart life, and that nothing which obscures or loses sight of the eternal source of life can regenerate or quicken;—to teach men to cry out, with St. Augustine, "*Fecisti nos ad te, Domine, et inquietum est cor nostrum donec requiescat in te:* Thou hast made us for thyself, O Lord, and our heart is unquiet until it rests in thee,"—this, however any one may be tempted to fence and juggle with the fact, is the truth on which all the rest depends.

Unfortunately it is a truth which there is much in the tasks and engagements of the Episcopate to obscure. A bishop is pre-eminently, at any rate in the popular conception of him, an administrator; and howsoever wide of the mark this popular conception may be from the essential idea of the office, it must be owned that there is much in a bishop's work in our day to limit his activities, and therefore his influence, within such a sphere.

To recognize his prophetic office as giving expression to that mission of the Holy Ghost of which he is pre-eminently the representative, to illustrate it upon a wider instead of a narrower field, to recognize and seize the greater opportunities for its exercise, to be indeed " a leader and commander " to the people, not by means of the petty mechanisms of officialism, but by the strong, strenuous, and unwearied proclamation of the truth; under all conditions to make the occasion some-how a stepping-stone to that mount of vision from which men may see God and righteousness and become sensible of the nearness of both to themselves,—this, I think you will agree with me, is no unworthy use of the loftiest calling and the loftiest gifts.

And such a use was his. A bishop-elect, walking with him one day in the country, was speaking, with not unnatural shrinking and hesitancy, of the new work toward which he was soon to turn his face, and said among other things, " I have a great dread, in the Episcopate, of perfunctoriness. In the administration, especially, of Confirmation, it seems almost impossible, in connection with its constant repetition, to avoid it."

He was silent a moment, and then said, " I do not think that it need be so. The office indeed is the same. But every class is different; and then—think what it is to them! It seems to me that that thought can never cease to move one."

What a clear insight the answer gave to his own ministry. One turns back to his first sermon,—that evening when, with his fellow-student in Virginia, he walked across the fields to the log-cabin where, not yet in Holy Orders, he preached it, and where afterward he ministered with such swiftly increasing power to a handful of negro servants. "It was an utter failure," he said afterward. Yes, perhaps; but all through the failure he struggled to give expression to that of which his soul was full; and I do not doubt that even then they who heard him somehow understood him.

We pass from those first words to the last,—those of which I spoke a moment ago,—the address to the choir-boys at Newton,—was there ever such an address to choir-boys before? He knew little or nothing about the science of music, and with characteristic candor he at once said so. But he passed quickly from the music to those incomparable words of which the music was the mere vehicle and vesture. He bade the lads to whom he spoke think of those who, long ago and all the ages down, had sung that matchless Psalter,—of the boys and men of other times, and what it had meant to them. And then, as he looked into their fresh young faces and saw the long vista of life stretching out before them, he bade them think of that larger and fuller meaning which was to come into those Psalms of David, when he,—was there some prophetic sense of how soon with him the end would be?—when he and such as he had passed away,—what new doors were to open, what deeper meanings were to be discerned, what nobler opportunities were to dawn, as the years hastened swiftly on toward their august and glorious consummation! How it all lifts us up as we read it, and how like it was to that " one sermon " which he forever preached!

And in saying so I do not forget what that was which some men said was missing in it. His, they tell us who hold some dry and formalized statement of the truth so close to the eye that it obscures all larger vision of it,—his, they tell us, was an " invertebrate theology." Of what he was and spoke, such a criticism is as if one said of the wind, that divinely-appointed symbol of the Holy Ghost, " it has no spine or ribs."

A spine and ribs are very necessary things; but we bury them as so much chalk and lime when once the breath has gone out of them! In the beginning we read " And the Lord God breathed into his nostrils the breath of life, and man became a living soul."

And all along since then there have been messengers of God into whom the same divine breath has been, as it were, without measure breathed, and who have been the quickeners and inspirers of their fellows. Nothing less than this can explain that wholly exceptional and yet consistent influence which he whom we mourn gave forth. It was not confined or limited by merely personal or physical conditions, but breathed with equal and quickening power through all that he taught and wrote. There were multitudes who never saw or heard him, but by whom nevertheless he was as intimately known and understood as if he had been their daily companion.

Never was there an instance which more truly fulfilled the saying, " The words that I speak unto you, they are spirit, and they are life." They reached down to the inmost need of empty and aching hearts and answered it. They spoke to that in the most sin-stained and wayward soul which is, after all, the image of the invisible God,—spoke to it, touched it, constrained it. " What has this fine-bred Boston scholar," plain men asked, when we bade him come to us and preach in our Trinity—" what has such an one to say to the business men of Wall Street?" But when he came, straightway every man found out that he had indeed something to say to him,—a word of power, a word of hope, a word of enduring joy and strength!

A kindred thinker of large vision and rare insight, New England born and nurtured like himself,* speaking of him not long after his death, said:

" There are three forms pertaining to the Christian truths: they are true as facts, they are true as doctrines intellectually apprehended, they are true as spiritual experiences to be realized. Bishop Brooks struck directly for the last. In the spirit he found the truth; and only as he could get it into a spiritual form did he conceive it to have power.

" It was because he assumed the facts as true in the main, refusing to insist on petty accuracy, and passed by doctrinal forms concerning which there might be great divergence of opinion, and carried his thought on into the world of spirit, that he won so great a hearing and such conviction of belief. For it is the

* The Rev. Theodore T. Munger, D.D.

spirit that gives common standing-ground; it says substantially the same thing in all men. Speak as a spirit to the spiritual nature of men, and they will respond, because in the spirit they draw near to their common source and to the world to which all belong.

"It was because he dealt with this common factor of the human and the divine nature that he was so positive and practical. In the spirit it is all yea and amen; there is no negative; in the New Jerusalem there is no night. We can describe this feature of his ministry by words from one of his own sermons: 'It has always been through men of belief, not unbelief, that power from God has poured into man. It is not the discriminating critic, but he whose beating, throbbing life offers itself a channel for the divine force,—he is the man through whom the world grows rich, and whom it remembers with perpetual thanksgiving.'"

And shall not you who are here to-day thank God that such a man was, though for so brief a space, your bishop? Some there were, you remember, who thought that those greater spiritual gifts of his would unfit him for the business of practical affairs. "A bishop's daily round," they said, "his endless correspondence, his hurried journeyings, his weight of anxious cares, the misadventures of other men, ever returning to plague him,—how can he bring himself to stoop and deal with these?"

But as in so much else that was transcendent in him, how little here, too, his critics understood him! No more pathetic proof of this has come to light than in that testimony of one among you who, as his private secretary, stood in closest and most intimate relations to him. What a story that is which he has given to us of a great soul—faithful always in the greatest? Yes, but no less faithful in the least. There seems a strange, almost grotesque impossibility in the thought that such an one should ever have come to be regarded as "a stickler for the canons."

But we look a little deeper than the surface, and all that is incongruous straightway disappears. His was the realm of a Divine Order,—his was the office of his Lord's servant. God had called him. He had put him where he was. He had set his Church to be his witness in the world, and in it, all his children, the greatest with the least, to walk in ways of reverent appointment. Those ways might irk and cramp him sometimes. They did: he might speak of them with sharp impatience and seeming disesteem sometimes. He did that too, now and then,—for he was human like the rest of us! But mark you this, my brothers, for, in an age which, under one figment or another, whether of more ancient or more modern license, is an age of much self-will,—we shall do well to remember it,— his was a life of orderly and consistent obedience to rule. He kept to the Church's plain and stately ways: kept to them and prized them too.

But all the while he held his soul wide open to the vision of his Lord! Up out of a routine that seemed to others that did not know or could not understand him, and who vouchsafed to him much condescending compassion for a bondage which he never felt, and of which in vain they strove to persuade him to complain,—up out of the narrower round in which so faithfully he walked, from time to time he climbed, and came back bathed in a heavenly light, with lips aglow with heavenly fire. The Spirit had spoken to him, and so he spoke to us. "The flesh profiteth nothing: it is the Spirit that quickeneth. The words that I speak unto you, they are spirit, and they are life."

And so we thank God, my brothers, not alone for his message, but that it was given to him to speak it as a bishop in the Church of God. We thank God that in a generation that so greatly needs to cry, as our "Te Deum" teaches us, "Govern us and lift us up!" he was given to the Church not alone to rule but to uplift.

What bishop is there who may not wisely seek to be like him by drawing forever on those fires of the Holy Ghost that set his lips aflame? Nay, what soul among us all is there that may not wisely seek to ascend up into that upper realm in which he walked, and by whose mighty airs his soul was filled? Unto the almighty and ever-living God we yield most high praise and hearty thanks for the wonderful grace and virtue declared in all his saints who have been the chosen vessels of his grace and the lights of the world in their several generations; but here and to-day especially for his servant, Phillips Brooks, sometime of this Commonwealth and this diocese, true prophet, true priest, true bishop, to the glory of God the Father.

Parkhurst, Charles H., an American clergyman, prominent in municipal reforms, born at Framingham, Mass., April 17, 1842. He studied theology and was pastor of a Congregational church at Lenox, Mass., 1874-80. Since the year last named he has been pastor of the Presbyterian church in Madison Square, New York City. He became president of the Society for the Prevention of Crime in 1891, and led in an attack upon the methods of the police department of the metropolis. He also took a prominent part in the Lexow investigation, which succeeded and has since been conspicuous in municipal reform movements in New York. He is an energetic, able speaker.

SERMON ON GARFIELD.

DELIVERED SEPTEMBER 25, 1881.

"Almost all things are by the law purged with blood."—Hebrews ix, 22.

EVERYTHING that is great and good has to be paid for. There is hardly anything in life that is pure gratuity. Life is toilsome, and if we are upon a path of ascent almost every step has to be taken irksomely and with pain. It is so arranged. The cross and then the crown.

That is God's thought, and so we find it wrought everywhere into the structure of life, individual and associate. In the market of the finer spiritual as well as in that of the coarser material commodities everything is stamped with its cost-mark.

Our prayers are sometimes only an attempt to obtain God's benefits at special rates, or to evade payment altogether. We court the health which the cup can give, but pray to be spared the cup: "Let this cup pass from me."

We want to be clothed in robes of white, but pray to be spared that tribulation out from which the white-robed saints of apocalyptic vision were come: purged (we ask to be), but by something other than blood. But "almost all things are by the law purged with blood."

That is one of those far-reaching thoughts of God, lodged away back in the old altar-ritual of the Hebrews, finer and truer than either priest or layman knew. Nowhere so true, of course, as upon Calvary: "Without shedding of blood is no remission." But the world is full of its little Calvaries. Every good thing is obtained by purchase, and every best thing is paid for in blood. Almost all things are purged with blood, and the pathway of life and the highway of history leads continuously over a new Golgotha.

There are qualities of character, individual and national, that are not wrought out by prosperity. Even "the Captain of our salvation was made perfect through sufferings." "Before I was afflicted I went astray."

Life gets continually broken in upon, therefore invaded, startled. Nothing ought so little to surprise us as a surprise. It keeps men's thoughts at a tension, and makes hearts plastic. Said Jeremiah: "Moab hath been at ease from his youth, and he hath settled on his lees, and hath not been emptied from vessel to vessel; therefore his taste remained in him, and his scent is not changed." "Hath settled on his lees."

It is a part of the holy discipline of God, then, to trespass upon the quiet of individual life and the serenity of national life. It makes men think, think deeply, think seriously; and serious thought easily becomes devout, and devout thought is redemption. It is not often that a joy reaches so deep a place in men's hearts as a sorrow does; defeat touches men in a way that victory does not. More heart, for some reason, gets put into a devout sigh than into a doxology. "Sorrow is better than laughter," said the Preacher, "for by the sadness of the countenance the heart is made better."

That is the meaning of tribulation; that is the deep philosophy underlying the event around which our thoughts cluster tearfully and prayerfully this morning. "Tearfully and prayerfully!" you see how easy and natural the sequence. Of course, we can do but a little in the way of understanding what in particular God means by this or by any other of his afflictive dispensations.

God is his own interpreter, not you or I. Each event has references forward and backward too reticent for us to detect or trace. We do not want to belittle the event or the holy author of it by translating it all out into the terms of our common thinking. We love to think of the sea as sloping down into the globe without trying to picture the deep, mysterious bottom upon which it rests; and of the mountains as spiring up into the everlasting blue without attempting to delineate that utmost finial of rock where the nether firmament passes into the upper.

And so of this great mountainous sorrow, for which

our hearts, even more than our streets and churches, are craped: we want to lay no profane hands upon its vastness, nor to make the event small by trying to make it near and intelligible.

An event, so vast that under the shadow of it the whole civilized and Christianized world to-day stands tearful and devout, is one whose truest meaning it lies beyond the scope of our ken either to detect or suspect. It lies deeply locked in the counsels of God. We do not understand it. "God is his own interpreter and he will make it plain." "*Will* make it plain." Not now, but then and there. And so we are content to leave it unexplained, inscrutable. We yield ourselves to the mystery of it, to be softened and chastened by it.

And yet the chastening, in order to be chastening, must lie along side of the thought of the divineness of this strange tragedy. A human and bad element there was in it certainly. But to have a holy discipline wrought in us by it, we shall have to recognize with exactly the same distinctness a divine and righteous element. We have got to feel that in it God teaches us, and stand face to face with him in the transaction. If it is explained as the pure outcome of impersonal historic forces, it fails to touch that spot in us when we cherish the sanctities.

Equally so if we treat it only as the fruitage of Guiteau's crazed brain or depraved heart. This is for us an infamous tragedy because man was in it, but a holy tragedy because God was in it. And our hearts cannot be sufficiently grateful that it is in this latter character, more than in the former, than men are feeling it and contemplating it, now in just these plaintive days through which we are moving; that the sense that God's hand was in the act has sweetened our hearts from all the bitterness incident to the remembrance that Guiteau's hand was in it.

And if, when the turf has begun to grow green over the dust of the dear and honored dead, if then with seriousness, but without show of malignity or of spite, and by quiet process of law, wisely applied and soberly executed, the criminal shall suffer what he shall then be adjudged to deserve, it will be the consummating touch put to a picture which in point of grandeur and moral sublimity is unmatched in the history of this or of any people. And so we have brought this matter in our hearts and in our discourse into the House of God this morning, for the reason that God is in the event and we want to find and feel him there.

Such a visitation as this, as we have seen, is the means by which God works in men tenderness of heart, and so opens the way for the cleansing and strengthening of character, individual and national. The months that have elapsed since the 2d of July have been long ones and tender. They have been strange months. They have worked strangely.

I do not know how to explain the temper of mind that prevails to-day, here, elsewhere. I looked, that waiting Monday afternoon, upon the cottage at Elberon without understanding why I was unmanned by it. I have read the sad story from day to day, gathering as it has each morning a new burden of pathos, without understanding the unbidden tears.

And it is so everywhere. Men are full of heart: their thoughts work quietly and deeply. I do not think there have been any two months in history that quite parallel them. Feelings have greatly fluctuated; and so our spirits have been strangely limbered, mellowed by them. We have become less and less embittered, but more and more burdened and stricken. Each new aspect of the case seems only to have been shaped in a way to let the blade down a little farther into the quick: no feature but what has given a little added tension to the strained chords of our sympathy.

For almost three months God has been steadily holding us all against the grinding-stone of a grave and anxious uncertainty. Mr. Garfield and his wife and children have somehow slipped, each of them, into a dear sort of membership in our own families. The sick-bed has been set up in each household.

We have also watched with him. In his affliction we have been afflicted. Our spirits have stood under his, trying to buoy it up. These months have in this way wrought in us a tenderness that only the eloquence of an event could have availed to do.

And now, friends, this singular mellowness of mind into which the tearful persuasiveness of the weeks has been gently leading us is capacity for all kinds of beautiful outgrowth. When, to-morrow afternoon, the world turns back once more from the newly-made grave in Lakeview the critical question will be: What will the world do with its sorrow?

What is going to become of its sorrow? Nothing dries sooner than a tear. Of course, the sorrow cannot remain sorrow. It is not in the nature of things. The heart could not bear it. Even nature is wise enough to dress in green its crumbling tenements of vegetable and stone. The decaying trunk converts itself into moss, and so frames life out of death and beauty out of despair.

And decayed hopes ought certainly to do as much. The sorrow cannot remain sorrow, but it can pass over into shapes that shall be fixed, and crystallize into jewels of high resolve and firm loyalty that shall be a permanent possession and a perpetual joy. And the vast possibilities of our sorrow are evidenced by certain practical results that the sorrow has already yielded. For our encouragement I want to notice two or three of these.

These last years have been a season in which irreligion and unfaith have been displaying themselves with rather more than usual resoluteness and bravado. Christian scholarship has taxed itself to the utmost to dislodge this unfaith. You have seen, perhaps, what is sometimes called a cloud-banner: a little pennon of mist that in certain conditions of the atmosphere will gather above a mountain summit, and cling there in the face of the boldest attempts of the sun to dissolve it or of the winds to dislodge it. It will not be brushed away. Shadowy and almost impalpable it maintains itself on its bleak watch-tower with a pertinacity at once grim and defiant.

But by-and-by subtle and invisible influences begin to pervade the sky: the wind shifts, perhaps, or the temper of the air is in some silent and stealthy way modified; and now the shapes of floating vapor soften their edges, their borders are combed out into a fleecy fringe, the cloud-banner is noiselessly furled, and the bare mountain peak stands out under the sunshine and the blue.

That is the very sublimity of gentleness. And it is in that way that God works, and has been working all about among us during these disciplinary months. He has not met scepticism with theism, as we do in our arguing; but the climate that was in men, and that by its very nature condensed into unfaith and unreligion, he gently displaced by another climate, in which unfaith just as easily dissolved.

And so by the breath of his spirit and the baptism of an event, he has accomplished by a persuasion aimed at the heart what Christian scholars have not availed to do with their noisier logic addressed to the head. "Man's necessity has been God's opportunity."

And so in the hour of their sad exigency, at the bidding of the government, at the instigation of the press, secular as well as religious, but most of all at the impulse of a holy and devout longing for God's deliverance, men slipped into the churches—even those to whom the church was an unwonted place—or in a still and unostentatious way cried "O God!" in the solitary sanctuary of their own spirits. And that is what the boasted atheism of the nineteenth century does! Cries up to God that he would save the sick man by the sea! There is gladness enough in that fact, of a nation bowed in prayer before our Christian God, almost to turn our Requiem into a Te Deum, and to make of our churches temples of thanksgiving, even though sable with the trappings of our woe.

Nor (most significant of all) has God's refusal to answer the nation according to the specific form of its request chilled by one degree the religious fervor with which the request was presented. If we can accord any confidence to the countenances that men are wearing, to the words they are speaking, to the thoughts to which they are giving expression through the medium of the press, home and foreign, the bitter cup has only chastened men into profounder devoutness, and, so far from embittering them toward God and belief in God, has only strengthened the texture of their faith and drawn them yet further beneath the shadow of the divine wing.

As it seems to me, it was one of the most thrilling passages in the whole dramatic story, that holy hush in the thronged streets of Washington, as the funeral cortège was moving toward the Capitol, when the Marine Band began slowly to play " Nearer, my God, to Thee! " And we shall turn away from the grave to-morrow, reflecting how blessed and profound is even the unconscious Christianity of the American people.

And then there are other results that have been already wrought that only show how the sweetest of flowers may unfold from the bitterest of buds. It has been an immensely nationalizing event. Around Mr. Garfield's bedside, and now around his grave, is no North, no South, no East, no West. Not since the war, and not since a long time before the war, have all the sections of our country come so distinctly under the pressure of one heart-beat. All the life-currents of our people, just now, are driven by a single pulse. We have prayed for him as a nation, we have watched with him as a nation, we are weeping over him as a nation, and now that he has passed yonder he shines with purest light among the stars of our national firmament.

In this way chords of national sympathy and fellowship have been struck that had almost forgotten to vibrate. We have learned that the music is not all out of the strings, and have discovered, it must seem, that if we are all to become thoroughly, permanently, and nationally one again it must be not along the avenue of our lower but along the avenue of our best impulses, tuned as now to a key-note high and grand enough to stir the best music that slumbers in every several heart of the nation.

And we have gotten a little closer to one another in a religious way, also, in these days of tender supplication and cross-bearing. There has been no sect in our prayers. We all came before the throne of mercy with only the thought of him we were praying for and Him we were praying to. For the time that was all there was in our religion. In these two facts we all touched one another. We all became in an unusual way members of one another. "To pray together" (so some one has said) "is the most touching paternity of hope and sympathy which man can contract on earth."

We have felt, kneeling together around our national altar, that there are lines along which even Protestant and Catholic, Jew and Gentile draw into coalition with one another. We have been reminded that cathedral, synagogue, and church all build down into the same soil, and all spin up into the same heaven.

The continents, too, have been made nearer. The bells on both sides of the Atlantic are tolling one requiem to-day, and the American and the English heart are drawing near to God in one prayer and one psalm. We lament sometimes the slow extension of the Kingdom of Christ, but when we contemplate the relations subsisting between nations, as a matter of course, in the old savage centuries, we are made to realize something of the achievements of the Gospel of Peace, that the subjects of one realm can with cordial tears supplicate the Throne of Grace in behalf of another realm, foreign to it, and rival with it.

And then this stress of mind, too, has been working within us deep and holy contempt for all kinds of political impurity. These months have been to us, in our political relations and ambitions, months of schooling. The country had been staggering under the burden of an army of office-seekers, scrambling for preferment. The shot fired in the depot at Washington was God's voice calling the nation to order. It was recognized as such, recognized abroad and recognized at home.

Business has gone on as usual since the 2d of July, but there has been very little politics. The people are not in a mood to bear it. The people have had a revelation; they have heard a voice. We have learned to recognize that the 2d of July was the legitimate outcome of what was just as actually existent before the 2d of July, only without having come yet to its final and loathsome demonstration. We have only been eating the fruit. It is bitter, and in that fruit we have learned to understand the essential quality of the tree. There are some things that do not advertise their essential badness till they have come to their growth.

Guiteau is simply the naked, filthy incarnation of political place-seeking. His case simply publishes the

possibilities of evil that lurk in every man that has a
mind to make country servant to his private interest.
The air has been cleared. Eyes have been opened.
We see in Guiteau the untinseled deformity of this
whole breed of political cormorants. In him the fact
has been shown to us without its disguises, and the
fact has been burned into the heart of the American
people by eighty days of waiting and weeping. "Almost all things are by the law purged with blood."
The precious blood has been shed, may it be applied
by us to the end that we may be cleansed.

And may this tenderness of the general heart go
on issuing—as it has already begun to do—go on issuing in completer consecration to country and to God,
prompting us to regard our civil obligations in the light
of Christian duties, to controvert every kind of political evil with Christian bravery and resoluteness, to
range ourselves with Christian alacrity on the side of
every force that makes for national righteousness, to
carry the interests of our country in tender and devout
hearts; especially to accord our hearty fellowship and
to yield our warmest sympathies to our new Executive
in the position of delicacy and difficulty in which he
now finds himself placed—these months have disciplined him just as they have disciplined us all—and to
prayerfully expect from him great and good things,
and to stand by him cordially in every effort of his
to administer this country justly and in the fear of God.

Above all, to hold ourselves in the mighty hand of
God; to recognize that above the catastrophes of life
and empire God abides in the quietness and strength of
his unfaltering purpose of wisdom and of grace, that

clouds may darken the earth but throw no shadow against the sky, and that enthroned above earthly vicissitudes and human administration, "the Lord reigneth."

Standing in imagination at the grave of the nation's dead, may we come more deeply than ever into the intimacies of God, and even while drinking the bitter cup have power and grace given unto us to say: "The Lord hath given, the Lord hath taken away: blessed be the name of the Lord."

Cummings, Amos J., an American politician and journalist, born at Conkling, N. Y., May 15, 1841. He entered a printing office at the age of twelve, remaining there till he joined the Federal Army in 1862. Retiring from military service as sergeant-major in 1864, he engaged in journalism, and until 1887 he occupied editorial positions upon " The Tribune " and " The Sun," in New York City. In that year he entered Congress, where he has since served continuously. He is the author of several books, such as " The Ziska Letters " and " The Sayings of Uncle Rufus."

ON THE NAVAL APPROPRIATION BILL.

DELIVERED IN THE HOUSE OF REPRESENTATIVES, MONDAY, APRIL 16, 1900.

MR. CHAIRMAN,—I would be untrue to myself if I did not congratulate the gentleman from Illinois who has just taken his seat upon the masterful showing which he has made in his report, and upon the conclusion of the arduous labors in committee that have accompanied the birth of this bill. That the committee itself did not come to a unanimous agreement is to me a matter of regret. I myself agree in some things with the minority and agree in others with the majority. But I believed it to be my duty, if I had any fight to make, to make it upon the floor of this House, as I have heretofore done, and I declined to sign the minority report.

Mr. Chairman, the past shows that a powerful navy for the American nation is a vital necessity. Without it we may become the prey of the robber nations of the earth; without a great navy, I will undertake to say, we to-day might be at war with Great Britain over the Alaska boundary. Her rapacity toward the Boers is due to her greed for gold; and there is as much gold in Alaska as in the Transvaal. It is the fact that we are prepared for war that saves us from trouble with the powers of Europe. From the days of the battle of Salamis down to the present a strong navy has been the safety of a maritime nation. It was the battle of Salamis that drove Xerxes from Greece, not the fight at the pass of Thermopylæ. It was the battle in the bay that sent him whirling back across the Hellespont into Asia, where he belonged.

When Hannibal invaded Italy and maintained himself there for seventeen years without re-enforcement, it was not the Roman legions that drove him to Africa; it was the Roman ships which conveyed Scipio's army there and forced Hannibal to follow it in a vain effort to defend Carthage. It was the navy that made Venice the supreme mistress of the commerce of the world for centuries. The Mediterranean Sea was practically a Venetian lake because of the Venetian navy.

It was her navy that afterward made Holland the mistress of the sea. And it was not until the English navy had been built to proper proportions that Van Tromp was compelled to pull down his broom and acknowledge its supremacy.

It was our navy that won the most brilliant victory in the Revolution. Admiral Paul Jones, in his fight with the " Serapis " and the " Countess of Scarborough " gave the Revolution an impetus that put behind our forefathers not only the sympathy of Europe, but substantial aid in the way of dollars and of French battleships.

Paul Jones, an American admiral, was the only man in either army or navy who had invaded England since the days of the battle of Hastings. The whole British coast was in alarm. He landed at different places and drew in plunder the same as the English themselves drew it in when they sacked the city of Pekin.

It was by the aid of the French navy that we achieved the final triumph of the American Revolution —the surrender of Cornwallis at Yorktown. Without the activity of the French fleet under the Comte de Grasse, Cornwallis would have escaped. A British fleet was hastening to his succor; but when its commander learned that a French fleet of superior force was already in the Chesapeake, it turned back to New York.

It was Nelson, and not Wellington, who was the leading factor in the downfall of Napoleon. The victories of the British navy at Aboukir, Copenhagen, Cape St. Vincent, and Trafalgar destroyed all his hopes. France was practically cut off from the rest of the world. Her commerce was utterly ruined, and she was compelled to feed upon herself until her resources were exhausted.

It was the American navy that gave us peace in the treaty of Ghent in the war of 1812. Hull had surrendered an American army at Detroit. Commodore Perry, within one hundred miles of that city, demolished a British fleet—the first time that American vessels had met an English fleet—and sent to Washington the immortal despatch, "We have met the enemy, and they are ours."

Scott had been driven back at Niagara and Lundy's Lane; Wilkinson had made a fiasco on the northern border; but the guns of the American navy were heard on Lake Champlain, where Commodore McDonough sent the English fleet to the bottom.

Washington, your own proud capital, had been captured by the British, and this building burned, our monuments defaced, the White House destroyed, your President became a fugitive in the forests of Virginia, but the victories of Decatur, of Commodore Stewart, of Bainbridge, and of old Isaac Hull in the "Constitution" were a sufficient recompense for the destruction of the city of Washington.

In only one instance in that war did the army achieve a victory, and that was at the Saranac, for the battle of New Orleans, it will be remembered, was fought long after the treaty of peace was signed.

The total destruction of the Turkish navy by the allied fleets of Navarino, rescued Greece from the clutches of the followers of the Prophet and restored to her her freedom.

It was the American navy that gave us the victory in the war with Mexico. Taylor had marched across the Nueces, across the Colorado, across the Rio Grande; he had taken Monterey; he had reached the plains of Buena Vista and wiped out Santa Anna's army; but it was Scott who went to the city of Mexico through the aid of the American navy, which bombarded the castle of San Juan de Ulloa and gave him a landing place at Vera Cruz.

It was the American navy that sounded the knell of doom for the Confederacy when gallant old Farragut broke the iron barrier, passed the forts of Jackson and St. Philip, and captured the city of New Orleans. And it was all done before McClellan left the Peninsula. The Confederacy was split in twain when the Mississippi was opened. The fate of the Confederacy was sealed the instant the ports of the South were declared under blockade by President Lincoln. If the Confederacy had had a navy, and if things had been more equal both on sea and on land, we should have had two nations in existence to-day where there is only one.

It was the navy, I may add, that won the Spanish war. I believe that if Schley and Sampson had been left to their own inspiration, or had received the orders that Dewey received, they would have gone into Santiago harbor without sending an army down there to storm San Juan and El Caney.

It was the navy, under Dewey, that destroyed the Spanish fleet and won the empire in the East; and it was the navy that finally brought proud Spain to her knees with her hands held upward, acknowledging her subjugation.

So, Mr. Chairman, I say that the navy is a vital necessity to the United States as well as to all other maritime nations. This vital necessity is recognized by the people of the country—north and south, east and west. The people to-day are clamoring for an increase of the navy because they know its usefulness, because they know it is a never-failing defender, because they know it is a never-failing aggressor, when war breaks out. In a multiplicity of ships there is safety.

Now, what have we done, and what are we doing, to carry out the wishes of the people? We have three battle-ships on the stocks, and no method of procuring armor for them. We have three more battle-ships and three armored cruisers authorized, and a string attached to each in the shape of a provision that they shall not be even contracted for unless the best armor manufactured can be obtained at $300 a ton. We propose to authorize in this bill the building of two more battle-ships, three more armored cruisers, and three protected cruisers. Shall there be a string attached to them also? Can men face their constituents after authorizing the construction of these battle-ships and cruisers, and then refusing to provide the money for furnishing the armor for them? Why, sir, it seems to me like voting for a declaration of war and refusing the funds necessary to carry on the war. I believe that the people demand to-day, not only the prompt construction of the ships already authorized, but also the construction of as many more vessels.

For nearly five years have some of these ships remained without armor. I well remember speeches on this floor in which we were told that we could get armor for $200 a ton. Very well; we tried it. No ships were built. The man wanted a twenty-year contract, with a pledge that a fleet of ships should be built each year, and went back on his promise; he could not furnish armor at $200 a ton. Then we reached a point where, after authorizing the construction of ships, we

attached a string to the authorization in another manner—this was June 10, 1896:

Provided, That the Secretary of the Navy is hereby
directed to examine into the actual cost of armor plate
and the price for the same which should be equitably
paid, and shall report the result of his investigation to
Congress at its next session, at a date not later than
January 1, 1897; and no contract for armor plate for
the vessels authorized by this act shall be made until
such report is made to Congress.

That was the condition then, and a similar condition
exists to-day. The ships are authorized by you, and
then you attach a string and by pulling it get no ships
at all. The ships are still unbuilt. We have gone
through a war since then, and not one of these ships
was built before war was declared, and not one was
available during the war. . . .

Mr. Chairman, at the next session of Congress you
provided that the price should not exceed $400 per ton
for armor inferior to the Krupp armor, but at the last
session of Congress you provided that superior armor
should not be obtained unless it could be had at $300 a
ton—an impossible price. If you pay $400 a ton for
the old harveyized armor, certainly the new Krupp
armor is worth at least as much, and yet you limited
the price to $300 a ton. In other words, you provide
that the best armor shall be furnished at $100 per ton
less than the sum you have expressed yourselves willing to pay for inferior armor. You practically determined, as I said before, that you would authorize the

ships, but you took special care to prevent the building of them. . . .

I think that it is time, Mr. Chairman, that this country understood that the lives of its sailors, its marines, and others connected with the naval service have been endangered and menaced when this government found itself involved in war by the action of Congress in regard to this question of armor plate. I say that the men who fought with Dewey at Manila and with Schley at Santiago are entitled to the best protection the government can give, by placing the best armor on its battle-ships that can be made, by metallic furniture, and by all other life-saving devices.

We authorize two battle-ships here to-day, and six cruisers, and here is the same old story and the same old string over and over again. We will not contract for them, gentlemen say, until we build an armor-plate factory and can manufacture the armor for them ourselves. We will delay the construction three years more, taking in the three battle-ships and three cruisers authorized in the last session, and the three battle-ships under contract, authorized in the first session of the Fifty-fifth Congress, thus making a total delay of eight years in the construction of some of these ships. On the score of alleged economy you are opposing expenditure that the world recognizes as an absolute necessity. . . .

Now, Mr. Chairman, I disagreed with the policy of the Naval Committee in some respects, but I propose to stand by it as far as my conscience will allow. I disagreed with the committee when they refused to provide for the building of gunboats. The Secretary of the Navy had asked for the construction of thirteen gunboats. When Admiral Dewey came before the committee he testified that he thought he would rather have battle-ships than gunboats. We had captured four Spanish gunboats when Manila was taken—that is, Dewey had raised the wrecks. Since then we have bought a lot of little gunboats—some not as large as canal-boats—from the Spanish government. Admiral Dewey, while before the committee, said he thought we did not want any more gunboats, and he would take two or three battle-ships in the place of them. Well, the committee gave him two battle-ships, although the Secretary had not asked for them; but while Secretary Long was before the committee he said he would have asked for them if he had thought he could get them.

Now, I believe in gunboats. I think that boats the size of the " Helena " and vessels of that class are the very thing that the nation needs. We must continue a protectorate over Cuba at least until they form a government, and it looks to me now as though they would not be able to form one for the next five years, and we must have ships for service on the coast of Porto Rico and among the islands of Hawaii. There is nothing so useful in such waters as gunboats. We certainly need them for the Philippines. Those bought and captured from the Spaniards may suffice for the present, as Admiral Dewey suggests. I am in favor of keeping these gunboats in the Philippines just as long as there is a rebel in arms in those islands.

When the islands are conquered, I am in favor of treating them exactly as we treat Cuba. They were both in rebellion against Spain, and of the two possibly the Filipinos were a little more gallant in fighting the Spaniards—at least fully as gallant as were the Cubans —and they are entitled to the same treatment. Sure it is that Aguinaldo and his Tagals supported Dewey's attack on Manila as heartily as did Garcia the assault of Shafter and Wheeler on Santiago. Gunboats are needed there, and are certainly needed elsewhere. I think it unwise to lop them off entirely in view of the recommendation of Secretary Long. We ought at least to split the difference with him and give him half of what he asked for.

I differed with the committee on the question of sheathed ships. While they took Dewey's word with regard to the battle-ships and gunboats, they refused to take his word as to sheathed ships. He said that a sheathed ship would run two years and maintain her speed without docking, whereas an unsheathed ship had to be docked at least once in every nine months. He acknowledged that the "Charleston" was lost on a sunken reef in the Philippine Islands because she was not sheathed. When asked whether, in his opinion, she could have been saved if she had been sheathed, he replied that at that same time a British war vessel ran upon an unknown reef and was pulled off in safety because she was sheathed. That seemed to me conclusive evidence that the battle-ships which we were authorizing in this bill should be sheathed.

But I compromised. We agreed to leave the matter to the Secretary of the Navy, and if the Secretary thinks it best to have them in the docks once in nine months instead of once every two years he may sit

5—6

down upon the project. I am willing to trust John D. Long, and I believe the people are willing to do so. . . .

Now, Mr. Chairman, the committee was unable to agree as to the question of building ships at the navy-yards. Well, there is a great deal to be said on both sides of this question. I thought that with three battle-ships and three armored cruisers not contracted for, and with two more battle-ships and six more cruisers, armored and protected, but not contracted for, we could afford at least to again try the experiment of building them in the navy-yards. It is a favorable time for doing so.

The Secretary of the Navy, however, is opposed to it. He says they will cost twice as much as vessels built elsewhere and take twice the time for construction. He also thought the yards would be more or less susceptible to political influences.

Possibly he is right. He undoubtedly knows far more about that than I do. I have no doubt that it will cost more to build these ships in the navy-yards than it would to build them under contract, and for this reason: The work of the government is done under the eight-hour system; the contractors work their men from nine to ten, eleven to twelve hours. So that of necessity it must cost more to build the ships in the navy-yards than it would under contract. But I took occasion to get a statement from Captain Sigsbee concerning the construction of vessels in the English, the French, and the German navy-yards. The period covered is approximately five years for France and Germany, and a little less for England, but in all cases the period for dockyard and private construction is the same. The rate of wages was comparatively the same in both the government and private yards. It took much longer to construct the vessels in the government than in the private yards. . . .

My friend from Illinois referred to the German navy. That navy is to-day within 2,700 tons of the strength of the American navy, and that is what made Admiral Diedrich so cocky in the Bay of Manila.

The Emperor of Germany is " some pumpkins; " he " feels his oats." For two years he has been struggling to surpass this country in the size of its navy, and to-day in the German Reichstag a bill is pending, which will undoubtedly pass, doubling the size of the German navy—increasing her tonnage over 400,000 tons. I think that is a strong argument in favor of our building the ships we have already authorized as soon as possible, and of authorizing the building of as many others as we can afford to pay for.

I was not unsusceptible to the inquiry made by the chairman of the great Committee on Appropriations, while my friend from Illinois was occupying the floor. He is one of the men who hold the purse-strings of the nation. He takes acount of stock in every session of Congress, and in view of the great volume of appropriations made at each session he wants to cut his cloth according to its length. He wants to know where " he is at," and he received the desired information, and in the same breath told you he was not opposed to your bill.

Nor are the people opposed to it. They will tolerate no more delay in this armor-plate matter. You can not take up a newspaper from the St. Croix to the Rio

Grande or from Puget Sound to Key Biscayne Bay
without finding paragraphs advocating the prompt increase of the navy. They recognize the fact that the
bombardment of New York by an enemy would entail
treble the cost of our entire navy.

I have always advocated its increase. No man in
this House rejoiced more than I rejoiced when men
from the South dominated the committee, and Mr.
Herbert, of Alabama, was made its chairman. Talk
about politics! You should have been here in the
Fifty-third Congress, when the leader of the minority,
the gentleman from Maine [Mr. Boutelle], used two
hours of the time of the committee in general debate,
taking in forty minutes of my time, using it in denunciation of the South, charging you with being inimical
to the navy. In the twenty minutes left I demonstrated the secret of your former enmity and prophe-
sied a great change. . . .

If we are to have an increased navy it is time to stop
talking and begin work. Authorizing it will not build
it; you must provide armor and do it promptly. Either
do this or stop the authorization of vessels. Do one
thing or the other. I believe that the people of the
country, ten to one, demand a decrease in the army and
an increase in the navy; and as long as I remain in this
House I intend to voice that demand.

Moody, Dwight L., a famous American evangelist, born at Northfield, Mass., February 5, 1837; died there, December 22, 1899. In early youth he was a clerk in a store, and, removing to Chicago in 1856, he soon engaged in missionary work there. A few years later he began to hold revival meetings, and, with the noted singer, Ira Sankey, he made several tours through the United States and Great Britain, holding revival services, often in the largest buildings available for that purpose, which were attended by vast throngs of people. He never entered the ministry, but at intervals throughout his life preached at huge revival meetings. He was not a thinker, and his oratory was unpolished, but his great earnestness lent impressiveness to what was said, and his influence over the emotional and unintellectual among his hearers was very great. Moody established schools at Northfield and Chicago, and was the author of several religious works.

WHAT THINK YE OF CHRIST?

I SUPPOSE there is no one here who has not thought more or less about Christ. You have heard about him, and read about him, and heard men preach about him. For eighteen hundred years men have been talking about him and thinking about him; and some have their minds made up about who he is, and doubtless some have not. And although all these years have rolled away, this question comes up, addressed to each of us, to-day, " What think ye of Christ? "

I do not think why it should not be thought a proper question for one man to put to another. If I were to ask you what you think of any of your prominent men, you would already have your mind made up about him. If I were to ask you what you thought of your noble Queen, you would speak right out and tell me your opinion in a minute.

If I were to ask about your prime minister, you would tell me freely what you had for or against him. And why should not people make up their minds about the Lord Jesus Christ, and take their stand for or against him? If you think well of him, why not speak well of him and range yourselves on his side? And if you think ill of him, and believe him to be an imposter, and that he did not die to save the world, why not lift up your voice and say you are against him? It would be a happy day for Christianity if men would just take sides—if we could know positively who was really for him and who was against him.

It is of very little importance what the world thinks of any one else. The Queen and the statesman, the peers and the princes, must soon be gone. Yes; it matters little, comparatively, what we think of them. Their lives can interest only a few; but every living soul on the face of the earth is concerned with this Man. The question for the world is, " What think ye of Christ? "

I do not ask you what you think of the Established Church, or of the Presbyterians, or the Baptists, or the Roman Catholics; I do not ask you what you think of this minister or that, of this doctrine or that; but I want to ask you what you think of the living person of Christ?

I should like to ask, Was he really the Son of God— the great God-Man? Did he leave heaven and come down to this world for a purpose? Was it really to seek and to save? I should like to begin with the manger, and follow him up through the thirty-three years he was here upon earth. I should ask you what you think of his coming into this world and being born in a manger when it might have been a palace; why he left the grandeur and the glory of heaven, and the royal retinue of angels; why he passed by palaces and crowns and dominion and came down here alone?

I should like to ask what you think of him as a teacher. He spake as never man spake. I should like to take him up as a preacher. I should like to bring you to that mountain-side, that we might listen to the words as they fall from his gentle lips. Talk about the preachers of the present day! I would rather a thousand times be five minutes at the feet of Christ than listen a lifetime to all the wise men in the world. He used just to hang truth upon everything. Yonder is a sower, a fox, a bird, and he just gathers the truth around them, so that you cannot see a fox, a sower, or a bird without thinking what Jesus said. Yonder is a lily of the valley, you cannot see it without thinking of his words, "They toil not, neither do they spin."

He makes the little sparrow chirping in the air preach to us. How fresh those wonderful sermons are, how they live to-day! How we love to tell them to our children, how the children love to hear! "Tell me a story about Jesus," how often we hear it; how the little ones love his sermons! No story-book in the world will ever interest them like the stories that he told. And yet how profound he was; how he puzzled the wise men; how the scribes and the Pharisees could never fathom him! Oh, do you not think he was a wonderful preacher?

I should like to ask you what you think of him as a physician. A man would soon have a reputation as a doctor if he could cure as Christ did. No case was ever brought to him but what he was a match for. He had but to speak the word, and disease fled before him. Here comes a man covered with leprosy.

"Lord, if thou wilt thou canst make me clean," he cries.

"I will," says the Great Physician, and in an instant the leprosy is gone. The world has hospitals for incurable diseases; but there were no incurable diseases with him.

Now, see him in the little home at Bethany, binding up the wounded hearts of Martha and Mary, and tell me what you think of him as a comforter. He is a husband to the widow and a father to the fatherless. The weary may find a resting-place upon that breast, and the friendless may reckon him their friend. He never varies, he never fails, he never dies. His sympathy is ever fresh, his love is ever free. O widow and orphans, O sorrowing and mourning, will you not thank God for Christ the Comforter?

But these are not the points I wish to take up. Let us go to those who knew Christ, and ask what they thought of him. If you want to find out what a man is nowadays, you inquire about him from those who know him best. I do not wish to be partial; we will go to his enemies, and to his friends. We will ask them, What think ye of Christ? We will ask his friends and his enemies. If we only went to those who liked him, you would say:

"Oh, he is so blind; he thinks so much of the man that he can't see his faults. You can't get anything out of him unless it be in his favor; it is a one-sided affair altogether."

So we shall go in the first place to his enemies, to those who hated him, persecuted him, cursed and slew him. I shall put you in the jury-box, and call upon them to tell us what they think of him.

First, among the witnesses, let us call upon the Pharisees. We know how they hated him. Let us put a few questions to them. "Come, Pharisees, tell us what you have against the Son of God, What do you think of Christ?" Hear what they say! "This man receiveth sinners." What an argument to bring against him! Why, it is the very thing that makes us love him. It is the glory of the gospel. He receives sinners. If he had not, what would have become of us? Have you nothing more to bring against him than this? Why, it is one of the greatest compliments that was ever paid him. Once more: "When he was hanging on the tree, you had this to say of him, 'He saved others, but he could not save himself and save us too.'" So he laid down his own life for yours and mine. Yes, Pharisees, you have told the truth for once in your lives! He saved others. He died for others. He was a ransom for many; so it is quite true what you think of him—He saved others, himself he cannot save.

Now, let us call upon Caiaphas. Let him stand up here in his flowing robes; let us ask him for his evidence. "Caiaphas, you were chief priest when Christ was tried; you were president of the Sanhedrim; you were in the council-chamber when they found him guilty; you yourself condemned him. Tell us; what did the witnesses say? On what grounds did you judge him? What testimony was brought against him?" "He hath spoken blasphemy," says Caiaphas. "He said, 'Hereafter shall ye see the Son of Man sitting on the right hand of power, and coming in the clouds of heaven.' When I heard that, I found him guilty of blasphemy; I rent my mantle and condemned him to death." Yes, all that they had against him was that he was the Son of God; and they slew him for the promise of his coming for his bride!

Now let us summon Pilate. Let him enter the witness-box.

"Pilate, this man was brought before you; you examined him; you talked with him face to face; what think you of Christ?"

"I find no fault in him," says Pilate. "He said he was the King of the Jews, [just as he wrote it over the cross]; but I find no fault in him." Such is the testimony of the man who examined him! And, as he stands there, the centre of a Jewish mob, there comes along a man, elbowing his way in haste. He rushes up to Pilate, and, thrusting out his hand, gives him a message. He tears it open; his face turns pale as he reads—"Have thou nothing to do with this just man, for I have suffered many things this day in a dream because of him." It is from Pilate's wife—her testimony to Christ. You want to know what his enemies thought of him? You want to know what a heathen thought? Well, here it is, "no fault in him;" and the wife of a heathen, "this just man!"

And now, look—in comes Judas. He ought to make a good witness. Let us address him. "Come, tell us, Judas, what think ye of Christ? You knew the master well; you sold him for thirty pieces of silver; you betrayed him with a kiss; you saw him perform those miracles; you were with him in Jerusalem. In Bethany, when he summoned up Lazarus, you were there. What think you of him?" I can see him as he comes into the presence of the chief priests; I can hear the money ring as he dashes it upon the table, "I have betrayed innocent blood!" Here is the man who betrayed him, and this is what he thinks of him! Yes, those who were guilty of his death put their testimony on record that he was an innocent man.

Let us take the centurion who was present at the execution. He had charge of the Roman soldiers. He had told them to make him carry his cross; he had given orders for the nails to be driven into his feet and hands, for the spear to be thrust in his side. Let the centurion come forward. "Centurion, you had charge of the executioners; you saw that the order for his death was carried out; you saw him die; you heard him speak upon the cross. Tell us, what think you of Christ?" Hark! Look at him; he is smiting his breast as he cries, "Truly, this was the Son of God!"

I might go to the thief upon the cross, and ask what he thought of him. At first he railed upon him and reviled him. But then he thought better of it: "This man hath done nothing amiss," he says.

I might go further. I might summon the very devils

themselves and ask them for their testimony. Have they anything to say of him? Why, the very devils called him the Son of God! In Mark we have the unclean spirit crying, " Jesus, thou Son of the most High God." Men say, " Oh, I believe Christ to be the Son of God, and because I believe it intellectually I shall be saved." I tell you the devils did that. And they did more than that, they trembled.

Let us bring in his friends. We want you to hear their evidence. Let us call that prince of preachers. Let us hear the forerunner; none ever preached like this man—this man who drew all Jerusalem and all Judæa into the wilderness to hear him; this man who burst upon the nations like the flash of a meteor. Let John the Baptist come with his leathern girdle and his hairy coat, and let him tell us what he thinks of Christ. His words, though they were echoed in the wilderness of Palestine, are written in the Book forever, " Behold the Lamb of God which taketh away the sin of the world!" This is what John the Baptist thought of him. " I bare record that he is the Son of God." No wonder he drew all Jerusalem and Judæa to him, because he preached Christ. And whenever men preach Christ, they are sure to have plenty of followers.

Let us bring in Peter, who was with him on the mount of transfiguration, who was with him the night he was betrayed. Come, Peter, tell us what you think of Christ. Stand in this witness-box and testify of him. You denied him once. You said, with a curse, you did not know him. Was it true, Peter? Don't you know him? " Know him!" I can imagine Peter saying: " It was a lie I told then. I *did* know him."

Afterward I can hear him charging home their guilt upon these Jerusalem sinners. He calls him "both Lord and Christ." Such was the testimony on the day of Pentecost. "God hath made that same Jesus both Lord and Christ." And tradition tells us that when they came to execute Peter he felt he was not worthy to die in the way his Master died, and he requested to be crucified with his head downward. So much did Peter think of him!

Now let us hear from the beloved disciple John. He knew more about Christ than any other man. He has laid his head on his Saviour's bosom. He had heard the throbbing of that loving heart. Look into his gospel if you wish to know what he thought of him.

Matthew writes of him as the Royal King come from his throne. Mark writes of him as the servant, and Luke of the Son of Man. John takes up his pen, and, with one stroke, forever settles the question of Unitarianism. He goes right back before the time of Adam. "In the beginning was the Word, and the Word was with God, and the Word was God." Look into Revelation. He calls him "the bright and the Morning Star." So John thought well of him—because he knew him well.

We might bring in Thomas, the doubting disciple. You doubted him, Thomas? You would not believe he had risen, and you put your fingers into the wound in his side. What do you think of him?

"My Lord and my God!" says Thomas.

Then go over to Decapolis and you will find Christ has been there casting out devils. Let us call the men of that country and ask what they think of him. "He hath done all things well," they say.

But we have other witnesses to bring in. Take the persecuting Saul, once one of the worst of his enemies. Breathing out threatenings he meets him. "Saul, Saul, why persecutest thou me?" says Christ. He might have added, "What have I done to you? Have I injured you in any way? Did I not come to bless you? Why do you treat me thus, Saul?" And then Saul asks, "Who art thou, Lord?"

"I am Jesus of Nazareth, whom thou persecutest." You, see he was not ashamed of his name; although he had been in heaven, "I am Jesus of Nazareth." What a change did that one interview make to Paul! A few years after we hear him say, "I have suffered the loss of all things, and do count them but dross that I may win Christ." Such a testimony to the Saviour!

But I shall go still further. I shall go away from earth into the other world. I shall summon the angels and ask what they think of Christ. They saw him in the bosom of the Father before the world was. Before the dawn of creation; before the morning stars sang together, he was there. They saw him leave the throne and come down to the manger. What a scene for them to witness! Ask these heavenly beings what they thought of him then. For once they are permitted to speak; for once the silence of heaven is broken. Listen to their song on the plains of Bethlehem, "Behold, I bring you good tidings of great joy, which shall be to all people. For unto you is born this day, in the city of David, a Saviour, which is Christ the Lord." He leaves the throne to save the world. Is it a wonder the angels thought well of him?

Then there are the redeemed saints—they that see him face to face. Here on earth he was never known, no one seemed really to be acquainted with him; but he was known in that world where he had been from the foundation. What do they think of him there? If we could hear from heaven we should hear a shout which would glorify and magnify his name. We are told that when John was in the Spirit on the Lord's Day, and being caught up, he heard a shout around him, ten thousand times ten thousand, and thousands and thousands of voices, "Worthy is the Lamb that was slain, to receive power, and riches, and wisdom, and strength, and honor, and glory, and blessing!" Yes, he is worthy of all this. Heaven cannot speak too well of him. Oh, that earth would take up the echo and join with heaven in singing, "Worthy to receive power, and riches, and wisdom, and strength, and honor, and glory, and blessing!"

But there is still another witness, a higher still. Some think that the God of the Old Testament is the Christ of the New. But when Jesus came out of Jordan, baptized by John, there came a voice from heaven. God the Father spoke. It was his testimony to Christ: "This is my beloved Son, in whom I am well pleased." Ah, yes! God the Father thinks well of the Son. And if God is well pleased with him, so ought we. If the sinner and God are well pleased with Christ, then the sinner and God can meet. The moment you say, as the Father said, "I am well pleased with him," and accept him, you are wedded to God. Will you not believe the testimony? Will you not believe this witness, this last of all, the Lord of hosts, the King of kings himself? Once more he repeats it, so that all may know it. With Peter and James and John, on the mount of transfiguration, he cries again, "This is my beloved Son; hear him." And that voice went echoing and re-echoing through Palestine, through all the earth from sea to sea; yes, that voice is echoing still, Hear him! Hear him!

My friend, will you hear him to-day? Hark! what is he saying to you? "Come unto me, all ye that labor and are heavy laden, and I will give you rest. Take my yoke upon you and learn of me; for I am meek and lowly in heart; and ye shall find rest unto your souls. For my yoke is easy, and my burden is light." Will you not think well of such a Saviour? Will you not believe in him? Will you not trust in him with all your heart and mind? Will you not live for him? If he laid down his life for us, is it not the least we can do to lay down ours for him? If he bore the Cross and died on it for me, ought I not to be willing to take it up for him? Oh, have we not reason to think well of him? Do you think it is right and noble to lift up your voice against such a Saviour? Do you think it is just to cry, "Crucify him! crucify him!"? Oh, may God help all of us to glorify the Father, by thinking well of his only-begotten Son.

Brooks, Phillips, a celebrated American clergyman and pulpit orator, born in Boston, Mass., December 13, 1835; died there, January 23, 1893. He studied theology, and, entering the Episcopal ministry, he was rector of the Church of the Advent, Philadelphia, 1859–60, and of Holy Trinity church, in the same city, 1862–69. In the last named year he was called to Trinity church, Boston, of which he continued the rector until elected to the bishopric of Massachusetts in 1891. While still in Philadelphia, he had acquired a more than local reputation as an eloquent, forcible preacher, and long before his death he had become the most eminent clergyman in the Episcopal Church, if not in the United States. As a pulpit orator he was well known in England also, having preached in many important churches there. He was a man of the broadest sympathies and untiring in the duties of his profession. His delivery was rapid, and his manner intensely earnest, while the magnetic quality of his preaching attracted crowds to hear him throughout his ministerial career. Some ten or more volumes of his sermons and addresses have been published.

ABRAHAM LINCOLN.*

" He chose David also his servant, and took him away from the sheepfolds; that he might feed Jacob his people, and Israel his inheritance. So he fed them with a faithful and true heart, and ruled them prudently with all his power."—Ps. lxxviii, 71–73.

WHILE I speak to you to-day, the body of the President who ruled this people is lying, honored and loved, in our city. It is impossible with that sacred presence in our midst for me to stand and speak of ordinary

* Sermon preached in Philadelphia while the body of the President was lying in the city.

topics which occupy the pulpit. I must speak of him to-day; and I therefore undertake to do what I had intended to do at some future time, to invite you to study with me the character of Abraham Lincoln, the impulses of his life, and the causes of his death. I know how hard it is to do it rightly, how impossible it is to do it worthily. But I shall speak with confidence because I speak to those who love him, and whose ready love will fill out the deficiencies in a picture which my words will weakly try to draw.

We take it for granted, first of all, that there is an essential connection between Mr. Lincoln's character and his violent and bloody death. It is no accident, no arbitrary decree of Providence. He lived as he did, and he died as he did, because he was what he was.

The more we see of events, the less we come to believe in any fate or destiny except the destiny of character. It will be our duty, then, to see what there was in the character of our great President that created the history of his life and at last produced the catastrophe of his cruel death. After the first trembling horror, the first outburst of indignant sorrow, has grown calm, these are the questions which we are bound to ask and answer.

It is not necessary for me even to sketch the biography of Mr. Lincoln. He was born in Kentucky fifty-six years ago, when Kentucky was a pioneer State. He lived, as boy and man, the hard and needy life of a backwoodsman, a farmer, a river boatman, and, finally, by his own efforts at self-education, of an active, respected, influential citizen, in the half-organized and manifold interests of a new and energetic community. From his boyhood up he lived in direct and vigorous contact with men and things, not as in older States and easier conditions with words and theories; and both his moral convictions and his intellectual opinions gathered from that contact a supreme degree of that character by which men knew him, that character which is the most distinctive possession of the best American nature, that almost indescribable quality which we call in general clearness or truth and which appears in the physical structure as health, in the moral constitution as honesty, in the mental structure as sagacity, and in the region of active life as practicalness.

This one character, with many sides, all shaped by the same essential force and testifying to the same inner influences, was what was powerful in him and decreed for him the life he was to live and the death he was to die. We must take no smaller view than this of what he was.

Even his physical conditions are not to be forgotten in making up his character. We make too little always of the physical; certainly we make too little of it here if we lose out of sight the strength and muscular activity, the power of doing and enduring, which the backwoods-boy inherited from generations of hard-living ancestors and appropriated for his own by a long discipline of bodily toil. He brought to the solution of the question of labor in this country not merely a mind, but a body thoroughly in sympathy with labor, full of the culture of labor, bearing witness to the dignity and excellence of work in every muscle that work had toughened and every sense that work had made

clear and true. He could not have brought the mind
for his task so perfectly unless he had first brought the
body whose rugged and stubborn health was always
contradicting to him the false theories of labor and
always asserting the true.

As to the moral and mental powers which distinguished him, all embraceable under this general descrip-
tion of clearness of truth, the most remarkable thing is
the way in which they blend with one another, so that
it is next to impossible to examine them in separation.
A great many people have discussed very crudely
whether Abraham Lincoln was an intellectual man or
not; as if intellect were a thing always of the same
sort, which you could precipitate from the other constituents of a man's nature and weigh by itself, and
compare by pounds and ounces in this man with another.

The fact is, that in all the simplest characters that
line between the mental and moral natures is always
vague and indistinct. They run together, and in their
best combinations you are unable to discriminate, in
the wisdom which is their result, how much is moral
and how much is intellectual. You are unable to tell
whether in the wise acts and words which issue from
such a life there is more of the righteousness that
comes of a clear conscience, or of the sagacity that
comes of a clear brain. In more complex characters
and under more complex conditions the moral and the
mental lives come to be less healthily combined. They
co-operate, they help each other less. They come even
to stand over against each other as antagonists, till we
have that vague but most melancholy notion which per-

vades the life of all elaborate civilization, that goodness and greatness, as we call them, are not to be
looked for together; till we expect to see and so do see
a feeble and narrow conscientiousness on the one hand,
and a bad, unprincipled intelligence on the other, divid-
ing the suffrages of men.

It is the great boon of such characters as Mr. Lincoln's that they reunite what God has joined together
and man has put asunder. In him was vindicated the
greatness of real goodness and the goodness of real
greatness. The twain were one flesh. Not one of all
the multitudes who stood and looked up to him for direction with such a loving and implicit trust can tell you
to-day whether the wise judgment that he gave came
most from a strong head or a sound heart. If you ask
them, they are puzzled. There are men as good as he,
but they do bad things. There are men as intelligent
as he, but they do foolish things. In him goodness and
intelligence combined and made their best result of
wisdom.

For perfect truth consists not merely in the right
constituents of character, but in their right and intimate conjunction. This union of the mental and moral
into a life of admirable simplicity is what we most
admire in children; but in them it is unsettled and unpractical. But when it is preserved into manhood,
deepened into reliability and maturity, it is that glori-
fied childlikeness, that high and reverend simplicity,
which shames and baffles the most accomplished astute-
ness, and is chosen by God to fill his purposes when he
needs a ruler for his people, of faithful and true heart,
such as he had who was our President.

Another evident quality of such a character as this will be its freshness or newness, if we may so speak. Its freshness or readiness,—call it what you will,—its ablity to take up new duties and do them in a new way, will result of necessity from its truth and clearness. The simple natures and forces will always be the most pliant ones. Water bends and shapes itself to any channel. Air folds and adapts itself to each new figure. They are the simplest and the most infinitely active things in nature.

So this nature, in very virtue of its simplicity, must be also free, always fitting itself to each new need. It will always start from the most fundamental and eternal conditions, and work in the straightest even although they be the newest ways, to the present prescribed purpose. In one word, it must be broad and independent and radical. So that freedom and radicalness in the character of Abraham Lincoln were not separate qualities, but the necessary results of his simplicity and childlikeness and truth.

Here, then, we have some conception of the man. Out of this character came the life which we admire and the death which we lament to-day. He was called in that character to that life and death. It was just the nature, as you see, which a new nation such as ours ought to produce.

All the conditions of his birth, his youth, his manhood, which made him what he was, were not irregular and exceptional, but were the normal conditions of a new and simple country. His pioneer home in Indiana was a type of the pioneer land in which he lived. If ever there was a man who was a part of the time and

country he lived in, this was he. The same simple respect for labor won in the school of work and incor-
porated into blood and muscle; the same unassuming
loyalty to the simple virtues of temperance and industry and integrity; the same sagacious judgment which
had learned to be quick-eyed and quick-brained in the
constant presence of emergency; the same direct and
clear thought about things, social, political, and religious, that was in him supremely, was in the people he
was sent to rule.

Surely, with such a type-man for ruler, there would
seem to be but a smooth and even road over which he
might lead the people whose character he represented
into the new region of national happiness and comfort
and usefulness, for which that character had been
designed.

But then we come to the beginning of all trouble.
Abraham Lincoln was the type-man of the country, but
not of the whole country. This character which we
have been trying to describe was the character of an
American under the discipline of freedom. There was
another American character which had been developed
under the influence of slavery. There was no one
American character embracing the land. There were
two characters, with impulses of irrepressible and
deadly conflict.

This citizen whom we have been honoring and prais-
ing represented one. The whole great scheme with
which he was ultimately brought in conflict, and which
has finally killed him, represented the other. Beside
this nature, true and fresh and new, there was another
nature, false and effete and old. The one nature found

itself in a new world, and set itself to discover the new ways for the new duties that were given it. The other nature, full of the false pride of blood, set itself to reproduce in a new world the institutions and the spirit of the old, to build anew the structure of the feudalism which had been corrupt in its own day, and which had been left far behind by the advancing conscience and needs of the progressing race.

The one nature magnified labor, the other nature depreciated and despised it. The one honored the laborer, and the other scorned him. The one was simple and direct; the other, complex, full of sophistries and self-excuses. The one was free to look all that claimed to be truth in the face, and separate the error from the truth that might be in it; the other did not dare to investigate, because its own established prides and systems were dearer to it than the truth itself, and so even truth went about in it doing the work of error. The one was ready to state broad principles, of the brotherhood of man, the universal fatherhood and justice of God, however imperfectly it might realize them in practice; the other denied even the principles, and so dug deep and laid below its special sins the broad foundation of a consistent, acknowledged sinfulness.

In a word, one nature was full of the influences of freedom, the other nature was full of the influences of slavery.

In general these two regions of our national life were separated by a geographical boundary. One was the spirit of the North, the other was the spirit of the South. But the Southern nature was by no means all a Southern thing. There it had an organized, established form, a certain definite, established institution about which it clustered. Here, lacking advantage, it lived in less expressive ways and so lived more weakly. There, there was the horrible sacrament of slavery, the outward and visible sign round which the inward and spiritual temper gathered and kept itself alive. But who doubts that among us the spirit of slavery lived and thrived? Its formal existence had been swept away from one State after another, partly on conscientious, partly on economical grounds, but its spirit was here, in every sympathy that Northern winds carried to the listening ear of the Southern slaveholder, and in every oppression of the weak by the strong, every proud assumption of idleness over labor which echoed the music of Southern life back to us.

Here in our midst lived that worse and falser nature, side by side with the true and better nature which God meant should be the nature of Americans, and of which he was shaping out the type and champion in his chosen David of the sheepfold.

Here then we have the two. The history of our country for many years is the history of how these two elements of American life approached collision. They wrought their separate reactions on each other. Men debate and quarrel even now about the rise of Northern Abolitionism, about whether the Northern Abolitionists were right or wrong, whether they did harm or good.

How vain the quarrel is! It was inevitable. It was inevitable in the nature of things that two such natures living here together should be set violently against each other. It is inevitable, till man be far more unfeeling and untrue to his convictions than he has always been, that a great wrong asserting itself vehemently should arouse to no less vehement assertion the opposing right.

The only wonder is that there was not more of it. The only wonder is that so few were swept away to take, by an impulse they could not resist, their stand of hatred to the wicked institution. The only wonder is that only one brave, reckless man came forth to cast himself, almost single-handed, with a hopeless hope, against the proud power that he hated, and trust to the influence of a soul marching on into the history of his countrymen to stir them to a vindication of the truth he loved. At any rate, whether the Abolitionists were wrong or right, there grew up about their violence, as there always will about the extremism of extreme reformers, a great mass of feeling, catching their spirit and asserting it firmly, though in more moderate degrees and methods.

About the nucleus of Abolitionism grew up a great American Anti-Slavery determination, which at last gathered strength enough to take its stand to insist upon the checking and limiting the extension of the power of slavery, and to put the type-man, whom God had been preparing for the task, before the world, to do the work on which it had resolved. Then came discontent, secession, treason. The two American natures, long advancing to encounter, met at last, and a whole country, yet trembling with the shock, bears witness how terrible the meeting was.

Thus I have tried briefly to trace out the gradual course by which God brought the character which he

designed to be the controlling character of this new
world into distinct collision with the hostile character
which it was to destroy and absorb, and set it in the
person of its type-man in the seat of highest power.
The character formed under the discipline of freedom
and the character formed under the discipline of slavery
developed all their difference and met in hostile conflict when this war began.

Notice, it was not only in what he did and was toward the slave, it was in all he did and was everywhere
that we accept Mr. Lincoln's character as the true result of our free life and institutions. Nowhere else
could have come forth that genuine love of the people
which in him no one could suspect of being either the
cheap flattery of the demagogue or the abstract philanthropy of the philosopher, which made our President, while he lived, the centre of a great household
land, and when he died so cruelly made every humblest
household thrill with a sense of personal bereavement
which the death of rulers is not apt to bring. Nowhere
else than out of the life of freedom could have come
that personal unselfishness and generosity which made
so gracious a part of this good man's character.

How many soldiers feel yet the pressure of a strong
hand that clasped theirs once as they lay sick and weak
in the dreary hospital! How many ears will never lose
the thrill of some kind word he spoke—he who could
speak so kindly—to promise a kindness that always
matched his word! How often he surprised the land
with a clemency which made even those who questioned his policy love him the more for what they
called his weakness,—seeing how the man in whom

God had most embodied the discipline of freedom not only could not be a slave, but could not be a tyrant! In the heartiness of his mirth and his enjoyment of simple joys; in the directness and shrewdness of perception which constituted his wit; in the untired, undiscouraged faith in human nature which he always kept; and perhaps, above all, in the plainness and quiet, unostentatious earnestness and independence of his religious life, in his humble love and trust of God—in all, it was a character such as only freedom knows how to make.

Now it was in this character rather than in any mere political position that the fitness of Mr. Lincoln to stand forth in the struggle of the two American natures really lay. We are told that he did not come to the Presidential chair pledged to the abolition of slavery. When shall we learn that with all true men it is not what they intend to do, but it is what the qualities of their natures bind them to do, that determines their career!

The President came to his power full of the blood, strong in the strength of freedom. He came there free, and hating slavery. He came there, leaving on record words like these spoken three years before and never contradicted. He had said:

" A house divided against itself cannot stand. I believe this Government cannot endure permanently, half slave and half free. I do not expect the Union to be dissolved; I do not expect the house to fall; but I expect it will cease to be divided. It will become all one thing or all the other."

When the question came, he knew which thing he

meant that it should be. His whole nature settled that question for him. Such a man must always live as he used to say he lived (and was blamed for saying it) "controlled by events, not controlling them." And with a reverent and clear mind, to be controlled by events means to be controlled by God.

For such a man there was no hesitation when God brought him up face to face with slavery and put the sword into his hand and said, "Strike it down dead!" He was a willing servant then. If ever the face of a man writing solemn words glowed with a solemn joy, it must have been the face of Abraham Lincoln, as he bent over the page where the Emancipation Proclamation of 1863 was growing into shape, and giving manhood and freedom as he wrote it to hundreds of thousands of his fellow men. Here was a work in which his whole nature could rejoice. Here was an act that crowned the whole culture of his life.

All the past, the free boyhood in the woods, the free youth upon the farm, the free manhood in the honorable citizen's employments—all his freedom gathered and completed itself in this. And as the swarthy multitudes came in, ragged, and tired, and hungry, and ignorant, but free forever from anything but the memorial scars of the fetters and the whip, singing rude songs in which the new triumph of freedom struggled and heaved below the sad melody that had been shaped for bondage; as in their camps and hovels there grew up to their half-superstitious eyes the image of a great Father almost more than man, to whom they owed their freedom,—were they not half right?

For it was not to one man, driven by stress of policy,

or swept off by a whim of pity, that the noble act was due. It was to the American nature, long kept by God, in his own intentions till his time should come, at last emerging into sight and power, and bound up and embodied in this best and most American of all Americans, to whom we and those poor frightened slaves at last might look up together and love to call him, with one voice, our Father.

Thus we have seen something of what the character of Mr. Lincoln was, and how it issued in the life he lived. It remains for us to see how it resulted also in the terrible death which has laid his murdered body here in our town among lamenting multitudes to-day. It is not a hard question, though it is sad to answer. We saw the two natures, the nature of slavery and the nature of freedom, at last set against each other, come at last to open war. Both fought, fought long, fought bravely; but each, as was perfectly natural, fought with the tools and in the ways which its own character had made familiar to it.

The character of slavery was brutal, barbarous, and treacherous; and so the whole history of the slave power during the war has been full of ways of warfare brutal, barbarous, and treacherous beyond anything that man bred in freedom could have been driven to by the most hateful passions. It is not to be marvelled at. It is not to be set down as the special sin of the war. It goes back beyond that. It is the sin of the system. It is the barbarism of slavery. When slavery went to war to save its life, what wonder if its barbarism grew barbarous a hundred-fold!

One would be attempting a task which once was almost hopeless, but which now is only needless, if he set himself to convince a Northern congregation that slavery was a barbarian institution. It would be hardly more necessary to try to prove how its barbarism has shown itself during this war. The same spirit which was blind to the wickedness of breaking sacred ties, of separating man and wife, of beating women till they dropped down dead, of organizing licentiousness and sin into commercial systems, of forbidding knowledge and protecting itself with ignorance, of putting on its arms and riding out to steal a State at the beleaguered ballot-box away from freedom—in one word (for its simplest definition is its worst dishonor), the spirit that gave man the ownership in man in time of peace has found out yet more terrible barbarisms for the time of war.

It has hewed and burned the bodies of the dead. It has starved and mutilated its helpless prisoners. It has dealt by truth, not as men will in a time of excitement, lightly and with frequent violations, but with a cool and deliberate and systematic contempt. It has sent its agents into Northern towns to fire peaceful hotels where hundreds of peaceful men and women slept. It has undermined the prisons where its victims starved, and made all ready to blow with one blast their wretched life away. It has delighted in the lowest and basest scurrility even on the highest and most honorable lips. It has corrupted the graciousness of women and killed out the truth of men.

I do not count up the terrible catalogue because I like to, nor because I wish to stir your hearts to passion. Even now, you and I have no right to indulge in personal hatred to the men who did these things. But we are not doing right by ourselves, by the President that we have lost, or by God who had a purpose in our losing him, unless we know thoroughly that it was this same spirit which we have seen to be a tyrant in peace and a savage in war that has crowned itself with the working of this final woe.

It was the conflict of the two American natures, the false and the true. It was slavery and freedom that met in their two representatives, the assassin and the President; and the victim of the last desperate struggle of the dying slavery lies dead to-day in Independence Hall.

Solemnly, in the sight of God, I charge this murder where it belongs, on slavery. I dare not stand here in his sight, and before him or you speak doubtful and double-meaning words of vague repentance, as if we had killed our President. We have sins enough, but we have not done this sin save as by weak concessions and timid compromises we have let the spirit of slavery grow strong and ripe for such a deed. In the barbarism of slavery the foul act and its foul method had their birth.

By all the goodness that there was in him; by all the love we had for him (and who shall tell how great it was); by all the sorrow that has burdened down this desolate and dreadful week,—I charge this murder where it belongs, on slavery, I bid you to remember where the charge belongs, to write it on the door-posts of your mourning houses, to teach it to your wondering children, to give it to the history of these times, that all times to come may hate and dread the sin that killed our noblest President.

If ever anything were clear, this is the clearest. Is there the man alive who thinks that Abraham Lincoln was shot just for himself; that it was that one man for whom the plot was laid? The gentlest, kindest, most indulgent man that ever ruled a State! The man who knew not how to speak a word of harshness or how to make a foe! Was it he for whom the murderer lurked with a mere private hate?

It was not he, but what he stood for. It was law and liberty, it was government and freedom, against which the hate gathered and the treacherous shot was fired. And I know not how the crime of him who shoots at law and liberty in the crowded glare of a great theatre differs from theirs who have levelled their aim at the same great beings from behind a thousand ambuscades and on a hundred battle-fields of this long war. Every general in the field, and every false citizen in our midst at home, who has plotted and labored to destroy the lives of the soldiers of the republic, is brother to him who did this deed. The American nature, the American truths, of which our President was the anointed and supreme embodiment, have been embodied in multitudes of heroes who marched unknown and fell unnoticed in our ranks. For them, just as for him, character decreed a life and a death. The blood of all of them I charge on the same head. Slavery armed with treason was their murderer.

Men point out to us the absurdity and folly of this awful crime. Again and again we hear men say, " It was the worst thing for themselves they could have done. They have shot a representative man, and the cause he represented grows stronger and sterner by his death. Can it be that so wise a devil was so foolish here? Must it not have been the act of one poor madman, born and nursed in his own reckless brain?"

My friends, let us understand this matter. It was a foolish act. Its folly was only equalled by its wickedness. It was a foolish act. But when did sin begin to be wise? When did wickedness learn wisdom? When did the fool stop saying in his heart, "There is no God," and acting godlessly in the absurdity of his impiety? The cause that Abraham Lincoln died for shall grow stronger by his death,— stronger and sterner. Stronger to set its pillars deep into the structure of our nation's life; sterner to execute the justice of the Lord upon his enemies. Stronger to spread its arms and grasp our whole land into freedom; sterner to sweep the last poor ghost of slavery out of our haunted homes.

But while we feel the folly of this act, let not its folly hide its wickedness. It was the wickedness of slavery putting on a foolishness for which its wickedness and that alone is responsible, that robbed the nation of a President and the people of a father. And remember this, that the folly of the slave power in striking the representative of freedom, and thinking that thereby it killed freedom itself, is only a folly that we shall echo if we dare to think that in punishing the representatives of slavery who did this deed, we are putting slavery to death.

Dispersing armies and hanging traitors, imperatively as justice and necessity may demand them both, are not killing the spirit out of which they sprang. The traitor must die because he has committed treason. The murderer must die because he has committed murder. Slavery must die, because out of it, and it alone, came forth the treason of the traitor and the murder of the murderer.

Do not say that it is dead. It is not, while its essential spirit lives. While one man counts another man his born inferior for the color of his skin, while both in North and South prejudices and practices which the law cannot touch, but which God hates, keep alive in our people's hearts the spirit of the old iniquity, it is not dead. The new American nature must supplant the old. We must grow like our President, in his truth, his independence, his religion, and his wide humanity. Then the character by which he died shall be be in us, and by it we shall live. Then peace shall come that knows no war, and law that knows no treason; and full of his spirit a grateful land shall gather round his grave, and in the daily psalm of prosperous and righteous living thank God forever for his life and death.

So let him lie here in our midst to-day, and let our people go and bend with solemn thoughtfulness and look upon his face and read the lessons of his burial. As he paused here on his journey from the Western home and told us what by the help of God he meant to do, so let him pause upon his way back to his Western grave and tell us with a silence more eloquent than words how bravely, how truly, by the strength of God, he did it. God brought him up as he brought David up from the sheepfolds to feed Jacob, his people, and Israel, his inheritance. He came up in earnestness and faith, and he goes back in triumph.

As he pauses here to-day, and from his cold lips bids us bear witness how he has met the duty that was laid on him, what can we say out of our full hearts but this—" He fed them with a faithful and true heart, and ruled them prudently with all his power." The " Shepherd of the People!" that old name that the best rulers ever craved. What ruler ever won it like this dead President of ours? He fed us faithfully and truly. He fed us with counsel when we were in doubt, with inspiration when we sometimes faltered, with caution when we would be rash, with calm, clear, trustful cheerfulness through many an hour when our hearts were dark. He fed hungry souls all over the country with sympathy and consolation. He spread before the whole land feasts of great duty and devotion and patriotism, on which the land grew strong. He fed us with solemn, solid truths. He taught us the sacredness of government, the wickedness of treason. He made our souls glad and vigorous with the love of liberty that was in his. He showed us how to love truth, and yet be charitable—how to hate wrong and all oppression, and yet not treasure one personal injury or insult. He fed all his people, from the highest to the lowest, from the most privileged down to the most enslaved. Best of all, he fed us with a reverent and genuine religion. He spread before us the love and fear of God just in that shape in which we need them most, and out of his faithful service of a higher Master who of us has not taken and eaten and grown strong? "He fed them with a faithful and true heart."

Yes, till the last. For at the last, behold him standing with hand reached out to feed the South with mercy and the North with charity, and the whole land with peace, when the Lord who had sent him called him and his work was done!

He stood once on the battle-field of our own State, and said of the brave men who had saved it words as noble as any countryman of ours ever spoke. Let us stand in the country he has saved, and which is to be his grave and monument, and say of Abraham Lincoln what he said of the soldiers who had died at Gettysburg. He stood there with their graves before him, and these are the words he said:

"We cannot dedicate, we cannot consecrate, we cannot hallow this ground. The brave men who struggled here have consecrated it far beyond our power to add or detract. The world will little note nor long remember what we say here, but it can never forget what they did here. It is for us, the living, rather to be dedicated to the unfinished work which they who fought here have thus far so nobly advanced. It is rather for us to be here dedicated to the great task remaining before us, that from these honored dead we take increased devotion to that cause for which they gave the last full measure of devotion; that we here highly resolve that these dead shall not have died in vain; and this nation, under God, shall have a new birth of freedom, and that government of the people by the people and for the people shall not perish from the earth.

May God make us worthy of the memory of Abraham Lincoln!

EDWARD EVERETT.

Everett, William, an American educator and public speaker, born at Watertown, Mass., October 10, 1839. He was the youngest son of the noted orator, Edward Everett, and, studying law after leaving the university, was admitted to the bar in 1866, but never practiced. In 1872 he entered the Unitarian ministry, but has never had charge of a parish. He was a professor of Latin in Harvard University, 1870–77, and principal of Adams Academy, at Quincy, Mass., 1872–93. He was a member of Congress, 1893–94, returning after a few years to his former mastership at Quincy. He has at times taken an active interest in politics, but has exercised entire freedom of action and displayed great independence of party control. He is an eloquent political speaker, fond of startling his listeners, and with a pungent, peppery manner of delivery.

PATRIOTISM.

ORATION DELIVERED JUNE 28, 1900.

I DO not see how any one can rise on this occasion without trembling. It has been illustrated by too many distinguished names, it has brought forth too many striking sentiments, not to give every orator the certainty that he will fall short of its traditions and the doubt if he will so disastrously. But of one thing I am sure; it behooves the speaker to-day to be candid: no elegant or inflated common-places, concealing one's real sentiments by the excuse of academic dignity of courtesy, ought to sully the honesty with which brethren speak to each other. The first, the only aim of every university is the investigation and propagation of truth; truth in the convictions and truth in the utterance.

My very first knowledge of the Phi Beta Kappa dates back to early childhood. In the year 1846 I was present at a portion of the Commencement exercises when the parts were sustained by Francis James Child, George Martin Lane, Charles Eliot Norton, and George Frisbie Hoar.

Those exercises were followed by a Commencement dinner whose good cheer proved too much for a boy not yet seven years old. It was a dinner at home; no one ever wanted to eat too much at the official Commencement dinner. I heard, therefore, at my bedside the next day the tale of Phi Beta Kappa, how Charles Sumner had held his audience for two hours relating the achievements of the four Harvard graduates who had lately died, Pickering, Stone, Allston, and Channing, winding up with the magnificent peroration transferred, I believe, from an earlier address, in which he appealed so earnestly for peace as the duty of our age and answered Burke's lament that the age of chivalry had gone by, the declaration that the age of humanity had come, that the coming time should take its name, not from the horse but from man.

I can not even think of Phi Beta without these names and these thoughts ringing in my ears and almost dictating my words.

It seems to me that an orator can hardly go wrong if he holds fast to our motto, " Philosophy the guide, or rather the sailing-master of life." There is little doubt that when this motto was first given to a secret fraternity, " veiled in the obscurity of a learned language," it meant that philosophy which rejects revelation, the philosophy of the encyclopædists of France.

Accordingly, when the veil was taken away from the mystic characters Phi Beta Kappa, it was declared that philosophy included religion. How many who accept membership in it to-day direct their voyage of life by philosophy or religion after it might not be safe to say. It cannot, however, be wrong, whatever our subject is, to steer our way in it with her at the helm.

I am not going to plunge into a discussion of what philosophy means. It has been used to mean many things, and to some it means nothing at all. When Wackford Squeers, who sixty years ago we all knew was of the immortals and who is now in danger of being forgotten, was asked by any parent a question in some occult branch of study, like trigonometry, he was wont to answer, " Sir, are you a philosopher?" And to the invariable negative he would then reply, " Ah, then I can't explain it to you."

As one of Wackford Squeers's humblest successors I feel there is something not absurd in his counter-question when I meet what are called practical men discussing what they call the practical problems of life.

He who, whether decked with a blue and pink ribbon or not, steers his course with philosophy as his guide, approaches all life's problems in another temper and another spirit; he is working by other roads to other ends from him who is guided by the passions and worships the idols of the hour. Philosophy has different meanings for different men but the gulf is infinite between those who accept it with any meaning and those who know it not, or know it only as an object of patronage or scorn.

The philosopher walks by principle, not merely by interest or passion; by the past and the future, not merely by the unseen and the eternal, not merely by the seen and temporal—by law and not only by accident. It is not, as sometimes fancied, that he does not see, and, seeing, does not heed these things; he does not, as Plato bids him, turn his back on what this world shows. He meets immediate duties; he lives with contemporary men; he deals with existing demands. But he does all this by the light and guidance of rules of which the servant of time and place knows nothing.

I claim for this the assent of all my brothers here as an intellectual fact; but I desire at the outset of what I say to rouse your thoughts to it as the dictate of emotion and of conscience. Philosophy, the study of causes in their deepest effects, beginning with the true use of terms and proceeding by sound reasoning, has the power to transmit and sanctify the most commonplace transactions, the most hackneyed words.

The master of all philosophy began his work by forcing his contemporaries to define the commonest subjects of conversation. I would, as his follower, ask you to apply that method to one of the favorite watchwords, one of the pressing duties of to-day, and see if philosophy has not something to define and correct in a field where her sway is scarcely admitted.

You cannot talk for ten minutes on any of what are rightly held to be the great interests of life without feeling how loosely we use their names. We seem not to be dealing with sterling coin, which has the same value everywhere and always, but with counters that, passing with a conventional value here and now, are worthless when we come to some great public or private crisis.

Education, business, amusement, art, literature, science, home, comfort, society, politics, patriotism, religion—how many men who use these words have any true conception of their force? How many simply mean that form of education, that line of business, that sect in religion, that party in politics, to which they are accustomed?

How many are led by this loose yet limited use of words into equally loose and equally narrow ways of action? How many need a Socrates to walk through the streets and force them to define their terms? And how many, if he did appear again, would be ready to kill him for corrupting the youth, and holding to a god different from those the country worships?

Patriotism—love of country—devotion to the land that bore us—is pressed upon us now as paramount to every other notion in its claims on head, hand, and heart. It is pictured to us not merely as an amiable and inspiring emotion, but as a paramount duty which is to sweep every other out of the way. The thought cannot be put in loftier or more comprehensive words than by Cicero, " Cari sunt parentes, cari liberi, cari familiares, propinqui; sed omnes omnium caritates una patria complexa est."

" Dear are parents, dear are children, dear are friends and relations; but all affections to all men are embraced in country alone."

The Greek, the Roman, the Frenchman, the German, talks about " fatherland," and we are beginning to copy them; though to my ear the English " mother country " is far more tender and true.

Cicero follows up his words by saying that for her no true son would, if need be, hesitate to die. And his words, themselves an echo of what the poets and orators whose heir he was had repeated again and again, have been re-echoed and reiterated in many ages since he bowed his neck to the sword of his country's enemy.

But to give life for their country is the least part of what men have been willing to do for her. Human life has often seemed a very trifling possession to be exposed cheaply in all sorts of useless risks and feuds. It has been the cheerful sacrifice of the things that make life worth living, the eager endurance of things far worse than death, which show the mighty power which love of country holds over the entire being of men.

Wealth that Crœsus might have envied has been poured at the feet of our mother, and sacrifices taken up which St. Francis never knew—ease and luxury, refined company, and cultivated employment have been rejected for the hardships and suffering of the camp— the sympathy and idolatry of home have been abandoned for the tenfold hardships and sufferings of a political career; and at the age when we can offer neither life nor living as of any value to one's country, those children and grandchildren which were to have been the old man's and the old woman's solace are freely sent forth in the cause of the country which will send back nothing but a sword and cap to be hung on the wall and never be worn by living man again.

Such are the sacrifices men have cheerfully made for the existence, the honor, the prosperity of their country.

But perhaps the power of patriotism is shown more strongly in what it makes them do than in what it makes them give up. You know how many men have been, as it were, born again by the thought that they might illustrate the name and swell the force of their country, achieving what they never would have aroused themselves to do for themselves alone.

I do not mean the feats of military courage and strategy which are generally talked of as the sum of patriotic endeavor. I recollect in our war being told by a very well-known soldier who is now a very well-known civilian that it was conceited for me or any other man to think in time of war he could serve his country in any way but in the ranks.

But in fact every art and every science has won triumphs under the stress of patriotism that it has hardly known in less enthusiastic days. The glow that runs through every line of Sophocles and Virgil, as they sung the glories of Athens and Rome, is reflected in the song of our own bards from Spenser and Shakespeare to this hour; the rush and sweep of Demosthenes and Cicero dwelling on the triumphs and duties of their native lands are only the harbingers of Burke and Webster on the like themes; the beauty into which Bramante and Angelo poured all their souls to adorn their beloved Florence was lavished under no other impulse than that which set all the science of France working to relieve her agriculture and manufactures from the pressure laid upon her by the strange vicissitudes of her Revolution.

Not all this enthusiasm has succeeded; there have been patriotic blunders as well as patriotic triumphs, but still it stands true that men are spurred on to make the best of themselves in the days when love of country glowed strongest in their hearts. It would seem as if all citizens poured their individual affections and devotions into one Superior Lake from which they all burst in one Niagara of patriotism.

I am ashamed, however, to press such a commonplace proposition before this audience and in this place, where the walls are as redolent of love of country as Faneuil Hall itself. The question is if philosophy, our chosen guide of life, has anything to say of this same love of country,—if she brings that under her rule, as she does so much else of life, supplementing, curtailing. correcting,—or whether patriotism may bid defiance to philosophy, claiming her submission as she claims the submission of every other human interest, and bidding her yield and be absorbed, or stand off and depart to her visionary Utopia, where the claims of practical duty and natural sentiment do not seek to follow her.

For indeed we are told now that patriotism is not merely a generous and laudable emotion, but a paramount and overwhelming duty, to which everything else which men have called duties must give way. If a monarch, a statesman, a soldier stands forth preeminent in exalting the name or spreading the bounds of his country, he is a patriot—and that is enough.

Such a leader may be as perjured and blasphemous as Frederick, or as brutal and stupid as his father; he may be as faithless and mean as Marlborough, or as dissolute and bloody as Julius Cæsar; he may trample on every right of independent natives and drive his countrymen to the shambles like Napoleon; he may be as corrupt as Walpole and as wayward as Chatham; he may be destitute of every spark of culture, or may prostitute the gifts of the Muses to the basest ends; he may have, in short, all manner of vices, curses, or defects; but if he is true to his country, if he is her faithful standard-bearer, if he strives to set and keep her high above her rivals, he is right, a worthy patriot.

And if he seems lukewarm in her cause, if, however wise and good and accomplished he may be in all other relations, he fails to work with all his heart and soul to maintain her position among the nations, he must be stamped with failure if not with curse.

For the plain citizen who does not claim to be a leader in peace or war, the duty is still clearer. He must stand by his country, according to what those who have her destiny in their control decide is her proper course. In war or in peace he is to have but one watchword.

In peace, indeed, his patriotic duty will chiefly be shown by obeying existing laws, wherever they may strike, even as Socrates rejected all thought of evading the unjust, stupid, and malignant sentence that took his life. But it is not thought inconsistent with that true love of country to let one's opinions be known about those laws, and about the good of the country in general, in time of peace.

In a free land like ours every citizen is expected to be ready with voice and vote to do his part in correcting what is amiss, in protesting against bad laws, and, as far as he may, defeating bad men whom he believes to be seeking his country's ruin.

Nay, a citizen of a free country who did not so criticise would be held to be derelict to that highest duty which free lands, differing from slavish despotisms, impose upon their sons.

But in time of war we are told that all this is changed. As soon as our country is arrayed against another under arms, every loyal son has nothing to do but to support her armies to victory; he may desire peace, but it must be "peace with honor," whatever that phrase of the greatest charlatan of modern times may mean. He must not question the justice or the expediency of the war; he must either fight himself or encourage others to fight. Criticism of the management of the war may be allowable; of the fact of the war, it is treason. And the word for the patriot is, "Our country, right or wrong."

Right here, then, as I conceive it, Philosophy raises her warning finger before the passionate enthusiast and says: "Hold!" In the name of higher thought, of deeper law, of more serious principle, to which every man here, every child of Harvard, every brother of this society is bound to listen, Philosophy says "Hold!" With the terror of the voice within, with the majesty of the voice from above to Americans now, and with the spirit of Socrates returning to earth, it bids them know what they mean by the words they use, or they may be crowning as a lofty emotion that which is only an unreasoning passion, and clothing with the robes of duty what is only a superstition.

This love of country, this patriotic ardor of ours, must submit to have Philosophy investigate her claims, to rule above all other emotions, not in the interest of any less generous emotion, not to make men more sordid or selfish, but simply because there is a rule called truth, and a measure called right, by which every human action is bound to be gauged, because all gods and men and fiends should league all their forces, and with the golden chain of Olympus to draw its glory down to their purposes they will only find themselves drawn upward subject to its unchanging laws, the weak members hanging in the air, and the vile ones hurled down to Tartarus.

What is this country—this mother country, this fatherland that we are bidden to love and serve and stand by at any risk and sacrifice? Is it the soil? the land? the plains and mountains and rivers? the fields, and forests, and mines? No doubt there is inspiration from this very earth—from that part of the globe which one nation holds, and which we call our country.

Poets and orators have dwelt again and again on the undying attractions to our own land, no matter what it is like, the Dutch marshes, the Swiss mountains, soft Italy, and stern Spain equally clutching on the hearts of their people with a resistless chain.

But a land is nothing without the men. The very same countries, whose scenery, tame or bold, charming or awful, has been the inspiration to gallant generations, may, as the wheel of time turns, fall to indolent savages, listless slaves, or sordid money-getters. Byron

has told us this in lines which the men of his own time
felt were instinct with creative genius, but which the
taste of the day rejects for distorted thoughts in distorted verse:

> "Clime of the forgotten brave!
> Whose land from plain to mountain cave
> Was Freedom's home or Glory's grave!
> Shrine of the mighty! can it be,
> That this is all remains of thee?
> Approach, thou craven, crouching slave;
> Say, is not this Thermopylæ?
> These waters blue that round you lave,
>   O servile offspring of the free—
> Pronounce what sea, what shore is this?
> The gulf, the rock of Salamis!
>   'T were long to tell and sad to trace,
> Each step from splendor to disgrace;
> Enough—no foreign foe could quell
> Thy soul, till from itself it fell;
> Yes; self-abasement paved a way
> To villain-bonds and despot sway."

It is the nation, not the land, which makes the patriot; if the nation degenerate, the land becomes only a
monument, not a dwelling: let the nation rouse itself
and the country may be a palace and a temple once
more.

But who are the men that made the nation? Are
they the whole of the population or a part only? are
they one party only among the people, which is ready
perhaps to regard the other party not as countrymen,
but as aliens? Are the country the men who govern
her and control her destinies, the king, the nobles, the
popular representatives, the delegates to whom power is
transmitted when the people resign it?

Once the king was the nation, with perhaps a few counsellors; patriotism meant loyalty to the sovereign; every man who on any pretext arrayed himself against the Crown was a disloyal rebel, an unpatriotic traitor; until at length God for his own purposes saw fit to array Charles the First against the people of England, when, after years of civil war, and twice as many years of hollow peace, and five times as many years when discussion was stifled or put aside, the world came to recognize that loyalty to one's king and love to one's country are as different in their nature as the light of a lamp and the light of the sun.

And yet, if a king understands the spirit and heart of his nation, he may lead it so truly in peace or in war that love of country shall be inseparable from devotion to the sovereign. Modern historians may load their pages as they please with revelations of the meanness, the falsehood, the waywardness of Queen Elizabeth; yet England believed in her and loved her; and if England rose from ruin to prosperity in her reign it was because her people trusted her. In her day, as for two centuries before, Scotland, where three different races had been welded together by Bruce to produce the most patriotic of peoples, had scarcely a true national existence, certainly nothing that men could cling to with affection and pride, because kings and commons were alike the prey of a poor, proud, selfish nobility who suffered nobody to rule, scarcely to live, but themselves; exempting themselves from the laws which they forced upon their country.

An American cries out at the idea of a trusted aristocracy seeking to drag the force and affection of a nation of vassals, and calling that patriotism. Then what will he say to the patriotism of some of those lands which have made their national name ring through the world for the triumphs and the sacrifices of which it is the emblem?

What was Sparta? What was Venice? What was Bern? What was Poland? Merely the fields where the most exclusive aristocracies won name and fame and wealth and territory only to sink their unrecognized subject citizens lower every year in the scale of true nationality.

Not one of these identified the nation with the people. Or does an American insist on a democracy where the entire people's voice speaks through rulers of its choosing? Does he prefer the patriotism of Athens, where thirty thousand democrats kept up an interminable feud with ten thousand conservatives, one ever plunging the city into rash expeditions, the other, as soon as its wealth gave it the upper hand, disfranchising, exiling, killing the majority of the people, because it could hire stronger arms to crush superior numbers?

What was the patriotism of the Italian cities when faction alternately banished faction, when Dante suffered no more than he would have inflicted had his side got the upper hand? What was the patriotism in either Greece or Italy, which confined itself to its own city, and where city enjoyed far more fighting against city than ever thinking of union to save the common race from bondage?

For years, for centuries, for ages, the nations that would most eagerly repeat such sentiments as Cicero's about love of country never dreamed of using the word in any sense that a philosopher, nay, that a plain, truth-telling man, could not convict at once of meanness and contradiction.

But we of modern times look back with pity and contempt on those benighted ages which had not discovered the great arcanum of representative government, whereby a free nation chooses the men to whom it intrusts its concerns; its presidents and its prime ministers, its parliaments and congresses and courts. Yet even this mighty discovery, whereby modern nations are raised so far above those poor Old World creatures, the Greeks and Romans and mediæval Italians, has not so far controlled factional passion that many countries do not live in a perpetual civil war which Athens and Corinth would have been ashamed of. We all know how our dear sister republics of Central and Southern America, which, as Mr. Webster said, looked to the great Northern Light in forming their constitutions, treat their elections as merely indications which of two parties shall be set up to be knocked down by rifles and bombshells, unless it retains its hold by such means.

But how with ourselves? How with England? How with France? How often do we regard our elected governors as really standing for the whole nation and deserving its allegiance.

In 1846 the President of the United States and his counsellors hurried us into a needless, a bullying, a wicked war. Fully a quarter of the country felt it was an outrage and nothing else. But appeals were made to stand by the government, against which our own merciless satirist directed the lines which must have forever tingled in the ears and the consciences of the men who supported what they knew was irretrievably wicked.

> " The side of our country must allus be took,
>   And President Polk, you know, he is our country;
>   And the angel who writes all our sins in a book,
>   Puts the debit to him and to us the percontry."

No, brethren! no president, no prime minister, no cabinet, no congress or parliament, no deftly organized representative or executive body is or can be our country. To pay them a patriot's affectionate allegiance is as illogical as loyalty to James II. or to the French National Convention. Mere obedience to law when duly enacted is one thing; Socrates may drink the hemlock rather than run away from the doom to which a court of his native city has consigned him; but when the tribunals of that country perpetrated such a mockery of justice, Plato and Xenophon were right in cherishing to their dying day a poignant sense of outrage, an implacable grudge against such a stepmother as blood-stained Athens.

But sometimes the voice of the whole people speaks unmistakably; its ruler is the true agent and representative of a united and determined people; the will of the nation is unquestioned; who are you, who am I, that we should dispute it and think ourselves wiser and better than all our countrymen? Is not the whole nation the mother, whom to disobey is the highest sin? No! the particular set of men who make up the nation at any time will die and pass away, and what will their sons think of what they made their country do?

In 1854 the Emperor Nicholas, whose thoughts were never far from Constantinople, picked an unintelligible quarrel with the Sultan of Turkey. The unprincipled adventurer who contrived to add new stains to the name of Napoleon Bonaparte saw his chance to win glory for the Gallic eagle; he plunged into war and entrapped England unto it with him.

The wise old statesman who was at the head of the English government knew the war was needless and wrong; he did his utmost to stop it; but his countrymen preferred to listen to the reckless Palmerston, and they lashed first themselves and then Aberdeen into war.

The whole nation went mad. John Bright told them the philosophic, the political, the Christian truth, and Palmerston insulted him on the floor of the House of Commons. Two years were consumed in the costly and pestilential siege of Sebastopol; a hollow peace was patched up, of which the only significant article was after a short interval impudently broken by Russia; the unspeakable Turk was given another thirty years' lease of life.

And now I do not believe there is one grown man in England among the sons and grandsons of those who fought the Crimean war who does not believe Aberdeen and Bright were right, that Palmerston and England were wrong; and that the war was a national blunder, a national sin, a national crime. When John Bright stood almost against the whole nation, he was neither self-conceited nor unpatriotic, but a great and good man speaking as the prophet of God.

Yes, a whole people may be wrong, and deserve at

best the pity of a real patriot rather than his active love. Our country is something more than the single procession which passes across its borders in one generation; it means the land with all its people in all their periods; the ancestors whose exertions made us what we are, and whose memory is precious to us; the posterity to whom we are to transmit what we prize, unstained as we received it; and he who loves his country truly and serves her rightly must act and speak not for the present generation alone, but for all that rightly live, every event in whose history is inseparable from every other. If we pray, as does the seal of Boston, that "God will be to us as he was to the fathers," then we must be to God what our fathers were.

But after Philosophy has forced the vociferous patriot to define what he means by his country, she has a yet more searching question to ask: What will you do and what will you suffer for this country you love? How shall your love be shown?

There is one of the old Greek maxims which says in four words of that divine language what a modern tongue can scarcely stammer in four times four: "Sparta is thine allotted home; make her a home of order and beauty." Whatever our country needs to make her perfect, that she calls on us to do.

I have run over to you some of the great sacrifices and great exertions which patriots have made to make their dear home perfect and themselves perfect for her sake. But everything done or renounced to make her perfect must recognize that she is not perfect yet; and what our country chiefly calls on us for is not mighty exertions and sacrifices, but those particular ones, small or great, which shall do her real good and not harm.

That her commerce should whiten every sea; that her soil should yield freely vegetable and mineral wealth; that she should be dotted with peaceful homes, the abode of virtue and love; that her cities should be adorned with all that is glorious in art; that famine and poverty and plague and crime should be fought with all the united energy of head and hand and heart; that historians and poets and orators should continue to make her high achievements and mighty aims known to all her children and to the world; that the oppressed of every land may find a refuge within her borders; that she may stand before her sister nations indeed a sister, loved and honored,—these are the commonplaces, tedious, if noble to recount, of what patriotism has sought to do in many ages.

Yet every one of these things when actually achieved, has had a worm at the core of the showy fruit, which has made their mighty authors but little better than magnificent traitors.

For every one of these has been achieved at the expense of other nations, as ancient, as glorious, as dear to their own children, as worthy of patriotic love as their triumphant antagonists; and every one has been achieved at the still worse price of corruption and tyranny at home.

Every country has in times mistaken material for moral wealth, and has grown corrupt as she grew great; and every country in time has fancied that she could not be great and honored while her sisters were great and honored too; and has gone to war with them hoping to enlarge her borders at their expense and to gain by their loss.

It is here, again, at this very point, that the philosopher calls upon the patriot to say what he means by his cry, "Our country, right or wrong," the maxim of one who threw away an illustrious life in that worst of wicked encounters, a duel.

If there are such words as right and wrong, and those words stand for eternal realities, why shall not a nation, why shall not her loving sons, be made to bow to the same law, the utterance of God in history and in the heart? Can a king, can a president, can a congress, can a whole nation, by its pride or its passions turn wrong into right; or what authority have they to trifle or shuffle with either?

We are told that if we ever find ourselves at war with another country, no matter how that war was brought on, no matter what folly or wickedness broke the peace, no matter how completely we might oppose and deprecate it up to the moment of its outbreak, no matter how, as truthful historians, we may condemn it after it is over, no matter how iniquitous or tyrannical our sense and our conscience tells us are the terms on which peace has been obtained, we ought, during the war, to be heartily and avowedly for it. "We must not desert the flag." Patriotism demands that we should always stand by our country as against every other.

And what are the patriots in our rival country to be doing the while? Are they to support the war against us whether they think it right or wrong? Are they cheerfully to pay all taxes? Are they to volunteer for every battle? Are they to carry on war to the knife or the last ditch? Is their love for their country to be as unreasoning, as purely a matter of emotion, as ours?

Certainly, if the doctrine of indiscriminate patriotism, "our country, right or wrong," is the true one. If France and Germany fight, no matter what the cause, every Frenchman must desire to see Germany humiliated, and every German to see France brought to her knees, and it is absolutely their duty to have all cognizance of right and wrong swallowed up in passionate loyalty.

Lord Aberdeen and Mr. Bright were right in deprecating the Crimean War up to the moment of its declaration; history says they were right now, but while the war lasted it was their duty to sacrifice their sense of right to help the government aims. Mr. Webster and Mr. Clay were right in pouring out their most scathing eloquence against the Mexican War; General Grant was right in recording in his memoirs that he believed it unjust and unnecessary; yet Mr. Webster and Mr. Clay only fulfilled patriotic duty in sending their sons to die, one by the sword and one by the fever, in the same army where Grant did his duty by fighting against his conception of right.

Brethren, I call this sentimental nonsense. It cannot be patriotic duty to say up to 1846 that our country will be wrong if she fights, to say after 1849 that she was wrong in fighting, but to hold one's tongue, and maintain her so-called cause in 1847 and 1848 though we know it is wrong all along.

And, observe, these patriots make no distinction between wars offensive and defensive, wars for aggression and conquest and wars for national existence. In any war, in all wars in which our country gets engaged, we must support her; her honor demands that we shall not back out.

Oh, Honor! that terrible word, the very opposite of Duty; unknown in that sense to the soldiers, the statesmen, the patriots of Greece and Rome; honor, the invention of the Gothic barbarians, which more than any other one thing has reduced poor Spain to her present low estate.

There was a time when individual men talked about their honor and stood up to be stabbed and shot at, whether right or wrong, to vindicate it. That infernal fiction, the honor of the duel, was on the point, sixty years ago, of drawing Macaulay into the field in defence of a few sarcastic paragraphs in a review which he admitted himself were not to be justified. It was very shortly after that, that Prince Albert came to England with his earnest, simple, modest character: he used all his influence to stop the practice and the very idea of duelling; and now all England recognizes that any and every duel is a sin, a crime, and a folly, and that the code of honor has no defence before God or man. When shall the day come when the nations feel the same about public war? When shall the words of our own poet find their true and deserved acceptance, not as a poetical rhapsody, but as practical truth?

> "Were half the power that fills the world with terror,
>   Were half the wealth bestowed on camp and courts,
>   Given to redeem the human mind from error,
>   There were no need of arsenals and forts.

" The warrior's name should be a name abhorred,
    And every nation that should lift again
  Its hand against its brother ; on its forehead
    Should bear forevermore the curse of Cain."

Brethren, if there is anything of which philosophy must say it is wrong that thing is war. I do not mean any particular school of philosophy, ancient or modern. But I mean, if any one studies the nature of God and man in the light of history, with a view to draw from that study rules of sound thought and maxims of right action, he must say war is wrong, an antiquated, blundering, criminal means of solving a national doubt by accepting the certainty of misery.

I began my address with Cicero's definition of patriotism. I now recall to you his sentence wrung from the heart of a man who had blazoned with his eloquence the fame of many great soldiers, and was not even himself without a spark of military ambition: " Ego sic judico, inquissimam pacem justissimo bello esse anteferendam."—" This is my judgment, that the most unfair peace is preferable to the justest war."

Granting—as I do not—that war is sometimes necessary; so cutting off a man's leg, or extirpating an organ may be necessary; but it is always a horrible thing all the same, and just as the conservative surgery of our age is at work day and night to avoid these destructive operations, so the statesmanship of the day ought to be at work, not specifically to secure arbitration, as if that was anything more than a possible method, but to stop war as an eternal shame.

And granting war is sometimes necessary: if it is

ever engaged in for any cause less than necessary, it is wrong; and the country is wrong that engages in it. A doubtful war, a war about which opinions are divided, is for that very reason not doubtfully evil, and the country that makes it is wrong.

Yes, brethren, a nation may be in the wrong, in every war one nation must be in the wrong, and generally both are; and if any country, yours or mine, is in the wrong, it is our duty as patriots to say so, and not support the country we love in a wrong because our countrymen have involved her in it.

In the war of our Revolution, when Lord North had the king and virtually the country with him, Fox lamented that Howe had won the battle of Long Island and wished he had lost it. What! an Englishman wish an English army to be defeated? Yes, because England was wrong, and Fox knew it and said so.

But there is a theory lately started, or rather an old one revived, that war is a good thing in itself; that it does a nation good to be fighting and killing the patriot sons of another nation, who love their country as we do ours. We are told that every strenuous man's life is a battle of one kind, and that the virile character demands some physical belligerency. Yes, every man's life must be to a great extent a fight, but this preposterous doctrine would make every man a prize-fighter.

They say war elicits acts of heroism and self-sacrifice that the country does not know in the lethargy of peace.

Heroism and self-sacrifice! There are more heroic and sacrificial acts going on in the works of peace than the brazen throat of war could proclaim in a twelvemonth. The track of every practising physician is marked by heroic disregard of life that Napoleon's Old Guard might envy. Every fire like that of Chicago, every flood like that of Johnstown, every plague and famine like that of India, are fields carpeted with the flowers of heroic self-sacrifice; they spring up from the very graves and ashes. And these flowers do not have growing up beside them the poisoned weeds of self-seeking or corruption which are sure to precede, to attend, to follow every war.

The dove of peace that brings the leaves of healing does not have trooping at her wings the vultures that treat their living soldiers like carrion. When Lucan has seen throughout the catalogue of the national miseries that followed the quarrel of Cæsar and Pompey, he winds them all up in the terrible words, *" multis utile bellum "*—" war profitable to many men."

There is now much questioning of the propriety of capital punishment; it is strongly urged that the State has no right to take the life even of a hardened criminal, whose career has shown no trace of humanity or usefulness, and has put the capstone of murder on every other crime.

And yet we are told it is perfectly right to take a young man of the highest promise, a blessing to all who knew him, the very man to live for his country, and send him to be cut down by a bullet or by dysentery in a cause he cannot approve.

But there is a still newer theory come up about war as applied to ourselves. It seems that we share with a very few other peoples in the world a civilization so high, and institutions so divine that it is our duty and our destiny to go about the globe swallowing up inferior peoples and bestowing on them, whether they will or not, the blessings of the American——constitution?—well, no! not of the American constitution, but of the American dominion——and that when we are once started on this work of absorption they are rebels who do not accept the blessings. Now, if this precious doctrine were true, it utterly annihilates the old notion of patriotism and love of country; for that notion called upon every nation, however small or weak or backward, to maintain to the death its independence against any other, however great or strong or progressive.

According to this Mohammedan doctrine, this " death or the Koran " doctrine, the Finns and Poles are not patriots because they object to being absorbed by Russia, and the Hamburgers are rebels for not accepting the beneficent incorporation into France graciously proffered to them by Marshal Davoust.

But I will not enlarge upon this delicate subject by modern Americanism. It is bad enough for the nations we threaten to absorb. It is worse for us, the absorbers. I will ask you to remember what befell a noble nation which took up the work of benevolently absorbing the world.

When Xerxes had been driven back in tears to Persia, his rout released scores of Greek islands and cities, in the loveliest of lands and seas, and inhabited by the highest and wisest of men. There is nothing in art or literature or science or government that did not take its rise from them. Their tyrant gone, they looked around for a protector.

They saw that Athens was mighty on the sea, and they heard that she was just and generous to all who sought her citadel. And they put themselves, their ships and treasure, in the power of Athens, to use them as she would for the common defense. And the league was scarcely formed, the Persian was but just crushed, when the islands began to find that protection meant subjection.

They could not bear to think that they had only changed masters, even if Aristides himself assigned their tribute; and some revolted. The rebellion was cut down, Athens went on expanding, she made her subject islands pay money instead of ships, she transferred the treasury to her own citadel; she spent the money of her allies in those marvellous adornments that have made her the crown of beauty for the world forever.

Wider and wider did the empire of the Athenian democracy extend. Five armies fought her battles in a single year in five lands; Persia and Egypt, as well as Sparta, feeling the valor of her soldiers.

And the heart of Athens got drunk with glory, and the brain of Athens got crazed with power, and the roar of her boasting rose up to heaven, joined with the wail of her deceived and trampled subjects. And one by one they turned and fell from her, and joined their arms to her rival, who promised them independence; and every fond and mad endeavor to retain her empire only sucked her deeper into the eddy of ruin; and at length she was brought to her knees before her rival and her victorious fleet, and her impregnable walls were destroyed with the cry that now began the freedom of Greece.

It was only the beginning of new slavery; enslaved by the faithless Sparta, who sold half the cities back to Persia. Patching up once more a hollow alliance with Athens, enslaved by Macedonia, enslaved by Rome, enslaved by the Turks, poor Greece holds at last what she calls her independence under the protection of the great civilizing nations who let her live because they cannot agree how to cut up her carcass if they slay her.

Brethren, even as Athens began by protection and passed into tyranny and then into ruin, so shall every nation be who interprets patriotism to mean that it is the only nation in the world, and that every other which stands in the way of what it chooses to call destiny must be crushed. Love your country, honor her, live for her, if necessary die for her, but remember that whatever you would call right or wrong in another country is right and wrong for her and for you; that right and truth and love to man and allegiance to God are above all patriotism; and that every citizen who sustains his country in her sins is responsible to humanity, to history, to philosophy, and to Him to whom all nations are as a drop in the bucket, and the small dust on the balance.

Hill, Benjamin H., an American politician and orator, born in Jasper county, Ga., September 14, 1823; died at Atlanta, Ga., August 16, 1882. After his admission to the Georgia bar he entered upon the exercise of his profession at La Grange, in his native state, and, being sent to the State Legislature in 1851, was for ten years a leader of the Whigs in that body. He opposed the principle of secession until his State had formally passed an ordinance of secession, when he acquiesced in its decision. He was a conspicuous supporter of the Confederacy thereafter, serving in the Confederate Senate throughout its existence. At the close of the Civil War he was imprisoned for a short time by the Federal authorities. In 1870 he advised the people of his State to accept the political situation in an important "Address to the People of Georgia." He entered Congress as a representative in 1875, and in 1877 was elected to the United States Senate. Hill was a constitutional lawyer of marked ability, and both in court and in Congress distinguished himself by his eloquence. Among his best known speeches are his reply to Blaine in the House of Representatives, his Senate speech against Mahone, and his address on "The Perils of the Nation," delivered in 1868.

ON THE PERILS OF THE NATION.

DELIVERED BEFORE THE YOUNG MEN'S DEMOCRATIC UNION, OCTOBER 8, 1868.

PEOPLE OF THE NORTH,—In deference to the earnest wishes of a committee from the Young Men's Democratic Union Club, and the request of personal friends, some of whom differ with me in political views, I depart from my original intention not to make a speech in the North, and appear before you this evening.

I do not come to ask any favor for the Southern people. The representative, however, of that people who have experienced burdens of despotic power, and the insecurity of anarchy, I come, all the more earnestly, to address you in behalf of imperilled constitutional free government. Will you hear me without passion?

The South—exhausted by a long war and unusual losses—needs peace; desires peace; begs for peace. The North—distrustful, if not vindictive—demands guarantees that the South will keep the peace she so much needs.

In countries where wars have been more frequent, the important fact is well established by experiment, that magnanimity in the conqueror is the very highest guaranty of contented submission by the conquered. It is to be regretted that you seem not to have learned this lesson. A people who will not be magnanimous in victory are not worthy to be, and will not always remain, victors.

In the next place, if you of the North would only open your eyes and see the plainest truth of the century—that the Southern people fought for what they believed to be their right—you would find at once a sufficient guarantee for peace. The South believed honestly, fought bravely, and surrendered frankly; and in each of these facts she presents the most ample title to credit. Why will you not see and admit the fact which must go into history, that the Southern people honestly believed they had a right to secede? Some of the wisest framers of the constitution taught that doctrine. Many of the ablest men in the North, as well as in the South, of every generation, have taught this doctrine. Some of your own States made the recognition of that right, the recognition of their acceptance of union. Even your own Webster—your orator without a rival among you, dead or living—taught that this right existed for cause—certainly for much less cause than now exists. Will you, then, persist in saying that the Southern people are all traitors for exercising, or attempting to exercise, what such men and such States taught was a right? Will you say they did not honestly believe such teachers? Was it their intent to commit treason?

Here lies the whole cause of our continued troubles. The North will not admit what all other people know, and what all history must concede—that the South honestly believed in the right of secession. As a result of this infidelity to such plain fact, you assume that the Southern people are criminals. This idea is the sum of all your politics and statesmanship. It must be abandoned. It must be repudiated thoroughly and promptly. There can never be any peaceful and cordial reunion possible while one half the nation regard the other half as criminals. How can you trust criminals? Why should you desire Union with criminals? If the Southern people are honest, their assent to the nonsecession construction of the constitution is a sufficient guarantee. If they are not honest, but criminals, no promise they could make ought to be trusted. Power is the only guaranty of fidelity in criminals, and if you cannot believe and cannot trust the South, you must, indeed, abandon the constitution and govern with power forever, or you must give up the South as unworthy to federate with you in an equal government of consent.

I speak frankly. If you cannot abandon this miserable theory and habit in your politics, in your religion, and in your schools, of regarding the Southern people as criminal traitors for attempting what good men, and wise men, and great men taught was their right, you will make peaceful reunion under free institutions utterly impossible.

You must hold them as friends, or let them go as foreigners, or govern them as subjects. If you govern them as subjects you must share the penalty, for the same government can never administer freedom to one half and despotism to the other half of the same nation.

Rise above your passions, then, and realize that herein is your guaranty: The South believed honestly, fought bravely, and surrendered frankly.

Again. The exhausted condition of the South ought to inspire you with confidence in her professions of a desire for peace. Are you afraid for her to recover strength? Take care lest the desperation of exhaustion prove stronger than the sinews of prosperity. Peace is not desirable without its blessings.

But you of the North will not try magnanimity: will insist that the Southern people are traitors; and that an exhausted people are dangerous, and you must have guaranties. In your papers, from your pulpits, behind your counters, on your streets, and along your highways, I hear the perpetual charge that the South fought to destroy the government, committed treason and murder, and every inhuman crime, and that she is still intractable, and rebellious, and dangerous, and insincere, and must concede, and give guaranties.

Well, I am here to show you that the South has made every concession that an honorable people would exact, or an honest people could make. . . .

People of the North, will you not rise above passion, and save your own honor, and our common free government by doing plain justice to a people who accepted your pledge, and trusted your honor?

I beg you to understand the facts of actual history before it is too late. I repeat and beg you to note what the South has already conceded as the results of the war:

First. The South conceded at Appomattox, that the arguments of the ablest statesmen America ever produced, in favor of the right of secession as a constitutional remedy, had been replied to in the only manner they could be effectually replied to, by physical force; and the South consented that this judgment, written by the sword, should have legal force and effect.

Second. The South, by her own act, made valid the emancipation of her slaves in the only way in which that emancipation could be made valid, and thus gave up the property the North sold her, without compensation.

Third. The South has solemnly repudiated her debts, contracted in her defence, and has agreed to pay a full share of the debt contracted for her subjugation.

Fourth. The South has permitted without hindrance, the Congress to enter her States and establish tribunals unknown to the constitution, to govern a portion of their population in a manner different from the governments of the States.

Fifth. The South has agreed to make the negroes citizens and give them absolutely equal civil rights with the whites, and to extend to them every protection of law and every facility for education and improvement which are extended to the whites.

Sixth. In a word, I repeat, the South has agreed to everything which has been proposed by the civil or military governments of the United States and by every department of that government, except the single demand to disfranchise their own best men from their own State offices, at a time when their counsel are most needed, or to consent that negroes and strangers may disfranchise them.

For this, and for this only, all their other concessions are spit upon, and they are denounced as intractable, insincere, rebellious, and unwilling to accept the results of the war! Shame upon leaders who persist in such charges; and shame upon a people who will sustain such leaders! . . .

But what will the South do? I will tell you first what the South will not do, in my opinion.

The South will not secede again. That was her great folly—folly against her own interest, not wrong against you. Mark this: That folly will not be repeated. Even if the people of the South desire the disruption of the federal government, their statesmen have the sagacity to see that that result can more effectually come of this secession of the North from the constitution. Those ominous words " outside of the constitution " are more terribly significant than those

other words " secession from the Union." The former
is a secession having all the vices of the latter greatly
increased and none of its virtues. Certainly none of
its manliness, straightforward candor, and justifica-
tion. So note this: The South does not desire nor
seek disunion. If she desired it she does not deem
another secession necessary to bring it about. Disunion will come from Chicago, in spite of Southern opposition.

The South will not re-enslave the negro. She did
not enslave him in the first instance. That was your
work. The South took your slave-savage and gave
him the highest civilization ever reached by the negro.
You then freed him and kept the price of his slavery,
and you alone hold the property that was in human
flesh.

But the Southern whites will never consent to the
government of the negro. Never! All your money
spent in the effort to force it will be wasted. The
Southern whites will never consent to social and political equality with the negro. You may destroy yourselves in the effort to force it, and then you will fail.
You may send down your armies and exhaust the resources of the whole country for a century and pile up
the public debt till it lean against the skies; and you
may burn our cities and murder our people—our unarmed people—but you will never make them consent
to governments formed by negroes and strangers under the dictation of Congress by the power of the bayonet. Born of the bayonet, this government must live
only by the bayonet.

Now, I will tell you some things which, in my opinion, the South will do.

The South would accept the election of Mr. Seymour as a verdict of the Northern people that the general government was to be administered according to the constitution, and she would rejoice and come out of her sorrow strong, beautiful, and growing.

The South will accept the election of General Grant as a verdict by the Northern people that the constitution is a nullity and that they will that the general government be administered outside of it. But the South will then submit passively to your laws, but in her heart hope will still cleave to the constitution. It is her only port of safety from the storm of fanaticism, passion, and despotism.

The South surrendered secession as a constitutional remedy at Appomattox, but she did not surrender the constitution itself, nor the great principles of freedom it was intended to secure.

Whether Mr. Seymour or General Grant shall be elected, the Southern States—each State for itself—will quietly, peacefully, but firmly take charge of and regulate their own internal domestic affairs in their own way, subject only to the constitution of the United States. What then will you of the North do? What will President Grant do? Will you or he send down armies to compel those States to regulate their own affairs to suit you outside of the constitution? Will you?

It is high time this people had recovered from the passions of war. It is high time that counsel were taken from statesmen, not demagogues. It is high time that editors, preachers, and stump speakers had ceased slandering the motives and purposes of the South. It is high time the people of the North and the South understood each other and adopted means to inspire confidence in each other. It is high time the people of each State were permitted to attend to their own business. Intermeddling is the crime of the century. If it was folly in the South to secede it was crime in the North to provoke it. If it was error in the South to dissolve the Union it is crime in the North to keep it dissolved.

The South yields secession and yields slavery, and yields them for equal reunion. People of the North, now is the auspicious moment to cement anew and for still greater glory our common Union. But it must be cemented in mutual good will, as between equals and under the constitution. Such a Union the South pleads for. I care not what slanderers say, what fanaticism represents, or how selfish and corrupt hate and ambition pervert; I tell you there is but one desire in the South. From every heart in that bright land, from her cotton fields and grain farms, from her rich valleys and metal-pregnant mountains, from the lullabies of her thousands of rippling streams and moaning millions of her primeval forest-trees, comes up to you but this one voice—this one earnest, united voice: Flag of our Union, wave on; wave ever! But wave over freemen, not subject; over States, not Provinces; over a union of equals, not of lords and vassals; over a land of law, of liberty, and of peace, and not of anarchy, oppression, and strife!

People of the North, will you answer back in patriotic notes of cheering accord that our common constitution shall remain or in the discordant notes of sectional hate and national ruin that there shall be protection for the North inside of the constitution and oppression for the South outside of it?

If the latter then not only the Union, not only the constitution, but that grand, peculiar system of free federative governments so wisely devised by our fathers and known as the American system, and of which the constitution is but the instrument and the Union but the shadow—will die, must die, is dead!

Have you ever studied this American system of government? Have you compared it with former systems of free governments, and noted how our fathers sought to avoid their fatal defects? I commend this study to your prompt attention. To the heart that loves liberty it is more enchanting than romance, more bewitching than love, and more elevating than any other science. If history proves any one thing more than another it is that freedom cannot be secured in a wide and populous country except upon the plan of a federal compact for general interests, and untrammelled local governments for local interests.

Our fathers adopted this general plan with improvements in the details of profound wisdom which cannot be found in any previous system. With what a noble impulse of common patriotism they came together from distant States and joined their counsels to devise and perfect this system, henceforth to be forever known as the American system.

The snows that lodge on the summit of Mount Washington are not purer than the motives that begot it. The fresh dew-laden zephyrs from the orange groves of the South are not sweeter than the hopes its advent inspired. The flight of its own symbolic eagle, though he blew his breath upon the sun, could not be higher than its expected destiny! Alas, are these motives now corrupted? Are these hopes poisoned? And is this high destiny eclipsed, and so soon,—aye, before a century has brought to manhood its youthful visage? Stop before the blow is given and let us consider but its early blessings.

Under the benign influences of this promising American system of government our whole country at once entered upon a career of prosperity without a parallel in human annals. The seventy years of its life brought more thrift, more success, more individual freedom, more universal happiness with fewer public burdens than were ever before enjoyed or borne by any portion of the world in five centuries. From three millions of whites we became thirty millions. From three hundred thousand blacks we became four millions— a greater relative increase than of the whites with all the aid of immigration. From a narrow peopled slope along the dancing Atlantic we stretched with wide girth to the sluggish Pacific. From a small power which a European despotism, in jealousy of a rival, patronizingly took by the hand and led to independence, we became a power whose voice united was heard throughout the world and whose frown might well be dreaded by the combined powers of earth. Our granaries fed and our factories clothed mankind. The buffalo and his hunter were gone, and cities rose in the forests of the former, and flowers grew, and hammers rang, and prayers were said, in the playgrounds of the latter. Millions grew to manhood without seeing a soldier, or hearing a cannon, or knowing the shape or place of a bayonet! And is this happy, fruitful, peaceful system dying—hopelessly dying? Has it but twenty days more to live a struggling life?

People of the North, the answer is with you. Rise above passion, throw away corruption, cease to hate and learn to trust, and this dying system will spring to newer and yet more glorious life. The stake is too great for duplicity and the danger too imminent for trifling. The past calls to you to vindicate its wisdom; the present charges you with its treasures, and the future demands of you its hopes. Forget your anger and be superior to the littleness of revenge. Meet the South in her cordial proffers of happy reunion and turn not from her offered hand.

From your great cities and teeming prairies, from your learned altars and countless cottages, from your palaces on sea and land, from your millions on the waters and your multiplied millions on the plains, let one united cheering voice meet the voice that now comes so earnest from the South, and let the two voices go up in harmonious, united, eternal, ever-swelling chorus, Flag of our Union! wave on; wave ever! Aye, for it waves over freemen, not subjects; over States, not Provinces; over a union of equals, not of lords and vassals; over a land of law, of liberty, and peace, not of anarchy, oppression, and strife!

Hay, John, a distinguished American diplomatist and man of letters, born at Salem, Ind., October 8, 1838. He studied law and shortly after his admission to the bar in 1861 became an assistant secretary to President Lincoln. He served for a time in the Federal army during the Civil War and was subsequently secretary of legation at Paris and Madrid, and chargé d'affaires at Vienna. For six years he was one of the editors of the New York Tribune, and from 1879 to '1881, assistant secretary of State. He was appointed ambassador to Great Britain in 1897, and in September, 1898, was recalled in order to assume the office of secretary of state in the national cabinet. He has published several volumes of poems, and, with John Nicolay, a Life of Abraham Lincoln in ten volumes. He is a skilful diplomatist and an able, polished orator.

SECRETARY OF STATE'S TRIBUTE TO THE DEAD PRESIDENT.

THE JOINT MEMORIAL SESSION OF THE UNITED STATES SENATE AND THE HOUSE OF REPRESENTATIVES FEB 27, 1902.

" For the third time the Congress of the United States are assembled to commemorate the life and the death of a President slain by the hand of an assassin. The attention of the future historian will be attracted to the features which reappear with startling sameness in all three of these awful crimes: the uselessness, the utter lack of consequence of the act; the obscurity, the insignificance of the criminal; the blamelessness—so far as in our sphere of existence the best of men may be held blameless—of the victim. Not one of our

murdered Presidents had an enemy in the world; they
were all of such pre-eminent purity of life that no pretext could be given for the attack of passional crime;
they were all men of democratic instincts, who could
never have offended the most jealous advocates of
equality; they were of kindly and generous nature, to
whom wrong or injustice was impossible; of moderate
fortune, whose slender means nobody could envy.
They were men of austere virtue, of tender heart, of
eminent abilities, which they had devoted with single
minds to the good of the Republic. If ever men
walked before God and man without blame, it was
these three rulers of our people. The only temptation
to attack their lives offered was their gentle radiance—
to eyes hating the light that was offence enough.

" The stupid uselessness of such an infamy affronts
the common sense of the world. One can conceive
how the death of a dictator may change the political
conditions of an Empire; how the extinction of a nar-
rowing line of kings may bring in an alien dynasty.
But in a well-ordered Republic like ours, the ruler may
fall, but the State feels no tremor. Our beloved and
revered leader is gone—but the natural process of our
laws provides us a successor, identical in purpose and
ideals, nourished by the same teachings, inspired by the
same principles, pledged by tender affection as well as
by high loyalty to carry to completion the immense
task committed to his hands, and to smite with iron
severity every manifestation of that hideous crime
which his mild predecessor, with his dying breath, for-
gave. The sayings of celestial wisdom have no date;
the words that reach us, over two thousand years, out

of the darkest hour of gloom the world has ever known, are true to life to-day: ' They know not what they do.' The blow struck at our dear friend and ruler was as deadly as blind hate could make it; but the blow struck at anarchy was deadlier still.

THE PROBLEM OF ANARCHY.

" What a world of insoluble problems such an event excites in the mind! Not merely in its personal, but in its public aspects, it presents a paradox not to be comprehended. Under a system of government so free and so impartial that we recognize its existence only by its benefactions; under a social order so purely democratic that classes cannot exist in it, affording opportunities so universal that even conditions are as changing as the winds, where the laborer of to-day is the capitalist of to-morrow; under laws which are the result of ages of evolution, so uniform and so beneficent that the President has just the same rights and privileges as the artisan; we see the same hellish growth of hatred and murder which dogs equally the footsteps of benevolent monarchs and blood-stained despots. How many countries can join with us in the community of a kindred sorrow! I will not speak of those distant regions where assassination enters into the daily life of government. But among the nations bound to us by the ties of familiar intercourse—who can forget that wise and mild Autocrat who had earned the proud title of the Liberator? that enlightened and magnanimous citizen whom France still mourns? that brave and chivalrous King of Italy who only lived for his people? and, saddest of all, that lovely and sorrow-

ing Empress, whose harmless life could hardly have
excited the animosity of a demon.   Against that devil-
ish spirit nothing avails—neither virtue nor patriotism,
nor age nor youth, nor conscience nor pity.   We cannot even say that education is a sufficient safeguard
against this baleful evil—for most of the wretches
whose crimes have so shocked humanity in recent years
were men not unlettered, who have gone from the
common schools, through murder to the scaffold.

"Our minds cannot discern the origin nor conceive
the extent of wickedness so perverse and so cruel; but
this does not exempt us from the duty of trying to
control and counteract it.   We do not understand what
electricity is; whence it comes or what its hidden prop-
erties may be.   But we know it as a mighty force for
good or evil—and so with the painful toil of years men
of learning and skill have labored to store and to sub-
jugate it, to neutralize, and even to employ its destructive energies.   This problem of anarchy is dark and
intricate, but it ought to be within the compass of
democratic government—although no sane mind can
fathom the mysteries of these untracked and orbitless
natures—to guard against their aberrations, to take
away from them the hope of escape, the long luxury of
scandalous days in court, the unwholesome sympathy
of hysterical degenerates, and so by degrees to make
the crime not worth committing, even to these ab-
normal and distorted souls.

"It would be presumptuous for me in this presence
to suggest the details of remedial legislation for a
malady so malignant.   That task may safely be left
to the skill and patience of the National Congress,

which has never been found unequal to any such emergency. The country believes that the memory of three murdered comrades of yours—all of whose voices still haunt these walls—will be a sufficient inspiration to enable you to solve even this abstruse and painful problem, which has dimmed so many pages of history with blood and with tears.

A TYPICAL AMERICAN.

" Before an audience less sympathetic than this, I should not dare to speak of that great career which we have met to commemorate. But we are all his friends, and friends do not criticise each other's words about an open grave. I thank you for the honor you have done me in inviting me here, and not less for the kind forbearance I know I shall have from you in my most inadequate efforts to speak of him worthily.

" The life of William McKinley was, from his birth to his death, typically American. There is no environment, I should say, anywhere else in the world which could produce just such a character. He was born into that way of life which elsewhere is called the middle class, but which in this country is so nearly universal as to make of other classes an almost negligible quantity. He was neither rich nor poor, neither proud nor humble; he knew no hunger he was not sure of satisfying, no luxury which could enervate mind or body. His parents were sober, God-fearing people; intelligent and upright, without pretension and without humility. He grew up in the company of boys like himself, wholesome, honest, self-respecting. They looked down on nobody; they never felt it possible they could be looked down upon.   Their houses were the homes of probity, piety, patriotism.   They learned in the admirable school readers of fifty years ago the lessons of heroic and splendid life which have come down from the past.   They read in their weekly newspapers the story of the world's progress, in which they were eager to take part, and of the sins and wrongs of civilization with which they burned to do battle.   It was a serious and thoughtful time.   The boys of that day felt dimly, but deeply, that days of sharp struggle and high achievement were before them.   They looked at life with the wondering yet resolute eyes of a young esquire in his vigil of arms.   They felt a time was coming when to them should be addressed the stern admonition of the Apostle, "Quit you like men; be strong."

THE DAYS OF 1860.

"It is not easy to give to those of a later generation any clear idea of that extraordinary spiritual awakening which passed over the country at the first red signal fires of the war between the States.   It was not our earliest apocalypse; a hundred years before the nation had been revealed to itself, when after long discussion and much searching of heart the people of the colonies had resolved, that to live without liberty was worse than to die, and had therefore wagered in the solemn game of war 'their lives, their fortunes, and their sacred honor.'   In a stress of heat and labor unutterable, the country had been hammered and welded together; but thereafter for nearly a century there had been nothing in our life to touch the innermost fountain of feeling and devotion; we had had rumors of wars—even wars we had had, not without sacrifices and glory—but nothing which went to the vital self-consciousness of the country, nothing which challenged the nation's right to live. But in 1860 the nation was going down into the Valley of Decision. The question which had been debated on thousands of platforms, which had been discussed in countless publications, which thundered from innumerable pulpits, had caused in their congregations the bitter strife and dissension to which only cases of conscience can give rise, was everywhere pressing for solution. And not merely in the various channels of publicity was it alive and clamorous. About every fireside in the land, in the conversation of friends and neighbors, and deeper still, in the secret of millions of human hearts, the battle of opinion was waging; and all men felt and saw—with more or less clearness—that an answer to the importunate question: Shall the nation live? was due, and not to be denied. And I do not mean that in the North alone there was this austere wrestling with conscience. In the South as well, below all the effervescence and excitement of a people perhaps more given to eloquent speech than we were, there was the profound agony of question and answer, the summons to decide whether honor and freedom did not call them to revolution and war. It is easy for partisanship to say that the one side was right and that the other was wrong. It is still easier for an indolent magnanimity to say that both were right. Perhaps in the wide view of ethics one is always right to follow his conscience, though it lead him to disaster and death. But history is inexorable.

She takes no account of sentiment and intention; and in her cold and luminous eyes that side is right which fights in harmony with the stars in their courses. The men are right through whose efforts and struggles the world is helped onward, and humanity moves to a higher level and a brighter day.

"The men who are living to-day and who were young in 1860 will never forget the glory and glamor that filled the earth and the sky when the long twilight of doubt and uncertainty was ending and the time for action had come. A speech by Abraham Lincoln was an event not only of high moral significance, but of far-reaching importance; the drilling of a militia company by Ellsworth attracted national attention; the fluttering of the flag in the clear sky drew tears from the eyes of young men. Patriotism, which had been a rhetorical expression, became a passionate emotion, in which instinct, logic and feeling were fused. The country was worth saving; it could be saved only by fire; no sacrifice was too great; the young men of the country were ready for the sacrifice; come weal, come woe, they were ready.

M'KINLEY THE SOLDIER.

At 17 years of age William McKinley heard this summons of his country. He was the sort of youth to whom a military life in ordinary times would possess no attractions. His nature was far different from that of the ordinary soldier. He had other dreams of life, its prizes and pleasures, than that of marches and battles. But to his mind there was no choice or question. The banner floating in the morning breeze was the beckoning gesture of his country. The thrilling notes of the trumpet called *him*—him and none other—into the ranks. His portrait in his first uniform is familiar to you all—the short, stocky figure; the quiet thoughtful face; the deep, dark eyes. It is the face of a lad who could not stay at home when he thought he was needed in the field. He was of the stuff of which good soldiers are made. Had he been ten years older he would have entered at the head of a company and come out at the head of a division. But he did what he could. He enlisted as a private; he learned to obey. His serious, sensible ways, his prompt, alert efficiency soon attracted the attention of his superiors. He was so faithful in little things that they gave him more and more to do. He was untiring in camp and on the march; swift, cool and fearless in fight. He left the Army with field rank when the war ended, brevetted by President Lincoln for gallantry in battle.

" In coming years, when men seek to draw the moral of our great Civil War, nothing will seem to them so admirable in all the history of our two magnificent armies as the way in which the war came to a close. When the Confederate army saw the time had come, they acknowledged the pitiless logic of facts and ceased fighting. When the army of the Union saw it was no longer needed, without a murmur or question, making no terms, asking no return, in the flush of victory and fulness of might, it laid down its arms and melted back into the mass of peaceful citizens. There is no event since the nation was born which has so proved its solid capacity for self-government. Both sections share equally in that crown of glory. They had held a debate of incomparable importance and had fought it out with equal energy. A conclusion had been reached —and it is to the everlasting honor of both sides that they each knew when the war was over and the hour of a lasting peace had struck. We may admire the desperate daring of others who prefer annihilation to compromise, but the palm of common sense, and, I will say, of enlightened patriotism, belongs to the men like Grant and Lee, who knew when they had fought enough, for honor and for country.

M'KINLEY THE LAWYER.

" William McKinley, one of that sensible million of men, gladly laid down his sword and betook himself to his books. He quickly made up the time lost in soldiering. He attacked his Blackstone as he would have done a hostile intrenchment; finding the range of a country law library too narrow, he went to the Albany Law School, where he worked energetically with brilliant success; was admitted to the bar and settled down to practise—a brevetted veteran of 24— in the quiet town of Canton, now and henceforth forever famous as the scene of his life and his place of sepulture. Here many blessings awaited him: high repute, professional success, and a domestic affection so pure, so devoted and stainless that future poets, seeking an ideal of Christian marriage, will find in it a theme worthy of their songs. This is a subject to which the lightest allusion seems profanation; but it is impossible to speak of William McKinley without remembering that no truer, tenderer knight to his chosen lady ever lived among mortal men. If to the spirits of the just made perfect is permitted the consciousness of earthly things, we may be sure that his faithful soul is now watching over that gentle sufferer who counts the long hours in their shattered home in the desolate splendor of his fame.

" A man possessing the qualities with which nature had endowed McKinley seeks political activity as naturally as a growing plant seeks light and air. A wholesome ambition; a rare power of making friends and keeping them; a faith, which may be called religious, in his country and its institutions; and, flowing from this, a belief that a man could do no nobler work than to serve such a country—these were the elements in his character that drew him irresistibly into public life. He had from the beginning a remarkable equipment; a manner of singular grace and charm; a voice of ringing quality and great carrying power—vast as were the crowds that gathered about him, he reached their utmost fringe without apparent effort. He had an extraordinary power of marshalling and presenting significant facts, so as to bring conviction to the average mind. His range of reading was not wide; he read only what he might some day find useful; and what he read his memory held like brass. Those who knew him well in those early days can never forget the consummate skill and power with which he would select a few pointed facts and, blow upon blow, would hammer them into the attention of great assemblages in Ohio, as Jael drove the nail into the head of the Canaanite captain. He was not often impassioned; he rarely resorted to the aid of wit or humor; yet I never saw his equal in controlling and convincing a popular audience by sheer appeal to their reason and intelligence. He did not flatter or cajole them, but there was an implied compliment in the serious and sober tone in which he addressed them. He seemed one of them; in heart and feeling he *was* one of them. Each artisan in a great crowd might say: That is the sort of man I would like to be, and under more favoring circumstances might have been. He had the divine gift of sympathy, which, though given only to the elect, makes all men their friends.

M'KINLEY THE CONGRESSMAN.

" So it came naturally about that in 1876—the beginning of the second century of the Republic—he began, by an election to Congress, his political career. Thereafter for fourteen years this chamber was his home. I use the word advisedly. Nowhere in the world was he so in harmony with his environment as here; nowhere else did his mind work with such full consciousness of its powers. The air of debate was native to him; here he drank delight of battle with his peers. In after days, when he drove by this stately pile, or when on rare occasions his duty called him here, he greeted his old haunts with the affectionate zest of a child of the house; during all the last ten years of his life, filled as they were with activity and glory, he never ceased to be homesick for this hall. When he came to the Presidency, there was not a day when his Congressional service was not of use to him. Probably no other President has been in such full and cordial communion with Congress, if we may except Lincoln alone. McKinley knew the legislative body thoroughly, its composition, its methods, its habit of thought. He had the profoundest respect for its authority and an inflexible belief in the ultimate rectitude of its purposes. Our history shows how sure an executive courts disaster and ruin by assuming an attitude of hostility or distrust to the Legislature; and, on the other hand, McKinley's frank and sincere trust and confidence in Congress were repaid by prompt and loyal support and co-operation. During his entire term of office this mutual trust and regard—so essential to the public welfare—was never shadowed by a single cloud.

" He was a Republican. He could not be anything else. A Union soldier grafted upon a 'Clay Whig, he necessarily believed in the ' American System '—in protection to home industries; in a strong, aggressive nationality; in a liberal construction of the Constitution. What any self-reliant nation might rightly do, he felt this nation had power to do, if required by the common welfare and not prohibited by our written charter.

" Following the natural bent of his mind, he devoted himself to questions of finance and revenue, to the essentials of the national housekeeping. He took high rank in the House from the beginning. His readiness in debate, his mastery of every subject he handled, the bright and amiable light he shed about him, and above all the unfailing courtesy and goodwill with which he treated friend and foe alike—one of the surest signatures of a nature born to great destinies—made his service in the House a pathway of unbroken success and brought him at last to the all-important post of chairman of Ways and Means and leader of the majority. Of the famous revenue act which, in that capacity, he framed and carried through Congress, it is not my purpose here and now to speak. The embers of the controversy in the midst of which that law had its troubled being are yet too warm to be handled on a day like this. I may only say that it was never sufficiently tested to prove the praises of its friends or the criticisms of its opponents. After a brief existence it passed away, for a time, in the storm that swept the Republicans out of power. McKinley also passed through a brief zone of shadow, his Congressional district having been rearranged for that purpose by a hostile Legislature.

" Some one has said it is easy to love our enemies; they help us so much more than our friends. The people whose malevolent skill had turned McKinley out of Congress deserved well of him and of the Republic. Never was Nemesis more swift and energetic. The Republicans of Ohio were saved the trouble of choosing a Governor—the other side had chosen one for them. A year after McKinley left Congress he was made Governor of Ohio, and two years later he was re-elected, each time by majorities uphoped-for and overwhelming. He came to fill a space in the public eye which obscured a great portion of the field of vision. In two National Conventions, the Presidency seemed within his reach. But he had gone there in the interest of others and his honor forbade any dalliance with temptation. So his nay was nay—delivered with a tone and gesture there was no denying. His hour was not yet come.

M'KINLEY THE ORATOR.

"There was, however, no long delay. He became from year to year, the most prominent politician and orator in the country. Passionately devoted to the principles of his party, he was always ready to do anything, to go anywhere, to proclaim its ideas and to support its candidates. His face and his voice became familiar to millions of our people; and wherever they were seen and heard, men became his partisans. His face was cast in a classic mould; you see faces like it in antique marble in the galleries of the Vatican and in the portraits of the great Cardinal-statesmen of Italy; his voice was the voice of the perfect orator—ringing, vibrating, tireless, persuading by its very sound, by its accent of sincere conviction. So prudent and so guarded were all his utterances, so lofty his courtesy, that he never embarrassed his friends, and never offended his opponents. For several months before the Republican National Convention met in 1896 it was evident to all who had eyes to see that Mr. McKinley was the only probable candidate of his party. Other names were mentioned, of the highest rank in ability, character and popularity; they were supported by powerful combinations, but the nomination of William McKinley as against the field, was inevitable.

"The campaign he made will be always memorable in our political annals. He and his friends had thought that the issue for the year was the distinctive and historic difference between the two parties on the subject of the tariff. To this wager of battle the discussions

of the previous four years distinctly pointed. But no
sooner had the two parties made their nominations
than it became evident that the opposing candidate declined to accept the field of discussion chosen by the
Republicans, and proposed to put forward as the main
issue the free coinage of silver. McKinley at once accepted this challenge, and, taking the battle, for protection as already won, went with energy into the discussion of the theories presented by his opponents. He
had wisely concluded not to leave his home during the
canvass, thus avoiding a proceeding which has always
been of sinister augury in our politics; but from the
front porch of his modest house in Canton he daily
addressed the delegations which came from every part
of the country to greet him in a series of speeches so
strong, so varied, so pertinent, so full of facts briefly
set forth, of theories embodied in a single phrase, that
they formed the hourly text for the other speakers of
his party, and give probably the most convincing proof
we have of his surprising fertility of resource and flex-
ibility of mind. All this was done without anxiety or
strain. I remember a day I spent with him during that
busy summer. He had made nineteen speeches the day
before; that day he made many. But in the intervals
of these addresses he sat in his study and talked, with
nerves as quiet and a mind as free from care as if we
had been spending a holiday at the seaside or among
the hills.

M'KINLEY THE STATESMAN.

"When he came to the Presidency he confronted
a situation of the utmost difficulty, which might well

have appalled a man of less serene and tranquil self-confidence. There had been a state of profound commercial and industrial depression from which his friends had said his election would relieve the country. Our relations with the outside world left much to be desired. The feeling between the Northern and Southern sections of the Union was lacking in the cordiality which was necessary to the welfare of both. Hawaii had asked for annexation and had been rejected by the preceding administration. There was a state of things in the Caribbean which could not permanently endure. Our neighbor's house was on fire, and there were grave doubts as to our rights and duties in the premises. A man either weak or rash, either irresolute or headstrong, might have brought ruin on himself and incalculable harm to the country.

"Again I crave the pardon of those who differ with me, if, against all my intentions, I happen to say a word which may seem to them unbefitting the place and hour. But I am here to give the opinion which his friends entertained of President McKinley, of course claiming no immunity from criticism in what I shall say. I believe, then, that the verdict of history will be that he met all these grave questions with perfect valor and incomparable ability; that in grappling with them he rose to the full height of a great occasion, in a manner which redounded to the lasting benefit of the country and to his own immortal honor.

"The least desirable form of glory to a man of his habitual mood and temper—that of successful war—was nevertheless conferred upon him by uncontrollable events. He felt it must come; he deplored its necessity; he strained almost to breaking his relations with his friends, in order, first to prevent and then to postpone it to the latest possible moment. But when the die was cast, he labored with the utmost energy and ardor, and with an intelligence in military matters which showed how much of the soldier still survived in the mature statesman to push forward the war to a decisive close. War was an anguish to him; he wanted it short and conclusive. His merciful zeal communicated itself to his subordinates, and the war, so long dreaded, whose consequences were so momentous, ended in a hundred days.

"Mr. Stedman, the dean of our poets, has called him 'Augmenter of the State.' It is a proud title; if justly conferred, it ranks him among the few whose names may be placed definitely and forever in charge of the historic Muse. Under his rule Hawaii has come to us, and Tutuila; Porto Rica and the vast archipelago of the East. Cuba is free. Our position in the Caribbean is assured beyond the possibility of future question. The doctrine called by the name of Monroe, so long derided and denied by alien publicists, evokes now no challenge or contradiction when uttered to the world. It has become an international truism. Our sister republics to the south of us are convinced that we desire only their peace and prosperity. Europe knows that we cherish no dreams but those of world-wide commerce, the benefit of which shall be to all nations. The State is augmented, but it threatens no nation under heaven. As to those regions which have come under the shadow of our flag, the possibility of their being damaged by such change of circumstances was in the view of McKinley a thing unthinkable. To believe that we could not administer them to their advantage, was to turn infidel to our American faith of more than a hundred years.

M'KINLEY THE DIPLOMAT.

" In dealing with foreign Powers he will take rank with the greatest of our diplomatists. It was a world of which he had little special knowledge before coming to the Presidency. But his marvellous adaptability was in nothing more remarkable than in the firm grasp he immediately displayed in international relations. In preparing for war and in the restoration of peace he was alike adroit, courteous and far-sighted. When a sudden emergency declared itself, as in China, in a state of things of which our history furnished no precedent and international law no safe and certain precept, he hesitated not a moment to take the course marked out for him by considerations of humanity and the national interests. Even while the legations were fighting for their lives against bands of infuriated fanatics, he decided that we were at peace with China; and while that conclusion did not hinder him from taking the most energetic measures to rescue our imperilled citizens, it enabled him to maintain close and friendly relations with the wise and heroic Viceroys of the South, whose resolute stand saved that ancient empire from anarchy and spoliation. He disposed of every question as it arose with a promptness and clarity of vision that astonished his advisers, and he never had occasion to review a judgment or reverse a decision.

8—6

"By patience, by firmness, by sheer reasonableness, he improved our understanding with all the great Powers of the world, and rightly gained the blessing which belongs to the peacemakers.

M'KINLEY THE ECONOMIST.

"But the achievements of the nation in war and diplomacy are thrown in the shade by the vast economical developments which took place during Mr. McKinley's administration. Up to the time of his first election, the country was suffering from a long period of depression, the reasons of which I will not try to seek. But from the moment the ballots were counted that betokened his advent to power, a great and momentous movement in advance declared itself along all the lines of industry and commerce. In the very month of his inauguration steel rails began to be sold at $18 a ton—one of the most significant facts of modern times. It meant that American industries had adjusted themselves to the long depression—that through the power of the race to organize and combine, stimulated by the conditions then prevailing, and perhaps by prospect of legislation favorable to industry, America had begun to undersell the rest of the world. The movement went on without ceasing. The President and his party kept the pledges of their platform and their canvass. The Dingley bill was speedily framed and set in operation. All industries responded to the new stimulus and American trade set out on its new crusade, not to conquer the world, but to trade with it on terms advantageous to all concerned. I will not weary you with statistics, but one or two words seem necessary to show how the acts of McKinley as President kept pace with his professions as candidate. His four years of administration were costly; we carried on a war which, though brief, was expensive. Although we borrowed $200,000,000 and paid our own expenses without asking for indemnity, the effective reduction of the debt now exceeds the total of the war bonds. We pay $6,000,000 less in interest than we did before the war and no bond of the United States yields the holder 2 per cent. on its market value. So much for the Government credit; and we have $546,000,000 of gross gold in the Treasury.

"But, coming to the development of our trade in the four McKinley years, we seem to be entering the realm of fable. In the last fiscal year our excess of exports over imports was $664,592,826. In the last four years it was $2,354,442,213. These figures are so stupendous that they mean little to a careless reader—but consider! The excess of exports over imports for the whole preceding period from 1790 to 1897—from Washington to McKinley—was only $356,808,822.

"The most extravagant promises made by the sanguine McKinley advocates five years ago are left out of sight by these sober facts. The debtor nation has become the chief creditor nation. The financial centre of the world, which required thousands of years to journey from the Euphrates to the Thames and the Seine, seems passing to the Hudson between daybreak and dark.

"I will not waste your time by explaining that I do not invoke for any man the credit of this vast result. The captain cannot claim that it is he who drives the mighty steamship over the tumbling billows of the trackless deep; but praise is justly due him if he has made the best of her tremendous powers, if he has read aright the currents of the sea and the lessons of the stars. And we should be ungrateful if in this hour of prodigious prosperity we should fail to remember that William McKinley with sublime faith foresaw it, with indomitable courage labored for it, put his whole heart and mind into the work of bringing it about; that it was his voice which, in dark hours, rang out, heralding the coming light, as over the twilight waters of the Nile the mystic cry of Memnon announced the dawn to Egypt, waking from sleep.

M'KINLEY THE HARMONIZER.

" Among the most agreeable incidents of the President's term of office were the two journeys he made to the South. The moral reunion of the sections—so long and so ardently desired by him—had been initiated by the Spanish war, when the veterans of both sides, and their sons, had marched shoulder to shoulder together under the same banner. The President in these journeys sought, with more than usual eloquence and pathos, to create a sentiment which should end forever the ancient feud. He was too good a politician to expect any results in the way of votes in his favor, and he accomplished none. But for all that the good seed did not fall on barren ground. In the warm and chivalrous heart of that generous people, the echo of his cordial and brotherly words will linger long, and his name will be cherished in many a household where even yet the lost cause is worshipped.

"Mr. McKinley was re-elected by an overwhelming majority. There had been little doubt of the result among well-informed people; but when it was known, a profound feeling of relief and renewal of trust were evident among the leaders of capital and of industry, not only in this country, but everywhere. They felt that the immediate future was secure, and that trade and commerce might safely push forward in every field of effort and enterprise. He inspired universal confidence, which is the lifeblood of the commercial system of the world. It began frequently to be said that such a state of things ought to continue; one after another, men of prominence said that the President was his own best successor. He paid little attention to these suggestions until they were repeated by some of his nearest friends. Then he saw that one of the most cherished traditions of our public life was in danger. The generation which has seen the prophecy of the Papal throne—*Non videbis annos Petri*—twice contradicted by the longevity of holy men was in peril of forgetting the unwritten law of our Republic. 'Thou shalt not exceed the years of Washington. The President saw it was time to speak, and in his characteristic manner he spoke, briefly, but enough. Where the lightning strikes there is no need of iteration. From that hour, no one dreamed of doubting his purpose of retiring at the end of his second term, and it will be long before another such lesson is required.

M'KINLEY THE PATRIOT.

"He felt that the harvest time was come, to garner in the fruits of so much planting and culture, and he was determined that nothing he might do or say should be liable to the reproach of a personal interest. Let us say frankly he was a party man; he believed the politics advocated by him and his friends counted for much in the country's progress and prosperity. He hoped in his second term to accomplish substantial results in the development and affirmation of those policies. I spent a day with him shortly before he started on his fateful journey to Buffalo. Never had I seen him higher in hope and patriotic confidence. He was as sure of the future of his country as the Psalmist who cried ' Glorious things are spoken of thee, thou City of God.' He was gratified to the heart that we had arranged a treaty which gave us a free hand in the Isthmus. In fancy he saw the canal already built and the argosies of the world passing through it in peace and amity. He saw in the immense evolution of American trade the fulfilment of all his dreams, the reward of all his labors. He was—I need not say—an ardent protectionist, never more sincere and devoted than during those last days of his life. He regarded reciprocity as the bulwark of protection—not a breach, but a fulfilment of the law. The treaties which for four years had been preparing under his personal supervision he regarded as ancillary to the general scheme. He was opposed to any revolutionary plan of change in the existing legislation; he was careful to point out that everything he had done was in faithful compliance with the law itself.

" In that mood of high hope, of generous expectation, he went to Buffalo, and there, on the threshold of eternity, he delivered that memorable speech, worthy for its loftiness of tone, its blameless morality, its breadth of view, to be regarded as his testament to the nation. Through all his pride of country and his joy of its success runs the note of solemn warning, as in Kipling's noble hymn, ' Lest we Forget.'

" ' Our capacity to produce has developed so enormously and our products have so multiplied that the problem of more markets requires our urgent and immediate attention. Only a broad and enlightened policy will keep what we have. No other policy will get more. In these times of marvellous business energy and gain we ought to be looking to the future, strengthening the weak places in our industrial and commercial systems, that we may be ready for any storm or strain.

" 'By sensible trade arrangements which will not interrupt our home production we shall extend the outlets for our increasing surplus. A system which provides a mutual exchange of commodities is manifestly essential to the continued and healthful growth of our export trade. We must not repose in fancied security that we can forever sell everything and buy little or nothing.

" ' If such a thing were possible, it would not be best for us or for those with whom we deal. . . . Reciprocity is the natural outgrowth of our wonderful industrial development under the domestic policy now firmly established. . . . The period of exclusiveness is past. The expansion of our trade and commerce is the pressing problem. Commercial wars are unprofitable. A policy of goodwill and friendly trade relations will prevent reprisals. Reciprocity treaties are in harmony with the spirit of the times; measures of retaliation are not.'

"I wish I had time to read the whole of this wise and weighty speech; nothing I might say could give such a picture of the President's mind and character. His years of apprenticeship had been served. He stood that day past-master of the art of statesmanship. He had nothing more to ask of the people. He owed them nothing but truth and faithful service. His mind and heart were purged of the temptations which beset all men engaged in the struggle to survive. In view of the revelation of his nature vouchsafed to us that day, and the fate which impended over him, we can only say in deep affection and solemn awe: ' Blessed are the pure in heart, for they shall see God.' Even for that vision he was not unworthy.

M'KINLEY THE HEROIC.

"He had not long to wait. The next day sped the bolt of doom, and for a week after—in an agony of dread, broken by illusive glimpses of hope that our prayers might be answered—the nation waited for the end. Nothing in the glorious life that we saw gradually waning was more admirable and exemplary than its close. The gentle humanity of his words when he saw his assailant in danger of summary vengeance, ' Don't let them hurt him;' his chivalrous care that the news should be broken gently to his wife; the fine courtesy with which he apologized for the damage which his death would bring to the great Exhibition; and the heroic resignation of his final words, ' It is

God's way; His will, not ours, be done,' were all the
instinctive expressions of a nature so lofty and so
pure that pride in its nobility at once softened and en-
hanced the nation's sense of loss.   The Republic
grieved over such a son—but is proud forever of having produced him.   After all, in spite of its tragic
ending, his life was extraordinarily happy.   He had,
all his days, troops of friends, the cheer of fame and
fruitful labor; and he became at last,

> On fortune's crowning slope,
> The pillar of a people's hope,
> The centre of a world's desire.

"He was fortunate even in his untimely death, for
an event so tragical called the world imperatively to
the immediate study of his life and character, and thus
anticipated the sure praises of posterity.

"Every young and growing people has to meet, at
moments, the problems of its destiny.   Whether the
question comes, as in Egypt, from a sphinx, symbol of
the hostile forces of omnipotent nature, Who punishes
with instant death our failure to understand her meaning; or whether it comes, as in Jerusalem, from the
Lord of Hosts, who commands the building of His
temple, it comes always with the warning that the past
is past and experience vain: 'Your fathers, where
are they? and the prophets, do they live forever?'
The fathers are dead the prophets are silent; the questions are new, and have no answer but in time.

"When the horny outside case which protects the
infancy of a chrysalis nation suddenly bursts, and, in
a single abrupt shock, it finds itself floating on wings
which have not existed before, whose strength it has

never tested, among dangers it cannot foresee and is
without experience to measure every motion is a problem and every hesitation may be an error. The past
gives no clue to the future. The fathers, where are
they? and the prophets, do they live forever? We are
ourselves the fathers! We ourselves the prophets!
The questions that are put to us we must answer without delay, without help—for the sphinx allows no one
to pass.

"At such moments, which have already occurred
at least twice in the brief history of our own lives, we
may be humbly grateful to have had leaders simple
in mind, clear in vision — as far as human vision
can safely extend — penetrating in knowledge of
men, supple and flexible under the strains and
pressures of society, instinct with the energy of new
life and untried strength, cautious, calm, and, above
all, gifted in a supreme degree with the most surely
victorious of all political virtues—the genius of infinite patience.

FAME.

"The obvious elements which enter into the fame
of a public man are few and by no means recondite.
The man who fills a great station in a period of change,
who leads his country successfully through a time of
crisis; who, by his power of persuading and controlling others, has been able to command the best thought
of his age, so as to leave his country in a moral or
material condition in advance of where he found it—
such a man's position in history is secure. If, in addition to this, his written or spoken words possess the

subtle quality which carry them far and lodge them in men's hearts; and, more than all, if his utterances and actions, while informed with a lofty morality, are yet tinged with the glow of human sympathy, the fame of such a man will shine like a beacon through the mists of ages—an object of reverence, of imitation and of love. It should be to us an occasion of solemn pride that in the three great crises of our history such a man was not denied us. The moral value to a nation of a renown such as Washington's and Lincoln's and McKinley's is beyond all computation. No loftier ideal can be held up to the emulation of ingenuous youth. With such examples we cannot be wholly ignoble. Grateful as we may be for what they did, let us still be more grateful for what they were. While our daily being, our public policies, still feel the influence of their work, let us pray that in our spirits their lives may be voluble, calling us upward and onward.

"There is not one of us but feels prouder of his native land because the august figure of Washington presided over its beginnings, no one but vows it a tenderer love because Lincoln poured out his blood for it, no one but must feel his devotion for his country renewed, and kindled when he remembers how McKinley loved, revered and served it, showed in his life how a citizen should live and in his last hour taught us how a gentleman could die."

Higginson, Thomas Wentworth, an eminent American lecturer and essayist, born in Cambridge, Mass., December 22, 1823. He entered the Unitarian ministry early in his career, and after being pastor at Newburyport, Mass., 1847–50, he was pastor of an independent congregation at Worcester, in his native State, 1852–58. He was active in the anti-slavery movement, and during the Civil War was colonel of a Massachusetts regiment. He has been a member of the State Legislature and prominent in various reform movements, but the larger part of his time since the Civil War period has been devoted to literature, as the long list of his published works gives abundant evidence. He was long prominent in the lecture field, and at occasional social functions is always a favorite speaker. His addresses are always polished in style, and he possesses a particularly happy manner of delivery. His oration upon Grant and his plea for " Self Respect and Self Protection " are characteristic discourses.

DECORATION DAY ADDRESS AT MOUNT AUBURN CEMETERY, MAY 30, 1870.

WE meet to-day for a purpose that has the dignity and the tenderness of funeral rites without their sadness. It is not a new bereavement, but one which time has softened, that brings us here. We meet not around a newly-opened grave, but among those which nature has already decorated with the memorials of her love. Above every tomb her daily sunshine has smiled, her tears have wept; over the humblest she has bidden some grasses nestle, some vines creep, and the butterfly—ancient emblem of immortality—waves his little wings above every sod. To nature's signs of tenderness we add our own. Not " ashes to ashes, dust to dust," but blossoms to blossoms, laurels to the laureled.

The great Civil War has passed by—its great armies were disbanded, their tents struck, their camp-fires put out, their muster-rolls laid away. But there is another army whose numbers no presidential proclamation could reduce; no general orders disband. This is their camping-ground, these white stones are their tents, this list of names we bear is their muster-roll, their camp-fires yet burn in our hearts.

I remember this "Sweet Auburn" when no sacred associations made it sweeter, and when its trees looked down on no funerals but those of the bird and the bee. Time has enriched its memories since those days. And especially during our great war, as the nation seemed to grow impoverished in men, these hills grew richer in associations, until their multiplying wealth took in that heroic boy who fell in almost the last battle of the war. Now that roll of honor has closed, and the work of commemoration begun.

Without distinction of nationality, of race, of religion, they gave their lives to their country. Without distinction of religion, of race, of nationality, we garland their graves to-day. The young Roman Catholic convert, who died exclaiming "Mary! pardon!" and the young Protestant theological student, whose favorite place of study was this cemetery, and who asked only that no words of praise might be engraven on his stone—these bore alike the cross in their lifetime, and shall bear it alike in flowers to-day. They gave their lives that we might remain one nation, and the nation holds their memory alike in its arms.

And so the little distinctions of rank that separated us in the service are nothing here. Death has given the same brevet to all. The brillant young cavalry-general who rode into his last action, with stars on his shoulders and his death-wound on his breast, is to us no more precious than that sergeant of sharpshooters who followed the line unarmed at Antietam, waiting to take the rifle of some one who should die, because his own had been stolen; or that private who did the same thing in the same battle, leaving the hospital service to which he had been assigned. Nature has been equally tender to the graves of all, and our love knows no distinction.

What a wonderful embalmer is death! We who survive grow daily older. Since the war closed the youngest has gained some new wrinkle, the oldest some added gray hair. A few years more and only a few tottering figures shall represent the marching files of the Grand Army; a year or two beyond that, and there shall flutter by the window the last empty sleeve. But these who are here are embalmed forever in our imaginations; they will not change; they never will seem to us less young, less fresh, less daring, than when they sallied to their last battle. They will always have the dew of their youth; it is we alone who shall grow old.

And, again, what a wonderful purifier is death! These who fell beside us varied in character; like other men they had their strength and their weaknesses, their merits and their faults. Yet now all stains seem washed away; their life ceased at its climax, and the ending sanctified all that went before. They died for their country; that is their record. They found their way to heaven equally short, it seems to us from every battle-field, and with equal readiness our love seeks them to-day.

"What is a victory like?" said a lady to the Duke of Wellington. The greatest tragedy in the world, madame, except a defeat." Even our great war would be but a tragedy were it not for the warm feeling of brotherhood it has left behind it, based on the hidden emotions of days like these. The war has given peace to the nation; it has given union, freedom, equal rights; and in addition to that, it has given to you and me the sacred sympathy of these graves. No matter what it has cost us individually—health or worldly fortune—it is our reward that we can stand to-day among these graves and yet not blush that we survive.

The great French soldier, La Tour D' Auvergne, was the hero of many battles, but remained by his own choice in the ranks. Napoleon gave him a sword and the official title "First among the grenadiers of France." When he was killed, the emperor ordered that his heart should be entrusted to the keeping of his regiment— that his name should be called at every roll-call, and that his next comrade should make answer, "Dead upon the field of honor." In our memories are the names of many heroes; we treasure all their hearts in this consecrated ground, and when the name of each is called, we answer in flowers, "Dead upon the field of honor."

ORATION UPON GRANT.

DELIVERED AT THE MEMORIAL SERVICES HELD IN
CAMBRIDGE, MASSACHUSETTS, AUGUST 8, 1885.

IT was one of the most picturesque moments of the
history of Rome when, after the battle of Cannæ was
lost and the Roman army almost annihilated—while
Hannibal, the Carthaginian general, was measuring by
bushels the gold rings of the slain Roman knights
—the whole people of the city went out to greet with
honor their defeated general Terentius Varro, and to
bear to him a vote of thanks from the senate for " not
having despaired of the republic."

The vast obsequies celebrated all over the land to-day
are not in honor of a defeated general, but of a victorious one; yet the ground of gratitude is the same as
in that Roman pageant. Our Civil War, like that
between Rome and Carthage, began in defeat and was
transformed into victory, because he whom we cele-
brate did not despair of the republic. From the time
when his successes at Fort Donelson and Vicksburg
first turned the tide of adversity until the day when he
received Lee's surrender it was to him we looked.

Nor was this all. There was in all this something
more than mere generalship. Generalship is undoubtedly a special gift, almost amounting to genius—a
man is born to it, as he is for poetry, or chess-playing,
or commerce; and as in those other vocations, so in
this, his success in one direction does not prove him
equally strong in all. There are many ways in which
General Grant does not rank with the greatest of the

sons of men. He was wanting in many of the gifts and
even tastes which raise man to his highest; he did not
greatly care for poetry, philosophy, music, painting,
sculpture, natural science. The one art for which he
had genius is one that must be fleeting and perishable
compared to these; for the human race must in its progress outgrow war. But a remarkable personal quality
never can be ignored; if not shown in one way it will
be shown in another; and this personal quality Grant
had. Let us analyze some of its aspects.

He was great, in the first place, through the mere
scale of his work. His number of troops, the vast
area of his operations, surpassed what the world had
before seen. When he took 15,000 prisoners at Fort
Donelson, the capture was three times as large as when
Burgoyne surrendered, in the only American battle
thought important enough to be mentioned by Sir Edward Creasy in his "Fifteen Decisive Battles of the
World."

When, on July 4, 1863, he took Vicksburg, he received what was then claimed to be the greatest capture
of men and armament since the invention of gunpowder
and perhaps since the beginning of recorded history.
He captured 15 generals, 31,600 soldiers and 172 cannon. For victories less than this, Julius Cæsar was
made dictator for ten years, and his statue was carried
in processions with those of the immortal gods. Cæsar
at Pharsalia took about 24,000 prisoners; Napoleon at
Ulm, 23,000; Hannibal at Cannæ but 20,000. Yet
these in Grant's case were but special victories. How
great, then, his power when at the head of the armies
of the United States! Neither of these great com-

manders ever directed the movements of a million men.
The mere coarse estimate of numbers, therefore, is the
first measure of Grant's fame.

But mere numbers are a subordinate matter.   He
surpassed his predecessors also in the dignity of the
object for which he fought.   The three great generals
of the world are usually enumerated—following Macaulay—as being Cæsar, Cromwell and Napoleon.
Two of these fought in wars of mere conquest, and the
contests of the third were marred by a gloomy fanaticism, by cruelty and by selfishness. General Grant
fought to restore a nation, that nation being the hope of
the world. And he restored it. His work was as
complete as it was important. Cæsar died by violence;
Napoleon died defeated; Cromwell's work crumbled to
pieces when his hand was cold. Grant's career tri-
umphed in its ending; it is at its height to-day.

It was finely said by a Massachusetts statesman that
we did not fight to bring our opponents to our feet, but
only to our side. Grant to-day brings his opponents
literally to his side when they act as pall-bearers around
his coffin.

The next thing remarkable about him was the spirit
in which he fought. He belonged in his whole temperament to the Anglo-Saxon or Germanic type of generals, and not to the French or Latin type. It is said
that in the Duke of Wellington's despatches you never
find the word "glory," but always the word "duty,"
while in those of Napoleon Bonaparte you never find
the word "duty." but always "glory." Grant was in this
respect like Wellington. In his early western campaign he wrote to his father: "I will go on and do my

duty to the best of my ability, and do all I can to bring the war to a speedy close. I am not an aspirant to anything at the close of the war. . . . One thing I am well aware of: I have the confidence of every man in my command." Of course he had. Once convince men that your motive is duty and their confidence is yours.

When we come to the mere executive qualities involved in fighting, we find that Grant habitually combined in action two things rarely brought together—quickness and perseverance. That could be said of him which Malcolm McLeod said of Charles Edward, the Pretender: " He is the bravest man, not to be rash, and the most cautious man, not to be a coward, that I ever saw."

He did not have the visible and conspicuous dash of Sherman or Sheridan; he was rather the kind of man whom they needed to have behind them. But in quickness of apprehension and action, where this quality was needed, he was not their inferior, if they were even his equals. He owed to it his first conspicuous victory at Fort Donelson. Looking at the knapsacks of the slain enemy, he discovered that they held three days' rations, and knew, therefore, that they were trying to get away. Under this stimulus he renewed the attack and the day was won.

Moreover, it is to be noticed that he was, in all his action as a commander, essentially original—a man of initiative, not of routine. He was singularly free from the habit of depending on others. When in Egypt an official gave him an Arabian horse and advised that, at first, he should simply pace the horse up and down,

with one or two attendants to hold him, Grant, who
had at West Point been the best rider in his class, said
briefly, "If I can mount a horse I can ride him, and
all the attendants can do is to keep away." It was the
same with him through his military life; if he could
mount the horse he could ride it; and what caused all
to turn to him, as much as anything, was his knowledge that he was an original force, not an imitator or
dependant.

And to crown all these qualities was added one
more, that of personal modesty. When, at Hamburg,
Germany, he was toasted as "the man who had saved
the nation," he replied, "What saved the Union was the
coming forward of the young men of the country."
He put down the pride of the German officers, the most
self-sufficient military aristocracy of the world, by
quietly disclaiming the assumption of being a soldier
at all. He said to Bismarck: "I am more a farmer
than a soldier. I take little or no interest in military
affairs, and although I entered army thirty-five years
ago and have been in two wars—the Mexican as a
young lieutenant, and later [mark the exquisite moderation of that "and later"]—I never went into the
army without regret, and never retired without pleasure." Such a remark from the greatest captain of the
age disarmed even German criticism.

When we turn from the military life of Grant to his
civil life, we find him at great disadvantage and entering untried on a sphere where it is, perhaps, still too
early to judge him. He had been trained in the army,
a bad school for civil service through this reason, that
an army officer is obliged, if in command, to select his

subordinates, trust a great deal to them, stand by them under attack and not interfere very much with them till they lose his confidence and he drops them. It is almost impossible for him, as can be done in a counting room or a workshop, to watch his subordinates, check them, guide them and correct their mistakes from day to day. The chief drawbacks of President Grant's administration came from this habit, and now that it is past we can see that they left the man himself unstained. There were, undoubtedly, men of the highest character with whom he was brought in close contact whom he could not appreciate and with whom he could not well act. Thus he never did justice to Charles Sumner, but we may well admit, at this distance of time, that Sumner did not quite do justice to him.

There is no doubt, I suppose, that Grant would have died a happier man had he for a third time been raised to the Presidency. There is nothing strange in this. Nobody ever longed to be an ex-President, and anybody might honorably long to be set above even Washington by having a third Presidential term. To call this Cæsarism was idle; it was not in Grant to make one conscious step to impair the liberties of his country. Whether his third administration would not have damaged those liberties indirectly and unconsciously, we never shall know; the majority of Americans apparently either feared some such result, or found the precedent too dangerous to venture on. The step never was taken at any rate; and the nation is perhaps safer that it was not, but we must guard against connecting this ambition in Grant's case with anything base or unscrupulous.

He was never tried by this test of a third term of
power; but a third term of ordeal came to him in a
wholly unexpected way, and increased his hold upon
us all.   He told Bismarck, as we have seen, that he
never entered on a war without regret or retired from
it without pleasure.   But he was destined to enter
on just one more campaign—against pain and disease
combined with sudden poverty.   It was a formidable
coalition.   It is sometimes said that it is easier to die
well than to live well, but it is harder than either to
grow old, knowing that one's great period of action is
past, and weighed down with the double weight of
hopeless financial failure and irremediable bodily pain.
Either bankruptcy or physical torture has by itself
crushed many a man morally and mentally; but Grant's
greatest campaign was when he resisted them both.
Upon such a campaign as this he might well, as he
said, shrink from entering; but having been obliged to
enter upon it, he was still Grant.   Thousands of
Americans have felt a sense of nearness to him and a
sense of pride in him during the last few months such
as they never felt before.   He was already a hero in
war to us.   The last few months have made him a hero
of peace, *miles pacificus.*

It has already been said that the supreme generals of
the world were Cæsar, Cromwell, and Napoleon.
Grant was behind all three of these in variety of cultivation and in many of the qualities that make a man's
biography picturesque and fascinating.   He may be
said to have seemed a little prosaic, compared with any
one of these.   But in moral qualities he was above
them all; more truthful, more unselfish, more simple,

more humane. He fell short of Washington in this, that he was not equally great in war and statesmanship; but his qualities were within reach of all; his very defects were within reach of all; and he will long be with Washington and Lincoln the typical American in the public eyes. It is this typical quality after all that is most valuable. What we need most to know is not that exceptional men of rare gifts or qualities may arise here —they may arise anywhere—but that there is such an average quality among us that when a great personal leadership is wanted it will be forthcoming, after a few experiments. This is the secret of that popular preference always so obvious for an obscure origin in case of a great man. The preference is equally recognized among the philosophers; "the interest of history," says Emerson, "is in the fortunes of the poor." Indeed the deeper feeling of the whole world has always recognized this—it is to the proudest monarchy in Europe, the Castilian, that we owe the phrase, " the son of his own works"*—Grant was the son of his own works. His fame rests upon the broadest and surest of all pedestals, as broad as common humanity. He seems greatest because he was no detached or ideal hero, but simply the representative of us all.

* " El hijo de sus obras."

FOR SELF-RESPECT AND SELF-PROTEC-TION.

[Speech at the Annual Meeting of the American Woman Suffrage Association, held at Philadelphia, Pennsylvania, November 1, 1887.]

I HAVE the sensations of a revolutionary veteran, almost, in coming back to the city of Philadelphia and remembering our early meetings here in that time of storm, in contrasting the audiences of to-day with the audiences of that day, and in thinking what are the difficulties that come before us now as compared with those of our youth. The audiences have changed, the atmosphere of the community has changed; nothing but the cause remains the same, and that remains because it is a part of the necessary evolution of democratic society and is an immortal thing.

I recall those early audiences; the rows of quiet faces in Quaker bonnets in the foreground; the rows of exceedingly unquiet figures of Southern medical students, with their hats on, in the background. I recall the visible purpose of those energetic young gentlemen to hear nobody but the women, and the calm determination with which their boot-heels contributed to put the male speakers down. I recall their too assiduous attentions in the streets outside when the meetings broke up; and if there was any of that self-sacrifice which the chairman seems to imply, it did not refer to anything that actually took place inside the hall, although even the attempt on a man's part to get to the other end of his speech was sometimes attended with difficulties. The real test of chivalry, if there was one, consisted in the subsequent escorting through the streets of Lucy Stone and Susan B. Anthony in the Bloomer dresses of those days, in the midst of a somewhat uncomplimentary and peripatetic audience of small boys.

The times have changed. Much has come and gone since then. The Southern medical students have disappeared from the room, and almost, it may be, from Philadelphia. The change of fashion has swept away the Quaker bonnets in one direction and the Bloomer trousers in another.

The grand voices that cheered us then in great measure have passed away. The heroic, changeless, firm, granite attitude of Garrison, the fascinating eloquence of Phillips, and the womanly counsel of Lucretia Mott are all only noble memories for those who recall them; but the same cause fills this hall and these hearts to-day. The same cause is ours, fresher and younger because thirty years have gone by.

We need feel no anxiety about it. It comes before us to-day with no new arguments, no new illustrations, only with new tests and new methods. It comes, not with the vague and bodiless traditions of the past, but with the twenty-six thousand women voters of Kansas to-day behind it to strengthen it. It is the cause of the future, the cause of the American people, the inevitable, logical result of all our reasons, the recognition of which alone justifies us in calling ourselves Republicans. Its future is absolutely certain. Those who join themselves with it join to something that they can hold to. It is true of this, as Frederick Douglass said years ago of another organization, "This is the deck; all else is the sea."

I consider it, Mr. Chairman, a great merit of the cause, that as the time goes on, and as it widens so greatly the sphere of its adherents, it brings in a great variety of forces to suggest new arguments; it gives different points of view; different positions. We are not now that simple homogeneous body, all united on much the same arguments, all coming to the result in much the same way, that we were at the outset. It has developed, as the anti-slavery movement developed, a great variety of angles of incidence, a great variety of points of view; and the spirit and freshness and vigor of these meetings must come in a large degree from the freedom of those who stand on this platform to speak their own thought and approach the great question in their own way.

Who of us that served in the anti-slavery ranks does not remember those conflicts of opinion on the platform that seemed at times likely to rend the whole movement asunder? I remember dear old Stephen Foster, that man of iron. I remember with delight the time when he followed me in a speech in an anti-slavery convention at Worcester. He said at the outset, "I love my friend Higginson; but if there is anything I abhor, it is such sentiments, as he has been expressing."

That was the genuine thing; that was reform. Reformers are not always alike capable of that strict combination, that firm concentration, which makes conservatism so powerful. No liberal sect is ever found like the Roman Catholic Church in its power of cementing and organizing and binding. The force of reform is its individual enthusiasm, resulting from each person following out his own best view.

Reformers are like Esquimaux dogs. Do you know how Esquimaux dogs are fastened to the sledge? The owner of the dogs takes his sledge, catches his dog with difficulty, and fastens him by a single thong to the sledge. He catches another dog, puts his thong upon him and fastens him too. He has twenty dogs at last all harnessed to the sledge, each by his separate thong. Why does he waste his labor in that way? Because, whenever the experiment has been tried of putting Esquimaux dogs into a single combined harness, the trouble was, they turned around and ate each other up.

That is the trouble with reformers. If you try to make them think alike and act alike, destruction follows. Each for himself, each approaching his movement in his own way, and we have strength. I myself have tested the ability of the woman suffrage reformers to recognize this individuality of opinion; and those who know the recent history of this reform know it is a proof of the catholicity of this meeting that I have been invited to stand here among the speakers.

I believe myself that the woman suffrage reform has many points of view, and that in some points of view it is almost perilous to approach it. I believe that we never can safely rest the enfranchisement of any large number of people upon any attempt to predict with precision the specific or even the general tendency of the votes which they shall cast. I dread all prediction of that kind for the woman suffrage movement. I rejoiced to hear the first speaker [Mrs. Haggart] say this evening that if she knew that every bad woman in the country would be first at the polls, she still should advocate woman suffrage just the same.

If it were only mere policy, if it takes its chances of success only on the chance of a prediction, it is unsafe. It must rest on a principle to establish its permanent work and value.

I dare say that in many respects woman's voting would afford a better class of voters than the voters we have now, but I do not wish to enfranchise her for this reason. It might be a question then how long she would stay a better class after she had voted. I knew a man once who advocated woman suffrage on the ground that voting was necessarily demoralizing; that we had had men voting for a great while and they had brought the country to the verge of ruin; that women would unquestionably, in the course of fifty years, if enfranchised do the same thing, but that there would be fifty years in the meanwhile and that the country would last his time, which was all he cared for.

I distrust that line of argument. How do we know, it might be said, how much of the present virtue of women comes from the absence of voting? The argument proves to my mind too much. I believe that the majority of women would vote well. So we believed when we enfranchised the blacks, that the majority of them would vote well. But the thing we absolutely knew was and the only thing we knew, that whether they would vote well for the country or not the difference between their having the ballot and not having it meant for them freedom or slavery, and it was for that reason that we enfranchised them.

We took the chances of all the rest. Have they voted well? It is hard to say. They half ruined South Carolina financially. We know that. They voted against prohibition in Texas. We know that. That they would vote against civil service reform is exceedingly probable if they once knew clearly enough what it was. What we know is that because we enfranchised them they are still free, and that is enough for us to know. That stamps success upon their enfranchisement, although a thousand Senator Ingallses rise with their little voices at this late hour to protest against it and say it was a mistake.

So it is in regard to women. I believe and hope that the majority of women would vote as my friend, Mrs. Howe, thinks, for peace. But I know on the other hand that a Southern statesman said to me that the war was prolonged two years after the men would have given up, because the women of the South would not let them. That same man told me that in his opinion the practice of duelling at the South was sustained to this day not by the voices of the men but of the women.

Thus, while I believe that the vast majority of women would throw their influence for peace, I yet know the possibilities of a minority and I do not wish to rest their enfranchisement on that ground. I believe that the great majority of women would vote for honest government if they only understood it, if they would study it so as to understand it; but I cannot forget that all the ingenuity of Wall Street has never devised so perfectly ingenious and successful an instrument of fraud as the Woman's Bank of Boston, entirely the product of a woman's brain; and I do not wish to rest the demand for suffrage on the superior honesty of women.

I believe that women would be the custodians of public property, as they are the custodians of private property. You know that almost every young married man if he succeeds in making both ends meet on his limited income at the end of the first year owes it to his wife; and commonly ends in confessing that he lived more economically the first year of his marriage than the last year of his bachelorhood.

We may claim therefore that women are good, practical custodians of property; and yet I cannot forget that the Association of Collegiate Alumnæ has just published from the educated daughter of a member of Congress, a Pennsylvania woman, one of the most determined and desperate pleas in favor of German socialism that I have ever seen in print. And I cannot forget that it was a woman, Louise Michel, who uttered the other day the wish that on the day of the execution of the Chicago anarchists every court of justice in the world might have dynamite put under it and be exploded forever.

I do not therefore wish to claim woman suffrage on any basis of absolute prediction of what will be. In this I do not represent all of those who are with me. I may belong to a more conservative class of woman suffragists. I am sometimes told I am too conservative. I do not even dare to rest it on the ground as many do that the superior insight of women will make them better judges of public characters and enable them to penetrate more keenly the devices of scoundrels. I willingly believe that women may often have a good eye for a demagogue. The women of Kansas seem to have proved that when they disposed of Senator Ingalls.

But I am one of those who believe that in Massachusetts a service was rendered to the nation when we finally laid General Butler on the shelf; and I am not at all sure that the women of Massachusetts would have done it. I think we did a good thing, irrespective of party, when we put President Cleveland into the presidency, and I have been repeatedly told that if it had been left to women he never would have been chosen.

I do not venture therefore to rest the argument for women suffrage on the ground that women are a race of perfectly ideal saints who are to step up to our voting places and vote a millennium as soon as we enfranchise them. I do not know any speaker for woman suffrage who goes so far as that, though some might go further in that direction than I should. When George Eliot made one of her characters say, "I am not denying that women are foolish; God Almighty made 'em to match the men," I recognize the truth of it, and I recognize that those women, to match the men, have got to be enfranchised like the rest.

I believe, as I said, that every great extension of the franchise brings its dangers. Has there been a moment since the inauguration of our government that there has not been somebody to declare the failure of universal suffrage among men and say that our voting list was too large already? It is the price we pay for democratic government. We might have recognized it beforehand; indeed, it was recognized beforehand. Fisher Ames in comparing a monarchy and a republic, said: "A monarchy is a fine, well-built ship; it is beautiful to look at; it sails superbly. The difficulty is that sometimes it strikes a rock and then it goes down. But a republic," he said, "is a kind of a great clumsy raft. You can float anywhere on it; it will never sink but your feet are always in the water."

I have no expectation that the admission of women to the ballot will enable us to keep dry shod upon the raft, and I am as sure as I can be of anything in the future that when women are enfranchised they will have some of their own sins to answer for, and not be able to devote themselves entirely to correcting the sins of men.

So surely as you have women statesmen you will have women politicians; you will have women bosses, women wire-pullers, women intriguers. The talent that devised the Woman's Bank will be brought to bear, as far as its power goes, upon the bank of the nation. The power that advocates socialism now in the abstract would advocate it then in the concrete. All this is in the future. It is to be expected. No great extension of the suffrage, and there never was any so great as this, ever failed to bring with it risks and drawbacks on the way, but the result of those risks and drawbacks is a true republic, the result is a consistent democracy. The result is a nation in which a man can hear the glories of the republic sung, and not blush, as he has to now, at the thought that those boasts are built upon the disfranchisement of half the human race.

Why, in view of these incidental uncertainties, should women be enfranchised? That is the point where all suffragists, however they may differ as to methods of processes, come together at last. No matter how we may differ in details upon the platform you will find if you venture to take advantage of those differences that we are a good deal like those old-fashioned fighting Highlanders in Sir Walter Scott's story, of whom Bailie Nicol Jarvie declares that no matter how they may quarrel among themselves they are always ready to combine at last against " all honest folk that hae money in their pockets." Our combination is a mild one so far as the pockets go. It is incarnated in Miss Cora Scott Pond, the only person whom I have ever encountered in my long experience of reformers who could make a speech and ask for a little contribution and then take it up and make the audience feel grateful to her.*

That part of the duty we do well. We do well also the more strenuous and difficult parts, if, indeed, there is any part of a reform more difficult on the whole than raising money to carry it along.

I believe in woman suffrage for the sake of woman herself. I believe in it because I am the son of a woman and the husband of a woman and the father of a prospective woman. I remember that at one of the first woman suffrage meetings I ever attended one of the first speakers was an odd fellow from the neighboring town, considered half a lunatic. That didn't make much impression in those days when we were all considered a little crazy, but he was a little crazier than the rest of us. He pushed forward on the platform, seeming impatient to speak and throwing his old hat down by his side, he said, "I don't know much about this subject nor any other; but I know this, my mother was a

* Miss Pond's collection was being taken up during the speaker's remarks.

woman." I thought it was the best condensed woman suffrage argument I ever heard in my life.

Woman suffrage should be urged in my opinion not from any predictions that amount to certainty, that claim anything like certainty as to what women will do with their votes after they get them, but on the ground that by all the traditions of our government, by all the precepts of its early founders, by all the axioms that lie at the foundation of all our political principles, woman needs the ballot for herself, for self-respect on the one side and for self-protection on the other.

There was a time when whatever woman studied in school the idea of teaching her the principles of government, of her studying political economy, would have seemed an absurdity; it was hardly thought of. Her path lay outside of it. She was not brought in contact with it. There was no loss of self-respect in those days to her in finding that in every great system of government she was omitted, and that, as Tennyson says in his "Princess," in every great revolution

> " Millions of throats would bawl for civil rights;
>   No woman named,"

How is it now? Go into the nearest grammar school to-morrow and what may you happen upon? A mixed class of boys and girls reciting the constitution of the United States, or some one of the various manuals upon the history of politics or the organization of our government—reciting it together side by side, perhaps reciting it to a woman. Or you may go even into a college sometimes and find a whole class of young men reciting to their teacher in political economy out of a handbook written by a woman, Millicent Garrett Fawcett.

After those boys and girls have attained their maturity and voting day comes, then they separate as they come near the voting-place, and every boy goes inside the door to put what he has learned in the school, of that teacher, into practice; and the girls and their teacher pass along, powerless to express in action a single one of the principles they have been so studiously learning. I have watched that thing and wondered how women could bear it as they do; and at last I encountered one woman who seemed to me to take on the whole the most sensible view I ever encountered in the matter, who told me that again and again on election day she had gone out and walked up and down opposite the voting-place in her ward with tears streaming from her eyes to see every ignoramus and every drunkard in the neighborhood going in there to cast his vote, and she, a woman, unable to do anything to counteract it.

This is what I mean by a woman needing the ballot for self-respect. She comes to the centennial celebrations here—I forget just what the last one was that they had in Philadelphia but they have them every few years —she hears the great names cited, the great authorities, she goes home and looks up what those authorities said, how they defined civil government or how they defined freedom. She takes Benjamin Franklin for instance, "that eminent Philadelphian," as he is called in Philadelphia, "that eminent Bostonian who temporarily resided in Philadelphia," as they call him in Boston. She looks in his writings and she finds that great statesman saying, about 1770, so distinctly that words cannot make it clearer, that "they who have no voice nor vote in the electing of representatives do not enjoy liberty but are absolutely enslaved to those who have votes and to their representatives." And what is the woman to think of that?

Fifty years ago the man who was long considered the leading jurist of the West, Judge Timothy Walker, of Cincinnati, when asked "What is the legal position of woman in America?" said, "Write out as best you can the definition of legal slavery and when you have done that you have the legal position of a woman." The woman finds that; she sees such statements as that earlier or later. How can she feel? How can she help feeling that same loss of self-respect which a Jewish woman of the Jewish faith in old times could hardly help feeling when she heard men giving thanks to the Lord that they were not born women and heard women with humble voices saying, "I thank thee, Lord, that thou hast made me according to thy will?"

How could she help feeling as she would feel in a Mohammedan country when she found that in the great and most sacred mosques the edict was that no idiot, lunatic, or woman can enter here. The woman of old times who did not read books of political economy or attended public meetings could retain her self-respect; but the woman of modern times with every step she takes in the higher education finds it harder to retain that self-respect while she is in a republican government and yet not a member of it. She can study all the books that I saw collected this morning in the political economy alcove of the Bryn Mawr College; she can read them all; she can master them all; she can know more about them perhaps than any man she knows; and yet to put one thing she has learned there in practice by the simple process of putting a piece of paper into a ballot-box—she could no more do that than she could put out her slender finger and stop the planet in its course. That is what I mean by woman's needing woman suffrage for self-respect.

Then as to self-protection. In what does protection consist for us Americans? In the power of writing a remonstrance in the newspaper when the conductor of a train does not stop as he promised or when an ash barrel is not taken at the proper moment from before our back door? Is that the power that we have for self-protection? It is indeed the beginning of power. It is power because it has the ballot behind it; because the street department and the railroad department know that they have to do with that part of the community who have votes to back up what they say. Take away those votes and how little is the power.

The woman has the voice but not the vote. We know that there have been great changes in the position of woman, great improvements in the law in regard to women. What brought about those improvements? The steady labor of women like those on this platform, going before legislatures year by year and asking those legislatures to give them something they were not willing to give, the ballot; but as a result of it to keep the poor creatures quiet some law was passed removing a restriction. The old English writer, Pepys, in his diary, after spending a good deal of money for himself, finds a little left and buys his wife a new gown because he says, "It is fit the poor wretch should have something to content her." I have seen many laws passed for the advantage of women and they were generally passed on that principle.

I remember going before the legislature of Rhode Island once with Lucy Stone, and she unrolled with her peculiar persuasive power the wrong laws that existed in that Commonwealth in regard to women and after the hearing was over the chairman of the committee, a judge who has served for years on that committee, came down and said to her, "I have come to say to you, Mrs. Stone, that all you have said this morning is true, and that I am ashamed to think that I who have been chairman for years of this judiciary committee should have known in my secret heart that it was all true and should have done nothing to set those wrongs right until I was reminded of it by a woman."

Again and again I have seen that experience. Women with bleeding feet, women with exhausted voices, women with worn-out lives have lavished their strength to secure ordinary justice in the form of laws, which a single woman inside the State House, a single woman there armed with the position of member of the legislature and representing a sex who had votes could have got righted within two years.

Every man knows the weakness of a disfranchised class of men. The whole race of women is disfranchised and they suffer in the same way. It is not that men are so selfish. It is not that they intend to do so much wrong to women; but any of you who have served in a legislative body as I have know how difficult a thing it is to get attention for anything or any class of persons not represented on the floor; while a single person who stands on the floor clothed with his rights, with the other persons who have rights behind him, can command attention though he be in the smallest minority. A single naturalized citizen in the legislature can secure justice for all naturalized citizens. A single Roman Catholic member can secure justice for all Roman Catholic citizens; because though he may have been personally in the minority he represents votes behind him.

The woman represents no votes and she is weak. The best laws that are made for her in any State in the Union are no sure guarantee for her. They may be altered at any time so long as she is not there to speak for herself. Some Russian emperor, when he was told by an admirer, " Your Majesty, what do your people need of a constitution? Your Majesty is as good as a constitution to your people," said, " Then I am but a happy accident; that is all."

The best legislation women can get is nothing more than a happy accident unless women are there to defend it after they have got it. Again and again things have been given to them after the labor of years, and, perhaps, those same things have been taken from them.

In the legislature of New York women were vested with the power a few years ago to control their own offspring as against the will of a dead father. A year or two passed by, the law was revoked and the power was lost. For several years back in Massachusetts a married woman has had the right under the law to dispose by will of five thousand dollars' worth of real estate if held in her own name. The woman who had saved up her own earnings, who had made her own investments, who held real estate in her own name, could, to the extent of five thousand dollars, dispose of it by will.

The last legislature, as that keen observer, Mr. Sewell, tells us, by striking out a single word in a single statute, the word "intestate," took away that power and the woman no longer can dispose of her five thousand dollars. No attention was attracted, no agitation came because there was no woman there to take it up and call attention to it.

I served two years in the Massachusetts legislature and I remember that during one of those years there came up a bill which attracted very little attention in regard to the right of settlement in our towns. The point seemed a little complicated and I passed it by, being busy with other matters; but an official at the State House, Mr. H. B. Wheelwright, an official of the Board of State Charities, a man of great experience, came to me and said, " Do you understand that bill?" I said, " No. I was engaged on other matters and paid but little attention to it." He said, " Let me explain it to you." He sat down and explained it to me and showed me that should that bill pass hundreds of women in our factory towns in Massachusetts would fail of obtaining, as they had heretofore obtained under certain conditions, a settlement in those towns.

I asked those around me if they had noticed it. They had not. I found on investigation that the bill had come from the representatives of a certain town and that the whole bill was got up to meet a certain particular case. It was to relieve the overseers of the poor in that town from the duty of disposing of a single family; and for the sake of that, by this bill, thus quietly introduced, hundreds and perhaps thousands of women would suffer.

I took the points that he gave me, I made the statement, becoming simply his mouthpiece in the matter, and the bill was easily defeated. But had a single woman been on the floor herself to take note of the bills that came up that concerned her sex do you suppose a bill like that would have come as it did near to passage? If there is anything that is sure in public affairs it is that we can trust people to look after themselves.

I remember I was speaking of the ignorance of the men recently naturalized who had been before the Bureau of State Charities, and another State House official said to me, " There is not an emigrant however ignorant he may be who after he has lived six months in Massachusetts, fails to understand three sets of laws as well as you or I do; the settlement laws, the pauper laws, the penal laws. They understand it whether we do or not." Self-interest is what sharpens. When you get women voting and not till then will you have women substantially, and permanently protected.

It is for the self-respect and self-protection of women that I want woman suffrage. If they vote for good temperance laws, so much the better. If they make property secure, so much the better. But the real need of the suffrage is for women themselves. Self-respect and self-protection, these are what the demand rests upon; and in proportion as we concede to that demand we shall have a nation that also has for its reward self-protection and self-respect.

How long will women have to point out these things? How long will men with feebler voices, because less personal and less absorbingly interested, have to aid them in pointing them out? It is not enough to have our material successes. It is not enough to have the magnificent record of our long civil war and of the period of reconstruction that has followed. This nation won the respect of the world by its career in war. What it has now before it is so to legislate for equal justice as to retain the world's respect during coming centuries of happy peace.

Curtis, George William, a noted American journalist, essayist and public speaker, born in Providence, R. I., February 24, 1824; died at Livingston, Staten Island, N, Y., August 31, 1892. After spending some years in foreign travel, he was for a short time one of the editors of the "New York Tribune," and subsequently edited "Putnam's Monthly." In 1853 he entered the lecture field, in which he continued for a series of years with signal success. From 1856 onward he took a vital interest in political movements, and during an unsuccessful candidacy for Congress in 1864 he addressed audiences daily for six weeks. He became the political editor of "Harper's Weekly" in 1863, continuing to hold that position for the rest of his career, and he contributed the Easy Chair department of "Harper's Monthly" from the establishment of the periodical till shortly before his death. From 1880 he was president of the New York Association for Civil Service Reform. His political speeches were marked by great earnestness of purpose, as well as eloquence, and his lectures and occasional orations exhibit a polished, persuasive style.

ON THE SPOILS SYSTEM AND THE PROGRESS OF CIVIL SERVICE REFORM.*

TWELVE years ago I read a paper before this association upon reform in the Civil Service. The subject was of very little interest. A few newspapers which were thought to be visionary occasionally discussed it but the press of both parties smiled with profound indifference. Mr. Jenckes had pressed it upon an

* An address delivered before the American Social Science Association at its meeting in Saratoga, New York, September 8, 1881.

utterly listless Congress, and his proposition was regarded as the harmless hobby of an amiable man, from which a little knowledge of practical politics would soon dismount him. The English reform, which was by far the most significant political event in that country since the Parliamentary Reform Bill of 1832, was virtually unknown to us. To the general public it was necessary to explain what the Civil Service was, how it was recruited, what the abuses were, and how and why they were to be remedied. Old professional politicians, who look upon reforms as Dr. Johnson defined patriotism, as the last refuge of a scoundrel, either laughed at what they called the politics of idiocy and the moon, or sneered bitterly that reformers were cheap hypocrites who wanted other people's places and lamented other people's sins.

This general public indifference was not surprising. The great reaction of feeling which followed the war, the relaxation of the long-strained anxiety of the nation for its own existence, the exhaustion of the vast expenditure of life and money, and the satisfaction with the general success, had left little disposition to do anything but secure in the national polity the legitimate results of the great contest. To the country, reform was a proposition to reform evils of administration of which it knew little, and which, at most, seemed to it petty and impertinent in the midst of great affairs. To Congress, it was apparently a proposal to deprive members of the patronage which to many of them was the real gratification of their position, the only way in which they felt their distinction and power. To such members reform was a plot to deprive the bear of his honey, the dog of his bone, and they stared and growled incredulously.

This was a dozen years ago. To-day the demand for reform is imperative. The drop has become a deluge. Leading journals of both parties eagerly proclaim its urgent necessity. From New England to California public opinion is organizing itself in reform associations. In the great custom-house and the great post-office of the country—those in the city of New York—reform has been actually begun upon definite principles and with remarkable success, and the good example has been followed elsewhere with the same results. A bill carefully prepared and providing for gradual and thorough reform has been introduced with an admirable report in the Senate of the United States. Mr. Pendleton, the Democratic Senator from Ohio, declares that the Spoils System which has debauched the Civil Service of fifty millions of people must be destroyed. Mr. Dawes, the Republican Senator from Massachusetts, summons all good citizens to unite to suppress this gigantic evil which threatens the Republic. Conspicuous reformers sit in the Cabinet; and in this sorowful moment, at least, the national heart and mind and conscience, stricken and bowed by a calamity whose pathos penetrates every household in Christendom, cries to these warning words, " Amen! Amen!" Like the slight sound amid the frozen silence of the Alps that loosens and brings down the avalanche, the solitary pistol shot of the 2d of July has suddenly startled this vast accumulation of public opinion into conviction, and on every side thunders the rush and roar of its overwhelming descent, which will sweep away the host of evils bred of this monstrous abuse.

This is an extraordinary change for twelve years, but it shows the vigorous political health, the alert common sense, and the essential patriotism of the country, which are the earnest of the success of any wise reform. The war which naturally produced the lassitude and indifference to the subject which were evident twelve years ago had made reform, indeed, a vital necessity, but the necessity was not then perceived. The dangers that attend a vast system of administration based to its least detail upon personal patronage were not first exposed by Mr. Jenckes in 1867, but before that time they had been mainly discussed as possibilities and inferences. Yet the history of the old New York council of appointment had illustrated in that State the party fury and corruption which patronage necessarily breeds, and Governor McKean in Pennsylvania, at the close of the last century, had made " a clean sweep " of the places within his power. The spoils spirit struggled desperately to obtain possession of the national administration from the day of Jefferson's inauguration to that of Jackson's, when it succeeded. Its first great but undesigned triumph was the decision of the First Congress in 1789, vesting the sole power of removal in the President, a decision which placed almost every position in the Civil Service unconditionally at his pleasure. This decision was determined by the weight of Madison's authority. But Webster, nearly fifty years afterward, opposing his authority to that of Madison, while admitting the decision to have been final, declared it to have been wrong. The year

1820, which saw the great victory of slavery in the Missouri Compromise, was also the year in which the second great triumph of the spoils system was gained, by the passage of the law which, under the plea of securing greater responsibility in certain financial offices, limited such offices to a term of four years. The decision of 1789, which gave the sole power of removal to the President, required positive executive action to effect removal; but this law of 1820 vacated all the chief financial offices, with all the places dependent upon them, during the term of every President, who, without an order of removal, could fill them all at his pleasure.

A little later a change in the method of nominating the President from a Congressional caucus to a national convention still further developed the power of patronage as a party resource, and in the session of 1825--26, when John Quincy Adams was President, Mr. Benton introduced his report upon Mr. Macon's resolution declaring the necessity of reducing and regulating executive patronage; although Mr. Adams, the last of the Revolutionary line of Presidents, so scorned to misuse patronage that he leaned backward in standing erect. The pressure for the overthrow of the constitutional system had grown steadily more angry and peremptory with the progress of the country, the development of party spirit, the increase of patronage, the unanticipated consequences of the sole executive power of removal, and the immense opportunity offered by the four-years law. It was a pressure against which Jefferson held the gates by main force, which was relaxed by the war under Madison and the fusion of parties under Monroe, but which swelled again into a furious torrent as the later parties took form. John Quincy Adams adhered, with the tough tenacity of his father's son, to the best principles of all his predecessors. He followed Washington, and observed the spirit of the Constitution in refusing to remove for any reason but official misconduct or incapacity. But he knew well what was coming, and with characteristically stinging sarcasm he called General Jackson's inaugural address "a threat of reform." With Jackson's administration in 1830 the deluge of the spoils systems burst over our national politics. Sixteen years later, Mr. Buchanan said in a public speech that General Taylor would be faithless to the Whig party if he did not proscribe Democrats. So high the deluge had risen which has ravaged and wasted our politics ever since, and the danger will be stayed only when every President, leaning upon the law, shall stand fast where John Quincy Adams stood.

But the debate continued during the whole Jackson administration. In the Senate and on the stump, in elaborate reports and popular speeches, Webster, Calhoun, and Clay, the great political chiefs of their time, sought to alarm the country with the dangers of patronage. Sargent S. Prentiss, in the House of Representatives, caught up and echoed the cry under the administration of Van Buren. But the country refused to be alarmed. As the Yankee said of the Americans at the battle of White Plains, where they were beaten, "The fact is, as far as I can understand, our folks didn't seem to take no sort of interest in that battle." The reason that the country took no sort of interest in the discussion of the evils of patronage was evident. It believed the denunciation to be a mere party cry, a scream of disappointment and impotence from those who held no places and controlled no patronage. It heard the leaders of the opposition fiercely arraigning the administration for proscription and universal wrong-doing, but it was accustomed by its English tradition and descent always to hear the Tories cry that the Constitution was in danger when the Whigs were in power, and the Whigs under a Tory administration to shout that all was lost. It heard the uproar like the old lady upon her first railroad journey, who sat serene amid the wreck of a collision, and when asked if she was much hurt, looked over her spectacles and answered, blandly, "Hurt? Why, I supposed they always stopped so in this kind of travelling." The feeling that the denunciation was only a part of the game of politics, and no more to be accepted as a true statement than Snug the joiner as a true lion, was confirmed by the fact that when the Whig opposition came into power with President Harrison, it adopted the very policy which under Democratic administration it had strenuously denounced as fatal. The pressure for place was even greater than it had been twelve years before, and although Mr. Webster as Secretary of State maintained his consistency by putting his name to an executive order asserting sound principles, the order was swept away like a lamb by a locomotive. Nothing but a miracle, said General Harrison's attorney-general, can feed the swarm of hungry office-seekers.

Adopted by both parties, Mr. Marcy's doctrine that

the places in the public service are the proper spoils of a victorious party, was accepted as a necessary condition of popular government. One of the highest officers of the government expounded this doctrine to me long afterward. "I believe," said he, "that when the people vote to change a party administration they vote to change every person of the opposite party who holds a place, from the President of the United States to the messenger at my door." It is this extraordinary but sincere misconception of the function of party in a free government that leads to the serious defence of the Spoils System. Now, a party is merely a voluntary association of citizens to secure the enforcement of a certain policy of administration upon which they are agreed. In a free government this is done by the election of legislators and of certain executive officers who are friendly to that policy. But the duty of the great body of persons employed in the minor administrative places is in no sense political. It is wholly ministerial, and the political opinions of such persons affect the discharge of their duties no more than their religious views or their literary preferences. All that can be justly required of such persons, in the interest of the public business, is honesty, intelligence, capacity, industry, and due subordination; and to say that, when the policy of the government is changed by the result of an election from protection to free trade, every bookkeeper and letter carrier and messenger and porter in the public offices ought to be a free trader, is as wise as to say that if a merchant is a Baptist every clerk in his office ought to be a believer in total immersion. But the officer of whom I spoke undoubtedly expressed the general feeling. The necessarily evil consequences of the practice which he justified seemed to be still speculative and inferential, and to the national indifference which followed the war the demand of Mr. Jenckes for reform appeared to be a mere whimsical vagary most inopportunely introduced.

It was, however, soon evident that the war had made the necessity of reform imperative, and chiefly for two reasons: first, the enormous increase of patronage, and second, the fact that circumstances had largely identified a party name with patriotism. The great and radical evil of the spoils system was carefully fostered by the apparent absolute necessity to the public welfare of making political opinion and sympathy a condition of appointment to the smallest place. It is since the war, therefore, that the evil has run riot and that its consequences have been fully revealed. Those consequences are not familiar, and I shall not describe them. It is enough that the most patriotic and intelligent Americans and the most competent foreign observers agree that the direct and logical results of that system are the dangerous confusion of the executive and legislative powers of the government; the conversion of politics into mere place-hunting; the extension of the mischief to State and county and city administration, and the consequent degradation of the national character; the practical disfranchisement of the people wherever the system is most powerful; and the perversion of a republic of equal citizens into a despotism of venal politicians. These are the greatest dangers that can threaten a republic, and they are due to the practice of treating the vast system of minor public places which are wholly ministerial, and whose duties are the same under every party administration, not as public trusts, but as party perquisites. The English-speaking race has a grim sense of humor, and the absurdity of transacting the public business of a great nation in a way which would ruin both the trade and the character of a small huckster, of proceeding upon the theory—for such is the theory of the Spoils System—that a man should be put in charge of a locomotive because he holds certain views of original sin, or because he polishes boots nimbly with his tongue— it is a folly so stupendous and grotesque that when it is fully perceived by the shrewd mother-wit of the Yankee it will be laughed indignantly and contemptuously away. But the laugh must have the method, and the indignation the form, of law; and now that the public mind is aroused to the true nature and tendency of the Spoils System is the time to consider the practicable legal remedy for them.

The whole system of appointments in the Civil Service proceeds from the President, and in regard to his action the intention of the Constitution is indisputable. It is that the President shall appoint solely upon public considerations, and that the officer appointed shall serve as long as he discharges his duty faithfully. This is shown in Mr. Jefferson's familiar phrase in his reply to the remonstrance of the merchants of New Haven against the removal of the collector of that port. Mr. Jefferson asserted that Mr. Adams had purposely appointed in the last moments of his administration officers whose designation he should have left to his successor. Alluding to these appointments, he says: "I shall correct the procedure, and that done, return with joy to that state of things when the only question concerning a candidate shall be, Is he honest? Is he capable? Is he faithful to the Constitution?" Mr. Jefferson here recognizes that these had been the considerations which had usually determined appointments; and Mr. Madison, in the debate upon the President's sole power of removal, declared that if a President should remove an officer for any reason not connected with efficient service he would be impeached. Reform, therefore, is merely a return to the principle and purpose of the constitution and to the practice of the early administrations.

What more is necessary, then, for reform than that the President should return to that practice? As all places in the Civil Service are filled either by his direct nomination or by officers whom he appoints, why has not any President ample constitutional authority to effect at any moment a complete and thorough reform? The answer is simple. He has the power. He has always had it. A President has only to do as Washington did, and all his successors have only to do likewise, and reform would be complete. Every President has but to refuse to remove non-political officers for political or personal reasons; to appoint only those whom he knows to be competent; to renominate, as Monroe and John Quincy Adams did, every faithful officer whose commission expires, and to require the heads of departments and all inferior appointing officers to conform to this practice, and the work would be done. This is apparently a short and easy and constitutional method of reform, requiring no further legislation or scheme of procedure. But why has no President adopted it? For the same reason that the best of Popes does not reform the abuses of his Church. For the same reason that a leaf goes over Niagara. It is because the opposing forces are overpowering. The same high officer of the government to whom I have alluded said to me as we drove upon the Heights of Washington, "Do you mean that I ought not to appoint my subordinates for whom I am responsible?" I answered: "I mean that you do not appoint them now; I mean that if, when we return to the capital, you hear that your chief subordinate is dead, you will not appoint his successor. You will have to choose among the men urged upon you by certain powerful politicians. Undoubtedly you ought to appoint the man whom you believe to be the most fit. But you do not and cannot. If you could or did appoint such men only, and that were the rule of your department and of the service, there would be no need of reform." And he could not deny it. There was no law to prevent his selection of the best man. Indeed, the law assumed that he would do it. The Constitution intended that he should do it. But when I reminded him that there were forces beyond the law that paralyzed the intention of the Constitution, and which would inevitably compel him to accept the choice of others, he said no more.

It is easy to assert that the reform of the Civil Service is an executive reform. So it is. But the Executive alone cannot accomplish it. The abuses are now completely and agressively organized, and the sturdiest President would quail before them. The President who should undertake, single-handed, to deal with the complication of administrative evils known as the Spoils System would find his party leaders in Congress and their retainers throughout the country arrayed against him; the proposal to disregard traditions and practices which are regarded as essential to the very existence and effectiveness of party organization would be stigmatized as treachery, and the President himself would be covered with odium as a traitor. The air would hum with denunciation. The measures he should favor, the appointments he might make, the recommendations of his secretaries, would be opposed and imperilled, and the success of his administration would be endangered. A President who should alone undertake thoroughly to reform the evil must feel it to be the vital and paramount issue, and must be willing to hazard everything for its success. He must have the absolute faith and the indomitable will of Luther. "Here stand I; I can no other." How can we expect a President whom this system elects to devote himself to its destruction? General Grant, elected by a spontaneous patriotic impulse, fresh from the regulated order of military life and new to politics and politicians, saw the reason and the necessity of reform. The hero of a victorious war, at the height of his popularity, his party in undisputed and seemingly indisputable supremacy, made the attempt. Congress, good-naturedly tolerating what it considered his whim of inexperience, granted money to try an experiment. The adverse pressure was tremendous. "I am used to pressure," said the soldier. So he was, but not to this pressure. He was driven by unknown and incalculable currents.

He was enveloped in whirlwinds of sophistry, scorn, and incredulity. He who upon his own line had fought it out all summer to victory, upon a line absolutely new and unknown was naturally bewildered and dismayed. So Wellington had drawn the lines of victory on the Spanish Peninsula and had saved Europe at Waterloo. But even Wellington at Waterloo could not be also Sir Robert Peel at Westminster. Even Wellington, who had overthrown Napoleon in the field, could not also be the parliamentary hero who for the welfare of his country would dare to risk the overthrow of his party. When at last President Grant said, "If Congress adjourns without positive legislation on Civil Service reform, I shall regard such action as a disapproval of the system and shall abandon it," it was, indeed, a surrender, but it was the surrender of a champion who had honestly mistaken both the nature and the strength of the adversary and his own power of endurance.

It is not, then, reasonable, under the conditions of our government and in the actual situation, to expect a President to go much faster or much further than public opinion. But executive action can aid most effectively the development and movement of that opinion, and the most decisive reform measures that the present administration might take would be undoubtedly supported by a powerful public sentiment. The educative results of resolute executive action, however limited and incomplete in scope, have been shown in the two great public offices of which I have spoken, the New York Custom House and the New York Post-office. For nearly three years the entire practicability of reform has been demonstrated in those offices, and solely by the direction of the President. The value of such demonstrations, due to the Executive will alone, carried into effect by thoroughly trained and interested subordinates, cannot be over-estimated. But when they depend upon the will of a transient officer and not upon a strong public conviction, they are seeds that have no depth of soil. A vital and enduring reform in administrative methods, although it be but a return to the constitutional intention, can be accomplished only by the commanding impulse of public opinion. Permanence is secured by law, not by individual pleasure. But in this country law is only formulated public opinion. Reform of the Civil Service does not contemplate an invasion of the constitutional prerogative of the President and the Senate, nor does it propose to change the Constitution by statute. The whole system of the Civil Service proceeds, as I said, from the President, and the object of the reform movement is to enable him to fulfil the intention of the Constitution by revealing to him the desire of the country through the action of its authorized representatives. When the ground-swell of public opinion lifts Congress from the rocks, the President will gladly float with it into the deep water of wise and patriotic action. The President, indeed, has never been the chief sinner in the Spoils System, although he has been the chief agent. Even President Jackson yielded to party pressure as much as to his own convictions. President Harrison sincerely wished to stay the flood, but it swept him away. President Grant doubtfully and with good intentions tested the pressure before yielding. President Hayes, with sturdy independence, adhered inflexibly to a few points, but his party chiefs cursed and derided him. President Garfield—God bless and restore him!—frankly declares permanent and effective reform to be impossible without the consent of Congress. When, therefore, Congress obeys a commanding public opinion, and reflects it in legislation, it will restore to the President the untrammelled exercise of his ample constitutional powers according to the constitutional intention; and the practical question of reform is, How shall this be brought about?

Now, it is easy to kill weeds if we can destroy their roots, and it is not difficult to determine what the principle of reform legislation should be if we can agree upon the source of the abuses to be reformed. May they not have a common origin? In fact, are they not all bound together as parts of one system? The Representative in Congress, for instance, does not ask whether the interests of the public service require this removal or that appointment, but whether, directly or indirectly, either will best serve his own interests. The Senator acts from the same motives. The President, in turn, balances between the personal interests of leading politicians—President, Senators, and Representatives all wishing to pay for personal service and to conciliate personal influence. So also the party labor required of the place-holder, the task of carrying caucuses, of defeating one man and electing another, as may be ordered, the payment of the assessment levied upon his salary—all these are the price of the place. They are the taxes paid by him as conditions of receiving a personal favor. Thus the abuses have a common source, whatever may be the plea for the system from which they spring. Whether it be urged that the system is essential to party organization, or that the desire for place is a laudable political ambition, or that the Spoils System is a logical development of our political philosophy, or that new brooms sweep clean, or that any other system is un-American—whatever the form of the plea for the abuse, the conclusion is always the same, that the minor places in the Civil Service are not public trusts, but rewards and prizes for personal and political favorites.

The root of the complex evil, then, is personal favoritism. This produces Congressional dictation, Senatorial usurpation, arbitrary removals, interference in elections, political assessments, and all the consequent corruption, degradation, and danger that experience has disclosed. The method of reform, therefore, must be a plan of selection for appointment which makes favoritism impossible. The general feeling undoubtedly is that this can be accomplished by a fixed limited term. But the terms of most of the offices to which the President and the Senate appoint, and upon which the myriad minor places in the service depend, have been fixed and limited for sixty years, yet it is during that very period that the chief evils of personal patronage have appeared. The law of 1820, which limited the term of important revenue offices to four years, and which was afterward extended to other offices, was intended, as John Quincy Adams tells us, to promote the election to the presidency of Mr. Crawford, who was then Secretary of the Treasury. The law was drawn by Mr. Crawford himself, and it was introduced into the Senate by one of his devoted partisans. It placed the whole body of executive financial officers at the mercy of the Secretary of the Treasury and of a majority of the Senate, and its design, as Mr. Adams says, "was to secure for Mr. Crawford the influence of all the incumbents in office, at the peril of displacement, and of five or ten times an equal number of ravenous office-seekers, eager to supplant them." This is the very substance of the Spoils System, intentionally introduced by a fixed limitation of term in place of the constitutional tenure of efficient service; and it was so far successful that it made the custom house officers, district attorneys, marshals, registers of the land office, receivers of public money, and even paymasters in the army, notoriously active partisans of Mr. Crawford. Mr. Benton says that the four-years law merely made the dismissal of faithful officers easier, because the expiration of the term was regarded as "the creation of a vacancy to be filled by new appointments." A fixed limited term for the chief offices has not destroyed or modified personal influence, but, on the contrary, it has fostered universal servility and loss of self-respect, because reappointment depends, not upon official fidelity and efficiency, but upon personal influence and favor. To fix by law the terms of places dependent upon such offices would be like an attempt to cure hydrophobia by the bite of a mad dog. The incumbent would be always busy keeping his influence in repair to secure reappointment, and the applicant would be equally busy in seeking such influence to procure the place, and as the fixed terms would be constantly expiring, the eager and angry intrigue and contest of influence would be as endless as it is now. This certainly would not be reform.

But would not reform be secured by adding to a fixed limited term the safeguard of removal for cause only? Removal for cause alone means, of course, removal for legitimate cause, such as dishonesty, negligence, or incapacity. But who shall decide that such cause exists? This must be determined either by the responsible superior officer or by some other authority. But if left to some other authority the right of counsel and the forms of a court would be invoked; the whole legal machinery of mandamuses, injunctions, certioraris, and the rules of evidence would be put in play to keep an incompetent clerk at his desk or a sleepy watchman on his beat. Cause for the removal of a letter-carrier in the post-office or of an accountant in the custom house would be presented with all the pomp of impeachment and established like a high crime and misdemeanor. Thus every clerk in every office would have a kind of vested interest in his place because, however careless, slovenly, or troublesome he might be, he could be displaced only by an elaborate and doubtful legal process. Moreover, if the head of a bureau or a collector, or a postmaster were obliged to prove negligence, or insolence, or incompetency against a clerk as he would prove theft, there would be no removals from the public service except for crimes of which the penal law takes cognizance. Consequently, removal would be always and justly regarded as a stigma upon character, and a man removed from a position in a public office would be virtually branded as a convicted criminal. Removal for cause, therefore, if the cause were to be decided by any authority but that of the responsible superior officer, instead of improving, would swiftly and enormously enhance the cost, and ruin the efficiency, of the public service, by destroying subordination, and making every lazy and worthless member of it twice as careless and incompetent as he is now.

If, then, the legitimate cause for removal ought to be determined in public as in private business by the responsible appointing power, it is of the highest public necessity that the exercise of that power should be made as absolutely honest and independent as possible. But how can it be made honest and independent if it is not protected so far as practicable from the constant bribery of selfish interest and the illicit solicitation of personal influence? The experience of our large patronage offices proves conclusively that the cause of the larger number of removals is not dishonesty or incompetency; it is the desire to make vacancies to fill. This is the actual cause, whatever cause may be assigned. The removals would not be made except for the pressure of politicians. But those politicians would not press for removals if they could not secure the appointment of their favorites. Make it impossible for them to secure appointment, and the pressure would instantly disappear and arbitrary removal cease.

So long, therefore, as we permit minor appointments to be made by mere personal influence and favor, a fixed limited term and removal during that term for cause only would not remedy the evil, because the incumbents would still be seeking influence to secure reappointment, and the aspirants doing the same to replace them. Removal under plea of good cause would be as wanton and arbitrary as it is now, unless the power to remove were intrusted to some other discretion than that of the superior officer, and in that case the struggle for reappointment and the knowledge that removal for the term was practically impossible would totally demoralize the service. To make sure, then, that removals shall be made for legitimate cause only, we must provide that appointment shall be made only for legitimate cause.

All roads lead to Rome. Personal influence in appointments can be annulled only by free and open competition. By that bridge we can return to the practice of Washington and to the intention of the Constitution. That is the shoe of swiftness and the magic sword by which the President can pierce and outrun the protean enemy of sophistry and tradition which prevents him from asserting his power. If you say that success in a competitive literary examination does not prove fitness to adjust customs duties, or to distribute letters, or to appraise linen, or to measure molasses, I answer that the reform does not propose that fitness shall be proved by a competitive literary examination. It proposes to annul personal influence and political favoritism by making appointment depend upon proved capacity. To determine this it proposes first to test the comparative general intelligence of all applicants and their special knowledge of the particular official duties required, and then to prove the practical faculty of the most intelligent applicants by actual trial in the performance of the duties before they are appointed. If it be still said that success in such a competition may not prove fitness, it is enough to reply that success in obtaining the favor of some kind of boss, which is the present system, presumptively proves unfitness.

Nor is it any objection to the reformed system that many efficient officers in the service could not have entered it had it been necessary to pass an examination; it is no objection, because their efficiency is a mere chance. They were not appointed because of efficiency, but either because they were diligent politicians or because they were recommended by diligent politicians. The chance of getting efficient men in any business is certainly not diminished by inquiry and investigation. I have heard an officer in the army say that he could select men from the ranks for special duty much more satisfactorily than they could be selected by an examination. Undoubtedly he could, because he knows his men, and he selects solely by his knowledge of their comparative fitness. If this were true of the Civil Service, if every appointing officer chose the fittest person from those that he knew, there would be no need of reform. It is because he cannot do this that the reform is necessary.

It is the same kind of objection which alleges that competition is a droll plan by which to restore the conduct of the public business to business principles and methods, since no private business selects its agents by competition. But the managers of private business are virtually free from personal influence in selecting their subordinates, and they employ and promote and dismiss them solely for the interests of the business. Their choice, however, is determined by an actual, although not a formal, competition. Like the military officer, they select those whom they know by experience to be the most competent. But if great business houses and corporations were exposed to persistent, insolent, and overpowering interference and solicitation for place such as obstructs great public departments and officers, they too who resort to the form of competition, as they now have its substance, and they would resort to it to secure the very freedom which they now enjoy of selecting for fitness alone.

Mr. President, in the old Arabian story, from the little box upon the sea-shore, carelessly opened by the fisherman, arose the towering and haughty demon, ever more monstrous and more threatening, who would not crouch again. So from the small patronage of the earlier day, from a Civil Service dealing with a national revenue of only $2,000,000, and regulated upon sound business principles, has sprung the un-American, un-Democratic, un-Republican system which destroys political independence, honor, and morality, and corrodes the national character itself. In the solemn anxiety of this hour the warning words of the austere Calhoun, uttered nearly half a century ago, echo in startled recollection like words of doom: "If you do not put this thing down it will put you down." Happily it is the historic faith of the race from which we are chiefly sprung, that eternal vigilance is the price of liberty. It is that faith which has made our mother England the great parent of free States. The same faith has made America the political hope of the world. Fortunately removed by our position from the entanglements of European politics, and more united and peaceful at home than at any time

10—6

within the memory of living men, the moment is most auspicious for remedying that abuse in our political system whose nature, proportions, and perils the whole country begins clearly to discern. The will and the power to apply the remedy will be a test of the sagacity and the energy of the people. The reform of which I have spoken is essentially the people's reform. With the instinct of robbers who run with the crowd and lustily cry " Stop thief! " those who would make the public service the monopoly of a few favorites denounce the determination to open that service to the whole people as a plan to establish an aristocracy. The huge ogre of patronage, gnawing at the character, the honor, and the life of the country, grimly sneers that the people cannot help themselves and that nothing can be done. But much greater things have been done. Slavery was the Giant Despair of many good men of the last generation, but slavery was overthrown. If the Spoils System, a monster only less threatening than slavery, be unconquerable, it is because the country has lost its convictions, its courage, and its common-sense. " I expect," said the Yankee as he surveyed a stout antagonist, " I expect that you're pretty ugly, but I cal'late I'm a darned sight uglier." I know that patronage is strong, but I believe that the American people are very much stronger.

Ross, Jonathan, an American jurist, born at Water-
ford, Vt., April 30, 1826, In the earlier portion of his
career he taught school in his native State, and afterwards
studying law he was admitted to the bar in 1856, and entered
upon his profession at St. Johnsbury, Vt.   He had already
served three terms in the lower house of the State Legislature when in 1870 he entered the State Senate, and in the
same year he was elected to the State Supreme bench.   In
1890 he became chief justice of Vermont, and after the
death of Senator Morrill in 1898 Ross succeeded him in the
United States Senate.   In January, 1900, he delivered a
notable speech in the Senate on " The Island Possessions of
the United States."

THE NATION'S RELATION TO ITS ISLAND POSSESSIONS.

FROM SPEECH DELIVERED IN THE UNITED STATES
SENATE, JANUARY 23, 1900.

In regard to Cuba the duty is particular.   It is so
constituted by the resolutions antedating the war and
by the provisions of the treaty.   The preamble of the
joint resolution of Congress approved April 20, 1898,
counts upon the abhorrent conditions which have existed in that island for more than three years, shocking
to the moral sense of the people of the United States,
a disgrace to Christian civilization, culminating in the
destruction of the " Maine " with two hundred and
sixty-six of its officers and crew, and thereupon it is
solemnly resolved: (1) That the people of the island
are, and of right ought to be free and independent;
(2) That it is the duty of this government to demand,

and it does demand, that Spain at once relinquish its authority and government of the island; (3) Authorizes the President to use the entire land and naval forces and to call out the militia to enforce the demand; (4) The United States disclaims any disposition or intention to exercise sovereignty, jurisdiction, or control over the island except for the pacification thereof, and then asserts its determination to leave the government and control of the island to its people.

These were followed by the act approved April 25th, declaring that a state of war had existed between the United States and Spain since April 21st, and directing and empowering the President to use the entire land and naval forces and to call into the service the militia of the United States in the prosecution of the war. The President exercised the power conferred, obeyed the direction, prosecuted the war to a successful termination, resulting first in the protocol and then in the treaty ratified by the Senate, by which Spain relinquishes her sovereignty over Cuba, and the United States announces to the world that she is about to occupy and while the occupation continues she—

will assume and discharge the obligations that may, under international law, result from the fact of its occupation for the protection of life and property.

The United States is now in the exercise of such occupation. It has been claimed that she did not take sovereignty over the island; that on the relinquishment by Spain it vanished into thin air to some place unknown, or, as one eminent writer on international law has said, was in abeyance until the inhabitants of the island should be in condition to receive and exercise it. Sovereignty is supreme or paramount control in the government of a country. The United States is now and has been since the signing of the protocol in the exercise of this control in the government of the island. It has not been a divided control, as sometimes happens in the conflict of arms. Her control has been unquestioned and undisputed. I think the United States, upon the surrender of sovereignty over the island by Spain, immediately following the signing of the protocol, took sovereignty over the island, not as her own, nor for her benefit, nor for the people of the United States, but for the inhabitants of the island, for the specified and particular purpose of pacification of the island. What is meant by the pacification of the island? It may be difficult to determine.

Persons and nations may differ in regard to the state of things which must exist to have this accomplished. The Cubans may say that they are pacified, in a state of peace now, and therefore it is our duty to withdraw and allow them to set up such a government as they may choose. We may say that pacification means more than absence of a state of war; that, considering the state of things that had existed for three or more years, it means until the inhabitants shall have acquired a reliable, stable government. Are the Cubans capable of establishing and maintaining a stable government? Who shall decide? If that be the meaning, what kind of a government? A monarchy, a despotism abhorrent to the fundamental principles that have ruled and inspired this nation from its origin?

Who can tell? Then the announcement makes no provision for any return by such government when established for the expenditures and obligations incurred in prosecuting the war and administering the sovereignty. Is the United States to receive such compensation? She became a volunteer in the war, and announced herself such volunteer in taking the sovereignty until pacification is accomplished. As such the United States stands to-day before the civilized nations of the world. The inhabitants of Cuba are the beneficiaries of this voluntarily assumed duty, and when a difference arises between this government and them, whether the duty has been performed and whether this nation is to be compensated for the expense of its administration, have a right to arraign this nation at the bar of nations and demand that it give account of the stewardship which it voluntarily assumed. The determination of the rights of this nation and of the Cubans under this assumed duty may involve many nice questions and many difficulties.

Yet there are those who earnestly urge that Congress should make a declaration that the nation holds Puerto Rico and the Philippine Islands under the same undefined, yet in a sense particular, duty. In my judgment, such a course is beset with complications and difficulties. By adopting it the nation would court these and invite the inhabitants of the islands to engender perplexing questions and entanglements. Under the treaty the nation takes the sovereignty of Puerto Rico and of the Philippine Islands, under the general duty to use it in such a manner as Congress may judge will best subserve the highest interests of their inhabitants and the inhabitants of this nation. I would announce no other duty in regard to them. Many more complications and entanglements may arise in the discharge of the particular duty to Cuba than are likely to arise in the discharge of the general duty to Puerto Rico and the Philippine Islands.

It is urged that this nation should announce the policy of its purpose in the administration of the sovereignty. The flag of the nation has been planted on those islands. That is the emblem of its policy and ever has been, even when at half-mast, mourning the loss of her sons slain in its defence. The flag never did, and I hope never may, represent but one policy. That policy is individual manhood; the right to enjoy religious and civil liberty; the right of every man to believe in and worship God according to the dictates of his own conscience; the right to stand protected equally with every other man before the law in the enjoyment of freedom, of personal rights, and of property. Let the flag, as the representative of these principles, be planted and become dominant on and over every island and every inhabitant. No other, no better, policy can be proclaimed. In no other way can this Congress and nation discharge its duty to the people of the United States and to the people of the islands. Congress should proclaim this policy by its acts and make no attempt to do what it has no power to do—to pledge or limit the action of future Congresses. What future Congresses shall do is for them to determine and proclaim. It cannot be assumed that wisdom will die with the present Congress, nor that it is any part of its 'duty to proclaim what future Congresses shall do. Sufficient unto the day is the duty thereof.

If these principles are enforced as far as applicable to the government of these islands, the inhabitants will be blessed, whether they consent thereto in advance or not. In a representative government the right to govern is not derived from the consent of the governed until they arrive at a stage of advancement which will render them capable of giving an intelligent consent. Four fifths of the inhabitants of this country have given no consent except representatively. The consent of women, as a rule, and of minors is never required nor allowed to be taken. Wives and children are assumed to be represented by husbands and fathers. Boys are to be educated, trained, and ripened into manhood before they are capable of giving consent. Doubtless the boys of fifteen in this country are better prepared to give an intelligent consent than are the inhabitants of those islands. This is not their fault. After having lived for more than three hundred years under a government of oppression and practical denial of all rights it is not wonderful that they are not capable of judging how they should be governed. They are to be trained in these principles: first, by being allowed, under experienced leaders, to put them in practice in the simpler forms of government, and then be gradually advanced in their exercise as their knowledge increases.

All accounts agree that the administration of justice in the islands through the courts has been a farce; that no native could establish his rights or gain his cause, however righteous, against the Spaniards and priests;

that therein bribery and every form of favoritism and oppression prevailed. Under such training and abuse falsehood and deceit have become prevalent. These most discouraging traits of character cannot be changed in a generation, and never except by pure, impartial administration of justice through the courts, regardless of who may be the parties to the controversies. In my judgment, the people of this nation obtain more and clearer knowledge of their personal and property rights through the administration of justice in the courts than from all other sources.

All experience teaches that the requirements and impartial practice of the principles of civil and religious liberty cannot speedily be acquired by the inhabitants, left to their own way, under a protectorate by this nation. The experience of this nation in governing and endeavoring to civilize the Indians teaches this. For about a century this nation exercised in fact a protectorate over the tribes and allowed the natives of the country to manage their tribal and other relations in their own way. The advancement in civilization was very slow and hardly perceptible. During the comparatively few years that Congress has by direct legislation controlled their relations to each other and to the reservations the advancement in civilization has been tenfold more rapid. This is in accord with all experience. The untaught cannot become acquainted with the difficult problems of government and of individual rights and their due enforcement without skilful guides.

No practical educator would think of creating a body of skilled mechanics by turning the unskilled loose in a machine shop. He would place there trained super-

intendents and guides to impart information to their
untaught brains and to guide their unskilled hands. It
is equally true that they would never become skilled
without using their brains and hands in operating the
machines. So, too, if this nation would successfully
bring the inhabitants of these islands into the practice
of the principles of religious and civil liberty it must
both give them the opportunity to be taught in and
to practice them, first in their simpler forms and then
in their higher application, but under competent and
trained teachers and guides placed over them by this
nation. It is equally true that the laws and customs
now prevailing must neither be pushed one side nor
changed too suddenly. · They must be permeated gradually by the leaven of civil and religious liberty until
the entire population is leavened. To accomplish this
without mistake in the interest of the people of this
nation and of the inhabitants of the islands is a most
difficult task, demanding honesty, intelligence, and the
greatest care and good judgment. The task is rendered much more difficult because the people of the
islands have hitherto been governed by the application
of the direct opposite of these principles, and are com-
posed of great numbers of tribes, speaking different
dialects and languages and governed by different customs and laws.

The successful solution of this problem demands ac-
curate knowledge of the present conditions of the entire
population and of the different classes, of their respec-
tive habits, customs, and laws. As the principles of
civil and religious liberty are gradually intermingled
with their present customs, habits, and laws, changes

will be constantly going forward. An intimate knowledge of these changes will also be necessary for their successful government. Hence, as a first step to a successful discharge of this duty, Congress should create a department of government charged with the sole duty to become accurately acquainted with and to take charge of their affairs and place exact knowledge of them before Congress for its guidance. They should not, as now, be left in charge of departments overloaded and overworked.

The second step to be taken is to remove all civil appointments in the islands from the realm of politics. The nation will utterly fail in the discharge of its duty if the islands are made political footballs subject to change in government with every political change in the administration. The administration of the sovereignty must be intelligent, honest, and uninterrupted. A faithful, intelligent man with a full knowledge of the situation must not be displaced to give place to one ignorant of the conditions, however capable otherwise. The duty rests upon the entire nation. It must be discharged for the interest of the whole nation. There are honest, capable men in every political party. These should be sought out and given place in the administration of this sovereignty, as nearly as may be in proportion to the strength of the several political parties in the nation. Then when there is a political change in the administration there will be no inducement to make extensive changes in the administrative appointees of the sovereignty.

Difficult as is the administration of this sovereignty, if honestly and intelligently undertaken such administration, I believe, will be beneficial both to the people of this nation and to the inhabitants of the islands. Difficulties which have come as these have come—unsought—honestly and faithfully encountered, bring wisdom and strength. The struggle for nearly a century in this nation over slavery gave wonderful wisdom, strength and clearness of insight into the great principles which the nation is now called upon to apply to these oppressed islands. Stagnation is decay and ultimate death. Honest struggle, endeavor, and discussion bring light, growth, development, and strength. The primary object to be attained by the discharge of this duty is the elevation of the inhabitants of the islands physically, mentally, and morally; to make them industrious, honest, intelligent, liberty-loving, and law-abiding. This end attained, the secondary object—commercial and material growth among them and among the surrounding millions—will surely follow. The first unattained, the second, at best, will be spasmodic and of little worth.

The intelligent, thoughtful observer sees more in nature and in the ordering of the affairs of this world than the unguided plans and devices of men and nations. For him the wisdom of the Eternal shapes the affairs of men and of nations, sometimes even against their selfish plans and desires. For such, his hand planted the seed of individual manhood and for centuries watched over and cared for it in its slow growth amidst infinite sufferings, struggles, and conflicts, until at length planted on these shores, not entirely in its purity, but at last brought to full fruitage in the terrible struggles and conflicts which ended with the Civil

War. Under him no man, no nation, lives to itself alone. If it has received much, much must it give to the less favored. Under his guidance, I believe, the discharge of this great and difficult duty has fallen, unsought, to the lot of this nation. Then let the nation take up the duty which the Ruler of men and nations has placed upon it; go forward in an honest, unselfish, intelligent, earnest endeavor to discharge it for the highest interest of the nation and of the islands in the fear and under the direction of the Supreme Ruler, who guided the fathers and founders; and the nation will not, cannot, encounter failure.

Vance, Zebulon B., an American politician and orator, born in Buncombe county, N. C., May 13, 1830; died in Washington, D. C., April 14, 1894. After admission to the North Carolina bar in 1853 he settled at Asheville, in his native state, and the next year entered the State Legislature. He was sent to Congress in 1858, and, although opposed to secession, supported the action of his State in that matter, and served for a time in the Confederate Army. He was governor of North Carolina during much of the period of the war, but after the occupation of that State by the Union forces was imprisoned for some weeks in Washington. Elected to the United States Senate in 1870, he was refused admission, but on the removal of his political disabilities became a member of the Senate in 1879, continuing in that capacity until his death. In 1876 he had been governor of his State for a third time. Vance was one of the most popular Senators of his time, and was chairman of innumerable Congressional committees. He was conspicuously eloquent, and ardently championed the cause of free silver and tariff reform.

THE SLAVERY QUESTION.

FROM SPEECH DELIVERED IN THE HOUSE OF REPRESENTATIVES, MARCH 16, 1860.

THE scheme of removing and colonizing four million people is so utterly absurd in practice that it needs only to be suggested to exhibit its entire impracticability. Amalgamation is so odious that even the mind of a fanatic recoils in disgust and loathing from the prospect of intermingling the quick and jealous blood of the European with the putrid stream of African barbarism.

What, then, is best and right to be done with our slaves? Plainly and unequivocally, common sense says keep the slave where he is now—in servitude. The interest of the slave himself imperatively demands it. The interest of the master, of the United States, of the world, nay, of humanity itself, says, keep the slave in his bondage; treat him humanely, teach him Christianity, care for him in sickness and old age, and make his bondage light as may be ; but above all, keep him a slave and in strict subordination; for that is his normal condition; the one in which alone he can promote the interest of himself or of his fellows.

If this is not the language of political philosophy and true philanthropy, if this is not right, then are my most ardent convictions and the most generous impulses of my heart but shallow and false delusions; and I pray to be enlightened, as one who would, if possible, rise above all the surroundings of prejudice and section to view this great question solely by the pure and unflickering light of truth.

Such being our circumstances, and such our convictions, it is time for the opponents of slavery to know, and to be warned, that it is something more than pecuniary interest that binds us to that institution. It is not, as we are often tauntingly told, a desire for gain, or an aversion to physical labor, that makes us jealous of any interference with slavery.

The principle is more deeply seated than this. The general welfare and prosperity of our country, the very foundation of our society, of our fortunes, and, to a greater or less extent, the personal safety of our people, combine to make us defend it to the last extremity. And neither considerations of the Federal Union, nor any other good, will allow us to permit any direct interference with our rights in this respect.

But we are to be lulled to sleep, and our fear quieted, as to the purposes of the Republican party, by the oft-repeated assertions of your leaders, that you do not intend to interfere with it in the States. You say, again and again, that you only intend to prevent its extension into the Territories; and you complain that southern men will unjustly continue to charge you with interference with it inside the States. Mr. Seward, in his recent opiate, says:

" 3. That the capital States [by which he is supposed to mean slave States] do not practically distinguish between legitimate and constitutional resistance to the extension of slavery in the common Territories of the Union, and unconstitutional aggression against slavery established by local laws in the capital States."

And Mr. Wade has laid it down recently, as one of the grand principles of the Republican party, that there shall be no interference with slavery inside the States. I contend, sir, that to prohibit slavery in all the Territories, by an act of Congress, or to refuse to admit a new State because she recognizes slavery, would be a direct and unequivocal interference, about which common sense will admit of no sort of doubt.

In the first place, because it materially impairs the value of my property to restrain my power to remove it; and especially to make it no longer my property when I take it into what Mr. Seward himself acknowledges to be "the common territory." If your shoes and cotton fabrics were prohibited by Congress from entering the south, you would find their value impaired most woefully, and would justly regard it as an interference with the rights of trade.

In the second place, by surrounding the slave States with free territory, and building us in with an impassable wall, you would eventually force the abolition of slavery. Our population would become so dense, and our slaves so numerous, that we could not live; their value would depreciate to nothing, and we would not be able to keep them.

Do you not call this interference? If not, then what is it? A general desires to take a certain city; thinking it too strong to be won by storm, he sits down with his army before it, draws his lines of circumvallation, cuts off its supplies, and, shutting off all communication, waits patiently for famine and domestic insurrection to do their work. True, he says, "Don't be alarmed in there; I am not going to interfere with your internal affairs; I have no right to do that; in fact, one of the rules of war in my camp is, no interference with the internal affairs of this city; my only intention is that you shall not spread, as you are a very sinful people."

Yet that city, in spite of these protestations, would soon find itself subjugated and ruined. You are interfering with our rights in the most dangerous manner by thus seeking to violate one of the oldest and plainest principles of justice and reason—that you cannot do indirectly that which you are forbidden to do directly. The voice of the nation speaking through its representatives by a majority of four to one, North and South, affirmed this in 1838. In the twenty-fifth Congress, Mr. Atherton, of New Hampshire, moved a series of resolutions on this subject, the third of which sets forth—

" That Congress has no right to do that indirectly which it cannot do directly; and that the agitation of the subject of slavery in the District of Columbia or the Territories, as a means, and with the view of disturbing or overthrowing that institution in the several States is against the true spirit and meaning of the constitution, an infringement of the rights of the States affected, and a breach of the public faith upon which they entered into the Confederacy."

Upon this resolution the yeas were one hundred and sixty-four, and the nays forty. Well may you complain that the South will not distinguish between your resistance to the extension of slavery into the Territories and a direct interference with its existence in the States. The acutest minds can only see a different means of attaining the same result.

In the third place, your agitation and eternal harangues have a direct and inevitable tendency to excite our slaves to insurrection. I know that you deny not only an intention to do so, but the effect also.

But you speak in ignorance or disregard of history. It is unnatural to suppose that the noise of this great conflict will not reach the negro's ear, and that your violent professions of regard for his rights will not make him believe that those who shelter him when he runs away, will not also help him to cut his master's throat. The constant denunciation of his owners by your crazy fanatics will make him regard them as monsters, and will cause him to cherish the coals of rebellion until they burst forth into a consuming fire.

Wilberforce and Macaulay did not even intend to abolish slavery in the West Indies when they began their struggle for the rights of the negro—so they said—and they scouted the idea with horror that their agitation would lead to servile war. And yet, when the shrieks of murdered men and outraged women went up through the hot roar of conflagration throughout those lovely islands, the raging demons of lust and brutality bore upon their standards the name of Wilberforce, the philanthropist, beneath the effigy of a white woman kneeling at the feet of a negro, and on which was inscribed, "Liberty and white wives!"

And so strongly do these facts press upon you, as the legal result of your abolition teachings, that we have witnessed the mortifying spectacle of gentlemen rising on this floor and solemnly declaring that they were not in favor of servile insurrection!

But all this injustice will you do, and all these dangers to our wives and children will you incur, rather than permit slavery to enter another Territory, or permit it to come into the Union as a slave State, even though the unanimous voice of the people thereof so desired it. And this Territory, which you mock us by calling "common," what do you intend to do with it?

Sir, there are some districts in the south, in which

the widows of slain Mexican volunteers will outnumber
the whole forces which some of your northern States
had in the field during that war. And yet these widows
and their orphans are not permitted to enter, with their
property, upon these fair lands which their husbands
purchased with their blood. They have not even the
satisfaction of seeing them sold for the use of the public treasury. You thrust them aside; and, by what you
call a "homestead bill," propose to give them away to
those among you who cannot pay one shilling per acre
for homes.

The advocates of this agrarian iniquity unblushingly
avow that it will enable them to ship off the refuse
scum and redundant villainy of the cities of the north.
Your high-sounding catchwords of "homes for the
homeless" and "lands for the landless" can deceive
no one. Why not give also money to the moneyless,
and shoes to the barefoot? Why not imitate Rome,
when growing corrupt, and distribute largesses of
money and provisions among the people?

It would be the same, with the difference that Rome
robbed her provinces to feed her citizens, whilst you
would rob your citizens to feed the provinces. Nay,
you would feed the world; for every jail, workhouse,
and penitentiary in Europe would be emptied in our
Territories. The Atlantic Ocean would be bridged,
and swarms would pour across to enter into this land,
which is too good for southern slaveholders. The
good would come no faster, and of the bad we have
enough already. The old States lose their population
fast enough as it is, and no one should desire to increase
the depopulation. The true title of the bill, sir, should

read: "A bill to encourage foreign and domestic vagabondism, by granting quarter sections of the public land to each actual vagabond that cannot pay twelve-and-a-half cents per acre for a home."

I would finally beg to say to these anti-slavery gentlemen, that for purposes of present advantage they take but a limited view of the future of this great question. A world in arms could not abolish slavery in the southern States to-day, or, if once abolished, a world in arms would rise up and demand its restoration to-morrow. Our slaves are this moment more firmly fixed in their bondage than at any previous moment in our history. Their labor has become an indispensable necessity, not only to ourselves, but to the civilized world; and statesmen, whether British or American, know it.

Our united people will defend it with their blood in the Union, and should your whole society, yielding to a mad fanaticism, so trespass upon our rights as to drive us from the Union, we would find ourselves able to defend it as an independent nation. In fact, we have all the capacities for a separate and independent existence that are calculated to make a great and prosperous State. We produce all the great items of raw material necessary for manufactures; the well-watered valleys of the mountain regions in Virginia, Kentucky, Tennessee, and North Carolina present the most desirable seats for manufactories in the world.

The beautiful, healthful, and magnificent mountain region of western Carolina, which I am proud to represent on this floor, presents greater facilities itself for manufacturing than all New England put together.

The coal fields of my State would feed the glowing furnace for ages to come; and the fertile plains of the northwestern States do not furnish a finer region for the production of the common articles of food, than the great States of Kentucky, Tennessee, and North Carolina.

In fact, we combine everything within ourselves that is necessary for a separate and independent existence. Norfolk, which I believe is in any event destined to become a rival of New York and Liverpool, would then become the great port of entry for the south; and the opening up of the great regions of the west by the Southern Pacific Railroad, and the mingling of the waters of the Ohio with those of the Chesapeake Bay, by canal, would make her to rival the magnificence of Tyre and Sidon. In all these mutations, whilst we could flourish, your prosperity would be stricken down to the dust, and your dependence upon raw material would still hold you our obsequious dependent.

You talk now of forbearing to interfere with slavery among us, because of the delicacy of the question and the interest it involves to us; but you know that your own prosperity is still more dependent upon its existence. It is a tender regard for the goose that lays for you the golden egg, that makes you profess to be unwilling to lay hands upon it. You know that slave labor has built all your cities and towns, has erected your great warehouses, freights your rich navies, and carries wealth and happiness throughout all the bleak and sterile hills of New England.

You know that the shirt you wear, when you stand up to denounce the slaveholder; that the sugar that sweetens your tea, when you sit down to the evening and morning meal—nay, the very paper on which you indite your senseless philippics against the south, are the products of slave labor. You not only thus grow rich upon what you call an iniquity, but you owe your positions in this Hall to the prejudice which you feed and pamper against slavery, and which alone constitutes your whole stock in trade.

Think not, therefore, that you can prevent the extension of slavery, or abolish it where it is. For should you succeed, as you threaten, in cooping us up and surrounding us by Wilmot provisos, or by your homestead bills, in filling up the common Territories with northern and foreign squatters inimical to slavery, the time will come when the southern people, gathering up their households together, sword in hand, will force an outlet for it at the cannon's mouth.

Long years might intervene before this necessity came upon us, but come it certainly would, and we would then go forth and find other lands whose soil and climate were adapted to our institutions, from which you would not dare to attempt to expel us. But will you drive us to this course? Will the great conservative masses of the northern people, who are inheritors with us alike of the common glories of the past, and heirs-apparent of the unspeakable glories of our future, continue to urge this dire extremity upon their southern brethren?

Or will they not rather " be still, and behold how God will bring it to pass?" Will they not wait with patience for this great and all-absorbing problem to work itself out according to the immutable laws of climate, soil, and all the governing circumstances with which he has ever controlled the uprisings and the down-sittings of men?

In this way, and this only, as the waters of the great sea purify themselves, will the good of both the African slave and his European master be accomplished; without violence, without bloodshed, and without a disruption of the bonds which bind together this blood-bought and blood-cemented Union, which our fathers founded in the agony of the greatest of human struggles, and builded with prayers to Heaven for its perpetuity.

This way alone will enable us to avoid that dread day of disunion, of which I have thought in the bitterness of my spirit that I could curse it even as Job cursed his nativity: "Let that day be darkness; let not God regard it from above, neither let the light shine upon it. Let it not be joined unto the days of the year; let it not come into the number of the months. Let the stars of the twilight thereof be dark; let it look for light, but have none; neither let it see the dawning of the day."

Teller, Henry M., an American politician, born at Granger, N. Y., May 23, 1830. After a few years spent in teaching he studied law and was admitted to the bar, practising his profession in Illinois for a time and subsequently in Colorado. He was major-general of the Colorado militia, 1864–65, and in 1876 entered the United States Senate. During a part of the administration of President Arthur, from April, 1882, to March, 1885, Teller was Secretary of the Interior, but returned to the Senate in the last named year. He was re-elected in 1897 as an independent Silver Republican. His oratory is rather florid in character. One of his notable recent speeches was delivered in the Senate in March, 1900, on the bill for the relief of Porto Rico.

ON PORTO RICO.

[Speech delivered in the Senate, March 14, 1900, during the consideration of the bill temporarily to provide revenues for the relief of Porto Rico.]

MR. PRESIDENT,——Before we get through with this question of the power of the United States and what ought to be its policy there will be ample time, I know, for me to discuss it, and I will go directly to the bill, so that I may shorten my remarks within a proper time, in view of the fact that the senator from Washington has yielded the floor to me for a few moments.

In dealing with these new possessions my theory is that we may make them a part of the United States if we see fit. Now, if we conclude that we do not want to make them a part of the United States, I believe we have the same power to hold them, in a different relation, that Great Britain has. I have listened to all the discussion that has gone on here, and I can conceive of no reason why the sovereignty of the United States is limited to territory that they must make a part of the United States. They will be a part of the United States in one sense undoubtedly if we exercise a protectorate over them. They will be a dependency, and they will have a different relation to us from what the other Territories organized as incipient States have. If we choose, we can provide that the territory of Puerto Rico—I am speaking now of the geographical territory—shall be under the control and sovereignty of the United States, that the people of that island may make all the laws that we say they may make. We may give them absolute self-control, or, in my opinion, we may reserve the right to say to them, " There are certain things you cannot be allowed to do ; and if you do certain things, we will intervene and nullify your action."

Mr. President, from my standpoint, then, there is no difficulty in dealing with these possessions, and it becomes simply a question of policy. In this I am speaking for myself only. I do not represent any political organization, and I am not bound by any caucus or by any influences of that character. So far as I am concerned, I do not want to make Puerto Rico nor do I want to make the Philippines an integral part of the United States; I do not want to make their people citizens of the United States, with all the rights that citizenship of the United States ought to carry with it.

The relation that I would establish for those people is absolutely consistent with every tradition of our government and our people from the time we organized the government of the United States up to the present hour. If I had time, I could show historically that the fathers of this Republic contemplated that we should some day have colonies. It may be that it is not good policy to have colonies. That is another question. It may be—although I do not believe it—that it would be wise for us to get rid of Puerto Rico and return it to Spain, or to give it to the people of the island themselves. It may be that it would be wise for us to turn over the Philippine Islands to the anarchy and confusion which I believe would follow the withdrawal of the American troops from those islands at the present time. But I do not believe it.

I will admit that there will be some difficulties in dealing with those people. I foresaw that in the beginning, and I see it more clearly now than I did a year ago, as I believe everybody else does. But, as I said a long time since in this body, the American people will deal with this question in a spirit of fairness and in a spirit of courage. They are not going to be frightened by a contemplation of the fact that there are difficulties in front of them. If anybody can show a better way out of the difficulty than for us to hold those possessions, I am prepared to consider it. I am now considering, first, what is the duty that we owe, not to the Filipinos, not to the Puerto Ricans, but to the people of the United States? That is the paramount question. I believe we can deal with those people without doing any injustice to them or any injustice to ourselves. But we must have a policy; we must lay down a rule and follow it. What I complain of in the party in power is that it has not a policy, as it seems to me, on this question.

I do not know whether we are to have a colonial system or whether we are to make those people part and parcel of the United States. One or the other we must do. I regard the latter as infinitely more dangerous than the former. I would a great deal rather make Puerto Rico a colony than to make her a State; I would a great deal rather make the Philippine Islands a colony, a province, a dependency, or whatever you may choose to call it, than to make those islands into a State or to make their inhabitants citizens of the United States, with all the rights and privileges which follow, and which must ultimately mean, if they become citizens of the United States, that they shall stand before the law on an equality with all other citizens of the United States. If you make Puerto Rico a Territory, an incipient State, its people will have a right some day to expect to become a State of the Union; but if you hold them in tutelage and pupilage for an indefinite period as citizens of the United States, they will have a right to complain.

Mr. President, Puerto Rico is not a part of the United States to-day, neither are the Philippine Islands. In all the acquisitions of territorial property heretofore, we have had, before we acquired it, some relations established by treaty, or otherwise, with the people that we took under our control. When we took in Louisiana, we stipulated with France that we would make the people of that Territory citizens of the United States, entitled to all the rights, privileges, and immunities of citizens; when we took in Florida, we

'did the same with Spain; when we took in a portion
of Mexico, we did the same with Mexico; and when
we took in Alaska, we did the same with Russia.
When we acquired our new possessions, the commission that went over to Paris very wisely said that their
political status should be as Congress should determine.

In an early day, when Louisiana was taken in as a
part of the United States, it was questioned in the
House of Representatives, and even here, whether by
the treaty-making power alone that could be done.
In my judgment it could, because otherwise there
would be a restriction upon the treaty-making power,
which I think would be inconsistent with sovereignty.
But here we have no question. The people in these
possessions are not citizens to-day. The Filipinos are
not citizens nor are the Puerto Ricans. The bill now
pending before the Senate makes citizens of the inhabitants of Puerto Rico of the United States *ex industria*.
That feature alone, if there were no other in it, would
compel me to vote against the bill. I do not want
those people made citizens of the United States. I
want to extend to them all the privileges which are
consistent with their relations to this government, save
that of citizenship. I would extend to those territories
all the privileges, all the blessings which the constitution of the United States is, by some, supposed to have
conferred, but which I say are not conferred, but inherited, inhering in a free government. I would not
establish a relationship which would enable them to
participate with us in the election of a President and

to have their representatives on this floor or in the other House.

I am told by some senators here that this bill does make citizens of the people of Puerto Rico, but does not make Puerto Rico a part and parcel of the United States. If it is possible by language in a statute to make Puerto Rico a part of the United States, it is so made by this bill. In the first place, the people there are made citizens, their ports are made ports of the United States, and the writs of their courts run in the name of the people of the United States; we extend the internal revenue laws over them, the postal laws, and almost all other laws over them, except simply the laws as to the collection of duty on imports. We provide that their products coming into our ports shall pay duty.

Mr. President, if those people are to be a part and parcel of the United States, as they will be if this bill shall be enacted into law as it now stands, and as they will be if a considerable part of it should be stricken out, as I hear vague rumors that it may be, they will have such a relation, in my judgment, to the people of the United States that some of the provisions of this act will be absolutely indefensible and cannot be maintained in any case.

Mr. President, I am not going to waste time in speaking about the provision which puts a duty upon goods going into Puerto Rico. I think that was pretty well exploded here the other day, and I understand that it is liable to be abandoned. But the other question presents itself whether we have a right to put a duty on goods coming from Puerto Rico into the

United States. In my judgment that whole question must be solved by what is their relation to the people of the United States. If they are a part of the United States, if their people are citizens of the United States, you have no right to put a duty upon their goods. If they are not citizens of the United States, then it is a question of policy and not a question of justice ; but what right have the Puerto Ricans to insist now that they shall have free trade with us if they are not part and parcel of the United States ?

Mr. President, we are told that there is a great sugar interest and a great tobacco interest, or something of that kind, demanding that this duty shall be put on those people. I know nothing about that, and I do not care to consider it. It is not a question to be considered in determining this matter as to what influences are back of it. The question is, what is justice ? If they are citizens, as they will be under this bill, you have not any right to impose duties upon them, and it would be an act of gross injustice and one which cannot be legally maintained. If they are not citizens, you have as much right to put a duty upon them as you have to put it on English subjects who send their goods here from London.

A great number of people now in Puerto Rico who are clamoring for free trade with us are not citizens of that country at all, and the large sugar interests there are held by people who are not connected by any ties of citizenship with that country. English capitalists and other foreign capitalists are the owners of the sugar plantations. If we should accept the newspaper accounts we might suppose that every man in

Puerto Rico, poverty-stricken as many of them are, was engaged in shipping sugar and tobacco into the United States. There is not two per cent of the people of Puerto Rico who have any interest in shipping sugar here, and there is not two per cent of them who have any interest in shipping tobacco here. That is done by a few capitalists, and it is those who are interested in this subject. If you let them bring their sugar here at fifteen per cent of the regular tariff which the Cubans, for instance, must pay, the sugar and tobacco planters of Puerto Rico will make a great profit; and, with a two-years' accumulation of sugar in the hands of those rich people, they will be the ones who will be still more enriched and not the poverty-stricken people of that island. As suggested to me by the senator from Wisconsin [Mr. Spooner], the sugar people pay labor such wages as Americans would starve upon.

The great question to be considered all the time is, How can we treat these islands consistently with the traditions of the American people ? How can we do justice to them and justice to ourselves at the same time ? If we give to them practically self-government, they have no right to ask us for participation in the affairs of the general government; and anything that we may do for them, bad as this bill is—and I think it violates some of our traditions as it is—but, bad as it is, is it not better than anything that those people ever heretofore had or anything that they had any hope of having two years ago?

If we keep steadily in view the idea that if these people are capable of self-government, they shall have it—and I have no doubt of their ability to manage their own internal and domestic affairs practically without our supervision, although some senators say that is not the fact—if we yield that to them, we have not violated any principle of free government and of a free people; and all of this repeated newspaper clamor that we are about to do something extremely bad if we deny to those people full citizenship, it seems to me, is without any foundation whatever.

Mr. President, I had intended, as I said before, to go into very many phases of this case, and to touch upon even our relations with our Asiatic possessions; but I shall not do so now. I shall content myself with saying practically now what I have said—that this bill seems to me to be incongruous and unsatisfactory from any standpoint; I do not care whether it be from that of making Puerto Rico a part of the United States or making it a colony.

Knott, James Proctor, an American politician and orator, born at Lebanon, Ky., August 29, 1830. He began the study of law at sixteen, and removing to Missouri in 1850, was admitted to the bar there the next year. He entered the State Legislature in 1858, and was presently made State Attorney-General, but on his declining to take the test oath in 1861 he was disbarred. He returned to Kentucky the year after, and in 1866 was sent to Congress from that State. Re-elected in 1868, he made there a humorous speech on Duluth, which gave him a national reputation as a humorist. Knott sat again in Congress, 1875–83, and was Governor of Kentucky, 1883–87.

SPEECH ON "DULUTH."

DELIVERED IN THE HOUSE OF REPRESENTATIVES, JANUARY 21, 1871.

MR. SPEAKER,—If I could be actuated by any conceivable inducement to betray the sacred trust reposed in me by those to whose generous confidence I am indebted for the honor of a seat on this floor; if I could be influenced by any possible consideration to become instrumental in giving away, in violation of their known wishes, any portion of their interest in the public domain, for the mere promotion of any railroad enterprise whatever, I should certainly feel a strong inclination to give this measure my most earnest and hearty support; for I am assured that its success would materially enhance the pecuniary prosperity of some of the most valued friends I have on earth; friends for whose accommodation I would be willing to make almost any sacrifice not involving my personal honor or my fidelity as the trustee of an express trust.

And that act of itself would be sufficient to countervail almost any objection I might entertain to the passage of this bill, not inspired by the imperative and inexorable sense of public duty.

But, independent of the seductive influences of private friendship, to which I admit I am, perhaps, as susceptible as any of the gentlemen I see around me, the intrinsic merits of the measure itself are of such an extraordinary character as to commend it most strongly to the favorable consideration of every member of this House, myself not excepted, notwithstanding my constituents, in whose behalf alone I am acting here, would not be benefited by its passage one particle more than they would be by a project to cultivate an orange grove on the bleakest summit of Greenland's icy mountains.

Now, sir, as to those great trunk lines of railways, spanning the continent from ocean to ocean, I confess my mind has never been fully made up. It is true they may afford some trifling advantages to local traffic, and they may even in time become the channels of a more extended commerce. Yet I have never been thoroughly satisfied either of the necessity or expediency of projects promising such meagre results to the great body of our people. But with regard to the transcendent merits of the gigantic enterprise contemplated in this bill, I have never entertained the shadow of a doubt.

Years ago, when I first heard that there was somewhere in the vast *terra incognita,* somewhere in the bleak regions of the great northwest, a stream of water known to the nomadic inhabitants of the neighborhood as the river St. Croix, I became satisfied that the construction of a railroad from that raging torrent to some point in the civilized world was essential to the happiness and prosperity of the American people, if not absolutely indispensable to the perpetuity of republican institutions on this continent.

I felt, instinctively, that the boundless resources of that prolific region of sand and pine shrubbery would never be fully developed without a railroad constructed and equipped at the expense of the government, and perhaps not then. I had an abiding presentiment that, some day or other, the people of this whole country, irrespective of party affiliations, regardless of sectional prejudices, and " without distinction of race, color, or previous condition of servitude," would rise in their majesty and demand an outlet for the enormous agricultural productions of those vast and fertile pine barrens, drained in the rainy season by the surging waters of the turbid St. Croix.

These impressions, derived simply and solely from the " eternal fitness of things," were not only strengthened by the interesting and eloquent debate on this bill, to which I listened with so much pleasure the other day, but intensified, if possible, as I read over, this morning, the lively colloquy which took place on that occasion, as I find it reported in last Friday's " Globe." I will ask the indulgence of the House while I read a few short passages, which are sufficient, in my judgment, to place the merits of the great enterprise, contemplated in the measure now under discussion, beyond all possible controversy.

The honorable gentleman from Minnesota [Mr. Wilson] who, I believe, is managing this bill, in speaking of the character of the country through which this railroad is to pass, says this:

" We want to have the timber brought to us as cheaply as possible. Now, if you tie up the lands in this way, so that no title can be obtained to them—for no settler will go on these lands, for he cannot make a living—you deprive us of the benefits of that timber."

Now, sir, I would not have it by any means inferred from this that the gentleman from Minnesota would insinuate that the people out in this section desire this timber merely for the purpose of fencing up their farms so that their stock may not wander off and die of starvation among the bleak hills of St. Croix. I read it for no such purpose, sir, and make no comment on it myself. In corroboration of this statement of the gentleman from Minnesota, I find this testimony given by the honorable gentleman from Wisconsin [Mr. Washburn]. Speaking of these same lands, he says:

" Under the bill, as amended by my friend from Minnesota, nine tenths of the land is open to actual settlers at $2.50 per acre; the remaining one tenth is pine-timbered land, that is not fit for settlement, and never will be settled upon; but the timber will be cut off. I admit that it is the most valuable portion of the grant, for most of the grant is not valuable. It is

quite valueless; and if you put in this amendment of
the gentleman from Indiana you may just as well kill
the bill, for no man, and no company will take the
grant and build the road."

I simply pause here to ask some gentleman better
versed in the science of mathematics than I am, to tell
me if the timbered lands are in fact the most valuable
portion of that section of the country, and they would
be entirely valueless without the timber that is on them,
what the remainder of the land is worth which has no
timber on them at all?

But, further on, I find a most entertaining and instructive interchange of views between the gentleman
from Arkansas [Mr. Rogers], the gentleman from
Wisconsin [Mr. Washburn], and the gentleman from
Maine [Mr. Peters], upon the subject of pine lands
generally, which I will tax the patience of the House
to read:

" Mr. Rogers—Will the gentleman allow me to ask
him a question? "

" Mr. Washburn—Certainly."

" Mr. Rogers—Are these pine lands entirely worthless except for timber? "

" Mr. Washburn—They are generally worthless for
any other purpose. I am personally familiar with that
subject. These lands are not valuable for purposes of
settlement."

" Mr. Farnsworth—They will be after the timber is
taken off."

" Mr. Washburn—No, sir."

"Mr. Rogers—I want to know the character of these pine lands."

"Mr. Washburn—They are generally sandy, barren lands. My friend from the Green Bay district [Mr. Sawyer] is himself perfectly familiar with this question, and he will bear me out in what I say, that these timber lands are not adapted to settlement."

"Mr. Rogers—The pine lands to which I am accustomed are generally very good. What I want to know is, what is the difference between our pine lands and your pine lands?"

"Mr. Washburn—The pine timber of Wisconsin generally grows upon barren, sandy land. The gentleman from Maine [Mr. Peters] who is familiar with pine lands, will, I have no doubt, say that pine timber grows generally upon the most barren lands."

"Mr. Peters—As a general thing pine lands are not worth much for cultivation."

And further on I find this pregnant question, the joint production of the two gentlemen from Wisconsin.

"Mr. Paine—Does my friend from Indiana suppose that in any event settlers will occupy and cultivate these pine lands?"

"Mr. Washburn—Particularly without a railroad. Yes, sir, particularly without a railroad."

It will be asked after awhile, I am afraid, if settlers will go anywhere unless the government builds a railroad for them to go on.

I desire to call attention to only one more statement,

which I think sufficient to settle the question. It is one
made by the gentleman from Wisconsin [Mr. Paine],
who says:

" These lands will be abandoned for the present. It
may be that at some remote period there will spring up
in that region a new kind of agriculture, which will
cause a demand for these particular lands; and they
may then come into use and be valuable for agricultural purposes. But I know, and I cannot help thinking, that my friend from Indiana understands that, for
the present, and for many years to come, these pine
lands can have no possible value other than that arising
from the pine timber which stands on them."

Now, sir, after listening to this emphatic and unequivocal testimony of these intelligent, competent,
and able-bodied witnesses, who that is not as incredu-
lous as St. Thomas himself will doubt for a moment
that the Goshen of America is to be found in the sandy
valleys and upon the pine-clad hills of the St. Croix?
Who will have the hardihood to rise in his seat on this
floor and assert that, excepting the pine bushes, the
entire region would not produce vegetation enough in
ten years to fatten a grasshopper? Where is the patriot who is willing that his country shall incur the
peril of remaining another day without the amplest
railroad connection with such an inexhaustible mine of
agricultural wealth? Who will answer for the consequences of abandoning a great and warlike people, in
the possession of a country like that, to brood over the
indifference and neglect of their government? How

long would it be before they would take to studying the Declaration of Independence, and hatching out the damnable heresy of secession? How long before the grim demon of civil discord would rear again his horrid head in our midst, " gnash loud his iron fangs and shake his crest of bristling bayonets?"

Then, sir, think of the long and painful process of reconstruction that must follow, with its concomitant amendments to the constitution, the seventeenth, eighteenth, and nineteenth articles. The sixteenth, it is of course understood, is to be appropriated to those blushing damsels who are, day after day, beseeching us to let them vote, hold office, drink cocktails, ride a-straddle, and do everything else the men do. But, above all, sir, let me implore you to reflect for a single moment on the deplorable condition of our country in case of a foreign war, with all our ports blockaded, all our cities in a state of siege, the gaunt spectre of famine brooding like a hungry vulture over our starving land; our commissary stores all exhausted, and our famishing armies withering away in the field, a helpless prey to the insatiate demon of hunger; our navy rotting in the docks for want of provisions for our gallant seamen, and we without any railroad communication whatever with the prolific pine thickets of the St. Croix.

Ah, sir, I could very well understand why my amiable friends from Pennsylvania [Mr. Myers, Mr. Kelley, and Mr. O'Neill] should be so earnest in their support of this bill the other day; and, if their honorable colleague, my friend, Mr. Randall, will pardon the remark, I will say that I consider his criticism of their action on that occasion as not only unjust, but ungenerous. I knew they were looking forward with the far-reaching ken of enlightened statesmanship to the pitiable condition in which Philadelphia will be left unless speedily supplied with railroad connection in some way or other with this garden spot of the universe.

And besides, sir, this discussion has relieved my mind of a mystery that has weighed upon it like an incubus for years. I could never understand before why there was so much excitement during the last Congress over the acquisition of Alta Vela. I could never understand why it was that some of our ablest statesmen and most disinterested patriots should entertain such dark forebodings of the untold calamities that were to befall our beloved country unless we should take immediate possession of that desirable island. But I see now that they were laboring under the mistaken impression that the government would need the guano to manure the public lands on the St. Croix.

Now, sir, I repeat, I have been satisfied for years that, if there was any portion of the inhabited globe absolutely in a suffering condition for want of a railroad it was these teeming pine barrens of the St. Croix. At what particular point on that noble stream such a road should be commenced I knew was immaterial, and it seems so to have been considered by the draughtsman of this bill.

It might be up at the spring or down at the foot-log, or the water-gate, or the fish-dam, or anywhere along the bank, no matter where. But, in what direction should it run, or where it should terminate, were al-

ways to my mind questions of the most painful per-
plexity. I could conceive of no place on " God's green
earth " in such straitened circumstances for railroad
facilities as to be likely to desire or willing to accept
such a connection.

I knew that neither Bayfield nor Superior City
would have it, for they both indignantly spurned the
munificence of the government when coupled with such
ignominious conditions, and let this very same land
grant die on their hands years and years ago, rather
than submit to the degradation of a direct communication by railroad with the piney woods of the St.
Croix; and I knew that what the enterprising inhabitants of those giant young cities would refuse to take,
would have few charms for others, whatever their
necessities or cupidity might be.

Hence, as I have said, sir, I was utterly at a loss to
determine where the terminus of this great and indispensable road should be, until I accidentally overheard
some gentleman the other day mention the name of
" Duluth."

" Duluth ! " The word fell upon my ear with a peculiar and indescribable charm, like the gentle murmur
of a low fountain stealing forth in the midst of roses;
or the soft, sweet accents of an angel's whisper in the
bright joyous dream of sleeping innocence.

" Duluth ! " 'Twas the name for which my soul had
panted for years, as the hart panteth for the water-
brooks.

But where was " Duluth ? "

Never in all my limited reading, had my vision been
gladdened by seeing the celestial word in print. And

I felt a profound humiliation in my ignorance that its dulcet syllables had never before ravished my delighted ear. I was certain the draughtsman in this bill had never heard of it, or it would have been designated as one of the termini of this road. I asked my friends about it, but they knew nothing of it. I rushed to the library, and examined all the maps I could find. I discovered in one of them a delicate hair-like line, diverging from the Mississippi near a place marked Prescott, which, I supposed, was intended to represent the river St. Croix, but could nowhere find "Duluth."

Nevertheless, I was confident it existed somewhere, and that its discovery would constitute the crowning glory of the present century, if not of all modern times. I knew it was bound to exist in the very nature of things; that the symmetry and perfection of our planetary system would be incomplete without it. That the elements of maternal nature would since have resolved themselves back into original chaos, if there had been such a hiatus in creation as would have resulted from leaving out "Duluth!"

In fact, sir, I was overwhelmed with the conviction that "Duluth" not only existed somewhere, but that wherever it was it was a great and glorious place. I was convinced that the greatest calamity that ever befell the benighted nations of the ancient world was in their having passed away without a knowledge of the actual existence of "Duluth;" that their fabled Atlantis, never seen save by the hallowed vision of the inspired poesy, was in fact but another name for "Duluth;" that the golden orchard of the Hesperides was but a poetical synonym for the beer-gardens in the vicinity of "Duluth." I was certain that Herodotus had died a miserable death, because in all his travels and with all his geographical research he had never heard of "Duluth."

I knew that if the immortal spirit of Homer could look down from another heaven than that created by his own celestial genius upon the long lines of Pilgrims from every nation of the earth, to the gushing fountain of poesy, opened by the touch of his magic wand, if he could be permitted to behold the vast assemblage of grand and glorious productions of the lyric art, called into being by his own inspired strains, he would weep tears of bitter anguish, that, instead of lavishing all the stores of his mighty genius upon the fall of Ilion, it had not been his more blessed lot to crystallize in deathless song the rising glories of "Duluth."

Yes, sir, had it not been for this map, kindly furnished me by the legislature of Minnesota, I might have gone down to my obscure and humble grave in an agony of despair, because I could nowhere find "Duluth.." Had such been my melancholy fate, I have no doubt that with the last feeble pulsation of my breaking heart, with the last faint exhalation of my fleeting breath, I should have whispered, "Where is 'Duluth'?"

But, thanks to the beneficence of that band of ministering angels who have their bright abodes in the far-off capital of Minnesota, just as the agony of my anxiety was about to culminate in the frenzy of despair, this blessed map was placed in my hands; and, as I unfolded it, a resplendent scene of ineffable glory opened before me, such as I imagined burst upon the enraptured vision of the wandering peri through the opening gates of Paradise.

There, there, for the first time, my enchanted eye rested upon the ravishing word, "Duluth!" This map, sir, is intended, as it appears from its title, to illustrate the position of "Duluth" in the United States; but if the gentlemen will examine it I think they will concur with me in the opinion that it is far too modest in its pretensions. It not only illustrates the position of "Duluth" in the United States, but exhibits its relations with all created things. It even goes further than this. It hits the shadowy vale of futurity, and affords us a view of the golden prospects of "Duluth," far along the dim vista of ages yet to come.

If the gentlemen will examine it they will find "Duluth," not only in the centre of the map but represented in the centre of a series of concentric circles one hundred miles apart and some of them as much as four thousand miles in diameter, embracing alike in their tremendous sweep the fragrant savannas, the sunlit south, and the eternal solitudes of snow that mantle the icebound north. How these circles were produced is perhaps one of those primordial mysteries that the most skilled paleologist will never be able to explain. But the fact is, sir, "Duluth" is pre-eminently a central point, for I am told by gentlemen who have been so reckless of their own personal safety as to venture away into those awful regions where "Duluth" is supposed to be, that it is so exactly in the centre of the visible universe that the sky comes down at precisely the same distance all around it.

I find by reference to this map that " Duluth " is situated somewhere near the western end of Lake Superior, but as there is no dot or other mark indicating its exact location I am unable to say whether it is actually confined to any particular spot or whether " it is just lying around there loose."

I really cannot tell whether it is one of those ethereal creations of intellectual frostwork, more intangible than the rose-tinted clouds of a summer sunset; one of those airy exhalations of the speculator's brain which, I am told, are very fitting in the form of towns and cities along those lines of railroad, built with government subsidies, luring the unwary settler, as the mirage of the desert lures the famishing traveler on, until it fades away in the darkening horizon; or whether it is real *bona fide,* substantial city, all " staked off," with the lots marked with their owners' names, like that proud commercial metropolis recently discovered on the desirable shores of San Domingo. But however that may be I am satisfied " Duluth " is there, or thereabouts, for I see it stated here on the map that it is exactly thirty-nine hundred and ninety miles from Liverpool, though I have no doubt, for the sake of convenience, it will be moved back ten miles, so as to make the distance an even four thousand.

Then, sir, there is the climate of " Duluth," unquestionably the most salubrious and delightful to be found anywhere on the Lord's earth. Now I have always been under the impression, as I presume other gentlemen have, that in the region around Lake Superior it was cold enough for at least nine months of the year to freeze the smokestack off a locomotive.

But I see it represented on this map that "Duluth" is situated exactly half way betwen the latitudes of Paris and Venice, so that gentlemen who have inhaled the exhilarating air of the one or basked in the golden sunlight of the other may see at a glance that "Duluth" must be the place of untold delight, a terrestrial paradise, fanned by the balmy zephyrs of an eternal spring, clothes in the gorgeous sheen of ever-blooming flowers and vocal with the silvery melody of nature's choicest songsters.

In fact, sir, since I have seen this map I have no doubt that Byron was vainly endeavoring to convey some faint conception of the delicious charms of "Duluth" when his poetic soul gushed forth in the rippling strains of that beautiful rhapsody—

> "Know ye the land of the cedar and the vine,
> Whence the flowers ever blossom, the beams ever shine;
> Where the light wings of Zephyr, oppressed with perfume,
> Wax faint o'er the gardens of Gaul in her bloom;
> Where the citron and olive are fairest of fruit,
> And the voice of the nightingale never is mute;
> Where the tints of the earth and the hues of the sky,
> In color though varied, in beauty may vie?"

As to the commercial resources of "Duluth," sir, they are simply illimitable and inexhaustible, as is shown by this map. I see it stated here that there is a vast scope of territory, embracing an area of over two millions of square miles, rich in every element of material wealth and commercial prosperity, all tributary to "Duluth."

Look at it, sir [pointing to the map]. Here are inexhaustible mines of gold, immeasurable veins of silver, impenetrable depths of boundless forest, vast coal measures, wide-extended plains of richest pasturage— all, all embraced in this vast territory—which must, in the very nature of things, empty the untold treasures of its commerce into the lap of " Duluth."

Look at it, sir [pointing to the map] ; do you not see from these broad, brown lines drawn around this immense territory that the enterprising inhabitants of " Duluth " intend some day to inclose it all in one vast corral, so that its commerce will be bound to go there, whether it would or not? And here, sir [still pointing to the map], I find within a convenient distance the Piegan Indians, which, of all the many accessories to the glory of " Duluth," I consider by far the most inestimable. For, sir, I have been told that when the smallpox breaks out among the women and children of the famous tribe, as it sometimes does, they afford the finest subjects in the world for the strategical experiments of any enterprising military hero who desires to improve himself in the noble art of war, especially for any valiant lieutenant-general whose

> " Trenchant blade. Toledo trusty,
> For want of fighting has grown rusty,
> And eats into itself for lack
> Of somebody to hew and hack."

Sir, the great conflict now raging in the Old World has presented a phenomenon of military science unprecedented in the annals of mankind, a phenomenon that has reversed all the traditions of the past, as it has disappointed all the expectations of the present. A great and warlike people, renowned alike for their

skill and valor, have been swept away before the triumphant advance of an inferior foe like autumn stub-
ble before a hurricane of fire.

For aught I know the next flash of electric fire that
simmers along the ocean cable may tell us that Paris,
with every fibre quivering with the agony of impotent
despair, writhes beneath the conquering heel of her
loathed invader. Ere another moon shall wax and
wane the brightest star in the galaxy of nations may
fall from the zenith of her glory never to rise again.
Ere the modest violets of early spring shall ope their
beauteous eyes the genius of civilization may chant
the wailing requiem of the proudest nationality the
world has ever seen, as she scatters her withered and
tear-moistened lilies o'er the bloody tomb of butchered
France.

But, sir, I wish to ask if you honestly and candidly
believe that the Dutch would have overrun the French
in that kind of style if General Sheridan had not gone
over there and told King William and Von Moltke how
he had managed to whip the Piegan Indians?

And here, sir, recurring to this map, I find in the immediate vicinity of the Piegans " vast herds of buffalo " and " immense fields of rich wheat lands."

[Here the hammer fell. Many cries, " Go on! Go
on!"

The Speaker—Is there any objection to the gentleman from Kentucky continuing his remarks? The
chair hears none. The gentleman will proceed. Mr.
Knott continued :]

I was remarking, sir, upon these vast " wheat

fields" represented on this map, in the immediate neighborhood of the buffaloes and Piegans, and was about to say that the idea of there being these immense wheat fields in the very heart of a wilderness, hundreds and hundreds of miles beyond the utmost verge of civilization, may appear to some gentlemen as rather incongruous, as rather too great a strain on the "blankets" of veracity.

But to my mind there is no difficulty in the matter whatever. The phenomenon is very easily accounted for. It is evident, sir, that the Piegans sowed that wheat there and plowed it in with buffalo bulls. Now, sir, this fortunate combination of buffaloes and Piegans, considering their relative positions to each other and to "Duluth," as they are arranged on this map, satisfies me that "Duluth" is destined to be the best market of the world. Here, you will observe [pointing to the map], are the buffaloes, directly between the Piegans and "Duluth;" and here, right on the road to "Duluth," are the Creeks. Now, sir when the buffaloes are sufficiently fat from grazing on those immense wheat fields, you see it will be the easiest thing in the world for the Piegans to drive them on down, stay all night with their friends, the Creeks, and go into "Duluth" in the morning.

I think I see them now, sir, a vast herd of buffaloes, with their heads down, their eyes glaring, their nostrils dilated, their tongues out, and their tails curled over their backs, tearing along toward "Duluth," with about a thousand Piegans on their grass-bellied ponies yelling at their heels! On they come! And as they sweep past the Creeks they join in the chase, and away

they all go, yelling, bellowing, ripping and tearing
along amid clouds of dust until the last buffalo is safely
penned in the stockyards at " Duluth."

Sir, I might stand here for hours and hours and
expatiate with rapture upon the gorgeous prospects of
" Duluth," as depicted upon this map. But human life
is too short and the time of this House far too valuable
to allow me to linger longer upon this delightful theme.
I think every gentleman upon this floor is as well satisfied as I am that " Duluth " is destined to become
the commercial metropolis of the universe, and that
this road should be built at once. I am fully persuaded
that no patriotic representative of the American people,
who has a proper appreciation of the associated glories
of " Duluth " and the St. Croix, will hesitate a moment, that every able-bodied female in the land, between the ages of eighteen and forty-five, who is in
favor of " woman's rights," should be drafted and set
to work upon this great work without delay. Nevertheless, sir, it grieves my very soul to be compelled to
say that I cannot vote for the grant of lands provided
for in this bill.

Ah, sir, you can have no conception of the poignancy
of my anguish that I am deprived of that blessed privilege! There are two insuperable obstacles in the way.
In the first place my constituents, for whom I am acting here, have no more interest in this road than they
have in the great question of culinary taste now, perhaps, agitating the public mind of Dominica, as to
whether the illustrious commissioners, who recently
left this capital for that free and enlightened republic,
would be better fricasseed, boiled or roasted, and, in

the second place, these lands, which I am asked to give away, alas, are not mine to bestow! My relation to them is simply that of trustee to an express trust! And shall I ever betray that trust? Never, sir! Rather perish "Duluth!" Perish the paragon of cities! Rather let the freezing cyclones of the bleak northwest bury it forever beneath the eddying sands of the raging St. Croix.

Vest, George G., an American politician and orator, born at Frankfort, Ky., December 6, 1830. After pursuing the study of law, he removed to Missouri in 1856, and in 1860 took his seat in the State Legislature. This he soon relinquished in order to enter the Confederate Army, and subsequently he sat for two years in the Confederate Congress. Upon the close of the Civil War he resumed his legal practice, in Sedalia, Mo., and in 1878 he was chosen to the United States Senate, continuing a member of that body ever since. He is there known as one of its most vigorous debaters, having addressed the Senate on nearly all of the important measures which have come before it for more than twenty years.

ON INDIAN SCHOOLS.

SPEECH DELIVERED IN THE UNITED STATES SENATE, APRIL 7, 1900.

MR. PRESIDENT,—I shall not take the time of the Senate in discussing this oft-debated question as to the contract schools. My opinions have been so emphatically and repeatedly expressed that it is hardly necessary for me now to give information on that subject to any one who has taken any interest in the matter.

There are people in this country, unfortunately, who believe that an Indian child had better die an utter unbeliever, an idolater even, than to be educated by the Society of Jesus or in the Catholic church. I am very glad to say that I have not the slightest sympathy with that sort of bigotry and fanaticism. I was raised a Protestant; I expect to die one; I was never in a Catholic church in my life, and I have not the slightest sympathy with many of its dogmas ; but, above all, I have no respect for this insane fear that the Catholic church is about to overturn this government. I should be ashamed to call myself an American if I indulged in any such ignorant belief.

I look upon this as a man of the world, practical, I hope, in all things, and especially in legislation, where my sphere of duty now is. Unfortunately I am not connected with any religious organization. I have no such prejudice as would prevent me from doing what I believed to be my duty. I would give this question of the education of Indian children the same sort of consideration that I would if I were building a house or having any other mechanical or expert business carried on. I had infinitely rather see these Indians Catholics than to see them blanket Indians on the plains, ready to go on the warpath against civilization and Christianity.

I said a few minutes ago that I was a Protestant. I was reared in the old Scotch Presbyterian church; my father was an elder in it, and my earliest impressions were that the Jesuits had horns and hoofs and tails, and that there was a faint tinge of sulphur in the circumambient air whenever one crossed your path. Some years ago I was assigned by the Senate to duty upon the committee on Indian affairs, and I was assigned by the committee, of which Mr. Dawes was then the very zealous chairman, to examine the Indian schools in Wyoming and Montana. I did so under great difficulties and with labor which I could not now physically perform. I visited every one of them. I crossed that great buffalo expanse of country where you can now see only the wallows and trails of those

extinct animals, and I went to all these schools. I
wish to say now what I have said before in the Senate,
and it is not the popular side of this question by any
means, that I did not see in all my journey, which
lasted for several weeks, a single school that was doing
any educational work worthy the name of educational
work unless it was under the control of the Jesuits. I
did not see a single government school, especially these
day schools, where there was any work done at all.

Something has been said here about the difference
between enrollment and attendance. I found day schools
with 1,500 Indian children enrolled and not ten in attendance, except on meat days, as they called it, when
beeves were killed by the agent and distributed to the
tribe. Then there was a full attendance. I found
schools where there were old, broken-down preachers
and politicians receiving $1,200 a year and a house to
live in for the purpose of conducting these Indian day
schools, and when I cross-examined them, as I did in
every instance, I found that their actual attendance
was about three to five in the hundred of the enrollment. I do not care what reports are made, for they
generally come from interested parties. You cannot
educated the children with the day schools.

In 1850 Father De Smet, a self-sacrificing Christian
Jesuit, went, at the solicitation of the Flatheads, to
their reservation in Montana. The Flatheads sent two
runners, young men, to bring the black robes to educate them and teach them the religion of Christ. Both
of these runners were killed by the Blackfeet and never
reached St. Louis. They then sent two more. One of
them was killed, and the other made his way down the

Missouri River after incredible hardships and reached
St. Louis. Father De Smet and two young associates
went out to the Flathead reservation and established
the mission of St. Mary in the Bitter Root and St.
Ignatius on the Jocko reservation. The Blackfeet
burned the St. Mary mission, killed two of the Jesuits
and thought they had killed the other—Father Ravaille. I saw him when on this committee, lying in his
cell at the St. Mary's mission, paralyzed from the waist
down, but performing surgical operations, for he was
an accomplished surgeon, and doing all that he possibly
could do for humanity and religion. He had been
fifty-two years in that tribe of Indians. Think of it!
Fifty-two years. Not owning the robe on his back,
not even having a name, for he was a number in the
semi-military organization called the Company of
Jesus; and if he received orders at midnight to go to
Africa or Asia he went without question, because it
was his duty to the cause of Christ and for no other
consideration or reason.

Father De Smet established these two missions and
undertook to teach the Indian children as we teach our
children in the common schools by day's attendance.
It was a miserable failure. The Jesuits tried it for
years, supported by contributions from France, not a
dollar from the government, and they had to abandon
the whole system. They found that when the girls and
boys went back to the tepee at night all the work of
the day by the Jesuits was obliterated. They found
that ridicule, the great weapon of the Indian in the
tepee, was used to drive these children away from the
educational institutions established by the Jesuits.

When the girl went back to the tepee with a dress on like an American woman and attempted to speak the English language, and whom the nuns were attempting to teach how to sew and spin, and wash and cook, she was ridiculed as having white blood in her veins, and the result was that she became the worst and most abandoned of the tribe, because it was necessary in order to reinstate herself with her own people that she should prove the most complete apostate from the teachings of the Jesuits.

After nearly twenty years of this work by the Jesuits they abandoned it, and they established a different system, separating the boys and the girls, teaching them how to work, for that is the problem, not how to read or spell, nor the laws of arithmetic, but how to work and to get rid of this insane prejudice taught by the Indians from the beginning that nobody but a squaw should work, and that it degrades a man to do any sort of labor, or in fact to do anything except to hunt and go to war.

The hardest problem that can be proposed to the human race is how to make men self-dependent. There can be no self-respect without self-dependence, There can be no good government until a people are elevated up to the high plane of earning their bread in the sweat of their faces. When you come to educate negroes and Indians there is but one thing that will ever lift them out of the degradation in which long years of servitude and nomadic habits have placed them, and that is to teach them that the highest and greatest and most elevating thing in the human race is to learn how to work and to make themselves independent.

I take off my hat, metaphorically, whenever I think of this negro in Alabama—Booker Washington. He has solved that problem for his race, and he is the only man who has ever done it. Fred Douglass was a great politician, but he never discovered what was necessary for the negro race in this country. I have just returned from the south after a sojourn of five weeks upon the Gulf of Mexico.

The negro problem is the most terrible that ever confronted a civilized race upon the face of the earth. You cannot exterminate them; you cannot extradite them; you must make them citizens as they are and as they will continue to be. You must assimilate them. Exportation is a dream of the philanthropist, demonstrated to be such by the experiment in Liberia. Mr. Lincoln tried it, and took his contingent fund immediately after the war, shipped negroes to a colony in the West Indies, and those who were left from the fever after two years came back to the United States, and every dollar expended was thrown away. Washington, this negro in Alabama, has struck the keynote. It will take years to carry it out, and he has the prejudices of his own race and the prejudices of the ignorant whites against him; but he deserves the commendation of all the people, not only of the United States, but those of the civilized world.

Mr. President, the Jesuits have elevated the Indian wherever they have been allowed to do so without interference of bigotry and fanaticism and the cowardice of insectivorous politicians who are afraid of the A. P. A. and the votes that can be cast against them in their district and States. They have made him a Christian, and above even that have made him a workman able to support himself and those dependent upon him. Go to the Flathead reservation, in Montana, and look from the cars of the Northern Pacific Railroad, and you will see the result of what Father De Smet and his associates began and what was carried on successfully until the A. P. A. and the cowards who are afraid of it struck down the appropriation. There are now four hundred Indian children upon that reservation without one dollar to give them an hour's instruction of any kind. That is the teaching of many professors of the religion of Christ in the Protestant churches. I repudiate it. I would be ashamed of myself if I did not do it, and if it were the last accent I ever uttered in public life it would be to denounce that narrowminded and unworthy policy based upon religious bigotry.

This A. P. A. did me the greatest honor in my life during their last session in this city, two years ago. They passed a resolution unanimously demanding that I should be impeached because I said what I am saying now. Mr. President, the knowledge of the constitution of this country developed by that organization in demanding the impeachment of a United States senator for uttering his honest opinion in this chamber puts them beyond criticism. It would be cowardly and inhuman to say one word about ignorance so dense as that.

Mr. President, as I said, go through this reservation and look at the work of the Jesuits, and what is seen?

You find comfortable dwellings, herds of cattle and horses, intelligent, self-respecting Indians. I have been to their houses and found that under the system adopted by the Jesuits, the new system, as I may call it, after the failure of that which was attempted for twenty years, to which I have alluded, after they had educated these boys and girls and they had intermarried, the Jesuits would go out and break up a piece of land and build them a house, and that couple became the nucleus of civilization in the neighborhood. They had been educated under the system which prevented them from going back to the tepee after a day's tuition. The Jesuits found that in order to accomplish their purpose of teaching them how to work and to depend upon themselves it was necessary to keep them in school, a boarding school, by day and night, and to allow even the parents to see them only in the presence of the brothers or the nuns.

I undertake to say now—and every senator here who has passed through that reservation will corroborate my statement—that there is not in this whole country an object lesson more striking than that to be seen from the cars of the Northern Pacific Railroad, the fact that these Jesuits alone have solved the problem of rescuing the Indians from the degradation in which they were found.

Mr. President, these Jesuits are not there, as one of them told me, for the love of the Indian. Old Father Ravaille told me, lying upon his back in that narrow cell, with the crucifix above him, " I am here not for the love of the Indian, but for the love of Christ," without pay except the approval of his own conscience.

If you send one of our people, a clergyman, a politician even, to perform this work among the Indians, he looks back to the fleshpots of Egypt. He has a family, perchance, that he cannot take with him on the salary he receives. He is divided between the habits and customs and luxuries of civilized life and the self-sacrificing duties that devolve upon him in this work of teaching the Indians.

The Jesuit has no family. He has no ambition. He has no idea except to do his duty as God has given him to see it; and I am not afraid to say this, because I speak from personal observation, and no man ever went among these Indians with more intense prejudice against the Jesuits than I had when I left the city of Washington to perform that duty. I made my report to the secretary of the interior, Senator Teller, now on this floor, and I said in that report what I say here and what I would say anywhere and be glad of the opportunity to say it.

Mr. President, every dollar you give these day schools might as well be thrown into the Potomac River under a ton of lead. You will make no more impression upon the Indian children than if you should take that money and burn it and expect its smoke by some mystic process to bring them from idolatry and degradation to Christianity and civilization. If you can have the same system of boarding schools supported by the government that the Jesuits have adopted after long years of trial and deprivation, I grant that there might be something done in the way of elevating this race.

The old Indians are gone, hopelessly gone, so far as

civilization and Christianity are concerned. They look upon all work as a degradation and that a squaw should bear the burden of life. The young Indian can be saved. There are 3,000 of them to-day in the Dakotas—in South Dakota, I believe—who are voters, exercising intelligently, as far as I know, the right of suffrage. Go to the Indian Territory, where there are the Five Civilized Tribes, and you will see what can be done by intelligent effort, not with day schools, but with schools based upon the idea of taking the children and removing them from the injurious influence of the old Indians and teaching them the arts of civilization and of peace.

If I have ever done anything in my whole career in this chamber of which I am sincerely proud it is that upon one occasion I obtained an appropriation of $10,-000 for an industrial school at St. Ignatius, in Montana. A few years afterward, in passing through the Pacific coast, I stopped over to see that school. They heard I was coming and met me at the depot with a brass band, the instruments in the hands of Indian boys, and they played without discrimination Hail Columbia and Dixie. They had been taught by a young French nobleman whom I had met two years before at the mission, who had squandered the principal portion of his fortune in reckless dissipation in the salons of Paris and had suddenly left that sort of life and joined the company of Jesus and dedicated himself to the American missions. He was an accomplished musician, and he taught those boys how to play upon the instruments.

I went up to the mission and found there these In-

dian boys making hats and caps and boots and shoes
and running a blacksmith shop and carrying on a mill
and herding horses and cattle. The girls and boys,
when they graduated, intermarrying, became heads of
families as reputable and well-behaved and devoted to
Christianity as any we can find in our own States.
They were Catholics. That is a crime with some
people in this country.

Mr. President, are we to be told that a secret political organization in this country shall dictate to us
what we ought to do for this much-injured race whom
we have despoiled of their lands and homes and whom
God has put upon us as an inheritance to be cared for?
I accuse no senator here of any other motive than a
desire to do his public duty. I shall do mine, and I
should gladly vote for an amendment to this bill infinitely stronger than that of the senator from Arkansas. I would put this work, imperative upon us, in the
hands of those who could best accomplish it, as I would
give the building of my house to the best mechanic,
who would put up a structure that suited me and met
the ends I desired. If the Catholics can do it better
than anybody else, let them do it. If the Presbyterian,
the Methodist, the Congregationalist, or any other de-
nomination can do it, give the work to them; but to
every man who comes to me and says this is a union
of church and state, I answer him, " Your statement is
false upon the very face of it." Instead of teaching
the Indian children that they must be Catholics in order
to be good citizens, they are simply taught that work
is ennobling, and with the sense of self-dependence
and not of dependence upon others will come civiliza-

tion and Christianity. These are my feelings, Mr. President, and I would be glad if I could put them upon the statute books.

Watterson, Henry, born in Washington City, whilst his father was serving as a Representative in Congress from Tennessee, the 16th of February, 1840, and the elder Watterson continuing in public life, the succeeding twenty years were passed in the National Capital. Owing to defective vision young Watterson was educated mainly by private tutors, being carefully taught in music, for which he early showed decided aptitude. An accident to his left hand, quite disabling its action, diverted him from the piano, with which he had made excellent progress, first to literary and afterwards to newspaper work, and the War of 1861-65 found him well forward in his chosen pursuit. With the breaking out of hostilities between the sections he returned to Tennessee, entered the Confederate army and served variously as private soldier, Staff Officer and Chief of Scouts. During an interval of ten months he edited "The Rebel," at Chattanooga, a newspaper which, under his management, obtained great popularity and celebrity. After the War he resumed his journalistic work at Nashville, the Capital of Tennessee, where he married and whence (in 1868) he was called to Kentucky to succeed the famous George D. Prentice as editor of the "Louisville Journal." Here his career in reality began. Uniting the three English dailies of the Southern metropolis, he issued the "Courier-Journal," which has ever since stood foremost among American newspapers and without a rival among the newspapers of the South. Both as a speaker and a writer Mr. Watterson has occupied a commanding position before the country for thirty years. He has sat in seven National conventions, presiding over that of 1876, and serving as Chairman of the Platform Committee in those of 1880, 1884 and 1888. He was the orator on the occasion of the opening of the World's Fair at Chicago in 1892, and has delivered notable orations on many occasions of public importance. Mr. Watterson has resolutely declined office, though respond-

HENRY WATTERSON.

ing to the importunities of his party, and particularly of Mr. Tilden, its nominee for President, he accepted a seat in Congress during the stormy period of the disputed Presidential succession in 1876-77. He was a member of the Ways and Means Committee and of the Democratic Steering Committee. Few men of his time have occupied a larger measure of the public attention in the country at large, whilst in Kentucky he is often referred to as "the uncrowned king." Mr. Watterson never speaks that he does not attract universal attention and although an incisive partisan, his personal popularity is not limited to any party. He is an undoubting American, intrepid in his convictions and constant in his devotion to the higher standards and nobler ideals of his profession. During the last ten years he has been often spoken of as an available nominee for the Presidency by the more liberal and advanced wing of his party.

———

NATIONAL PROBLEMS DISCUSSED.

Delivered at the 25th anniversary banquet of the Boston Merchants Association, December 10, 1901.

In the event that I am ever a candidate for President of the United States, which Heaven forbid, I shall need the Electoral Vote of Massachusetts—or, rather let me say, that I never expect to become a candidate for that office until assured in advance of that vote—and, this being agreed upon, you will not think me taking unfair advantage of your hospitality, or making a self-seeking, electioneering use of it, when I say that I love Massachusetts. I love Massachusetts because Massachusetts loves liberty, and I love liberty.

If I am a crank about anything it is about my right at all times and under all circumstances to talk out in meeting. There is but one human being in this world whom I bow down to and obey, and she is not here this evening—she is at home—I came for pleasure—and, therefore, I am going to proceed just as though I were in reality Julius Cæsar!

Boston, I believe, is still in Massachusetts, and the Bostonese, I am told, possess the conceit of themselves. It is a handy thing to have about the house, and in your case happens to be founded on fact. I at least shall not deny your claim to many good things which have come to pass since the birth of Benjamin Franklin and on down to the completion of the Subway and the new Passenger Stations. And yet back in the neck of the woods where I abide there are those who think that Kentucky is "no slouch." A story is told of an old darky in slave-holding days who declared that his young master was the greatest man that ever lived. "Is he greater than Henry Clay?" "Yas, sir." "Greater than General Jackson?" "Yas, sir." "Well, come now, Uncle Ephraim, you won't say that he is greater than the Almighty?" Uncle Ephraim was stumped for a moment. "I won't say dat, sah; no, sah, but he bery young yit." Kentucky may not be all that Massachusetts is; but Kentucky is "bery young yit!"

You have here the accretions of nearly three centuries of thinking and doing. A single century ago the hunters of Kentucky were threading their way by the light of pine-knot and rifle-flash through the trackless canebrake and the perilous forest to plant the flag which you worship and I adore, upon the first stage of its westward journey around the world. During that War of Sections which extinguished African slavery and created a Nation, Massachusetts was united to a man. Kentucky was so divided that she sent an equal number of soldiers into both of the contending armies. Throughout the period succeeding the chaos of that great upheaval, whilst Massachusetts stood off at long range and took a speculative crack at all creation, Kentucky had to grapple with its realities; to bind up the wounds of the body-corporate; to recover the equipoise of the body-politic; to bury a lost cause and to repair the breaches among the combatants. We did it. We are still doing what is left of it for us to do. And, though we lack somewhat of the wealth which enables you to wish for a thing, and to have it, and, perhaps, the training and methods of order, which have come down to you from those bloody riots in which you will not deny that your fathers engaged—at Lexington and Concord and Bunker Hill—yea, in the streets of this very town— we are getting there, and let me repeat, Kentucky is young yet.

Not so young, however, that long before many of us here present were born she was not old enough to go partners with Massachusetts to help the manufacturers fleece the farmers under the pretension that high protective duties would develop our infant industries and make everybody rich.

I beg you will not be alarmed. I am not going to discuss the Tariff. Twenty-five years ago, I ventured in a modest Democratic platform, and in other simple, childlike ways, to advance the theory that "Custom House taxation," and I might have added all taxation, "shall be for revenue only;" in other words that the Government has no Constitutional right nor power in equity, to levy a dollar of taxation except for its own support, and that, when the sum required has been obtained, the tax shall stop. They called me names. They said I was a revolutionist. They even went the length of intimating that I was a Radical, and that, you know, down our way, is equivalent to telling a man he is a son-of-a-gun from Boston! Worse than all, I was heralded and stigmatized as a Free Trader. Hoary old infant industries, exuding the oleaginous substance of subsidy out of every pore, climbed upon their haunches and with tears in their eyes exclaimed, "What, would you deprive us children not only of our pap, but take from us the means of aiding the poor workingman to earn a living?" Being a person of tender sensibilities there were times when I wanted to creep off somewhere and weep. Lo! the scene shifts, and what do I see? I see the Republican Party, which was so aghast at the old-fashioned, allopathic treatment I prescribed, coming out as a full-fledged Free Trader on the homeopathic plan ; its hands full of protocolic pill boxes loaded with Reciprocity capsules; each capsule nicely sugared to suit the fancy of such infants as accept the treatment, each pill-box bearing the old reliable Protectionist label!

I should be disingenuous if I affected surprise. Indeed, the event fulfils a prophecy of my own. Many years ago, talking to a company of manufacturers at Pittsburg, I declared that the day was not far distant when Pennsylvania would be for Free Trade, whilst a Protectionist party would be growing in Kentucky; that with plants perfected, with trade-marks fixed and patents secure, Pennsylvania, seeking cheaper processes and wider markets, would say, "away with the Tariff," whilst the owners of raw-material, the coal barons and the iron lords of Kentucky, would cry out, "hold on, we don't want the robbing to stop until we have got our share of it."

I have lived to see—and I do not deny Protectionism its share of the credit—my contention being that it was bound to come and might have been had cheaper— I have lived to see the American manufacturer able to meet his foreign rival in every neutral market in Christendom, sure at least of recovering and controlling those markets that geographically belong to him; because, from a collar-button to a locomotive, the finished product of the American manufacturer to-day beats the world.

And this leads me to ask, if all of us are to turn Free Traders, where is the revenue needful to support the Government—economically administered, mind you, economically administered!—to come from? We are barred direct taxation. Henry George being dead, and Tom Johnson alone surviving, Massachusetts, the bell-wether of innovation, will have to wrestle with the Single Tax Problem even as long as she wrestled with the problem of Abolition; and, meanwhile, somehow, the Government must live. Is it possible that I must cross my own tracks, deny my own teaching and advocate a tariff with "incidental protection," enough to supply our poor President, and his advisers, and our poor Congress, and other of our impecunious employes in the public service with the means of keeping out of the poor-house? Shall there be another scandal about another liaison between Massachusetts and Kentucky, another league between the Puritan and the blackleg, another era of bargain, intrigue and corruption as a consequence of our foregathering here to-night? Can it be that it was for this that you would lure the star-eyed one away from the cold pedestal whereon, like Niobe, she stands, all tears, to these gilded halls and festive scenes? I was warned before I left home, that "those Yankees are mighty cute," and I am afraid that, when I get back, the wise ones will shake their heads and wonder what kind of walking it was between Boston Common and the head-waters of the Beargrass!

Forgive the levity. But, what a comedy the thing we call Government, what a humbug the thing we call Politics! And yet, after all, how inevitable! I have seen some real battles in my time; but more sham battles, and I do declare that I much prefer the sham battles to the real battles. I shall always contend that politics is not war; that party lines are not lines of battle. I believe that we shall never approach the ideal in Government until we have forced public men to speak the truth and hew to the line in public affairs, even as in private affairs, the same laws of honor holding good in both; and, whilst I would no more exclude sentiment than I would stop the circulation of blood, many lessons of dear-bought experience admonish me that we are as a rule nearest to being in error when we are most positive and emphatic; that grievous injustice and injury are perpetrated by the misrepresentation and abuse which are so freely visited upon public men for no other cause, or offence, than a difference of opinion; and that intolerance, the devil's hand-maiden, in our private relations, embraces the sum of all viciousness in affairs of Church and State.

Among men of sense and judgment, of heart and conscience, the subjects of real difference must needs be few and infrequent. Even these may be often accommodated without hurt to any interest, all Government being more or less a bundle of compromises. It is that we do in the aggregate what no one of us would dream of doing in severalty; the point turning, perhaps, upon the division of responsibility, but more upon the pressure which in excited times the wrong-headed and stout of will impose upon the more moderate, the better tempered and better advised. The press—particularly the Yellow Press—is doing a noble work toward the correction of this evil; because already the people are beginning to believe nothing they read in the newspapers, and after a while, tiring of an endless, daily circuit of misinformation, they will begin to demand a journalism less interesting and more trustworthy; and, believe me, whenever they make this requisition—whenever they discriminate between the organ of fact and the organ of fancy—there shall not be wanting editors who will prefer to grow rich telling the truth than to die poor telling lies. We may not have reached yet the summit of human perfectibility, where we can hold our own with the merchants of Boston, but even among the members of my profession the self-sacrificing spirit lives apace, and the time will come when the worst of us will scorn the scoop that is no longer profitable!

You have been told, and many of you doubtless believe that life is less secure in Kentucky than in China, or even in Chicago; and, but a little while ago a Kentucky mother was represented as thanking the One Above that her boy was bravely fighting in the Philippines instead of having to face the perils of the deadly roof-tree at home. You have been told that justice cannot be had in our courts of law. You have been told that, because we have some surviving prejudice against bringing the black man and brother into the bosom of our families, we are his enemies and would take unfair advantage of his ignorance and poverty. None of these things are true. They are the figments of a bigotry that obstinately refuses to see both sides. There is an equal quantum of human nature in Kentucky and in Massachusetts. There are as many church bells in the Bluegrass country as in the Bay State country, and they send the same sweet notes to Heaven and sound exactly alike. The one community, like the other, may be trusted to do its part by humanity and its duty to the State; nor can the one help the other except by generous allowance for infirmities that under the same conditions are common to both and by manly sympathy in the cause of liberty and truth, which was, and is, and ever shall be, the glory of our whole country and the fulfillment, under God, of its sublime destiny.

We live in untoward times. We have witnessed wondrous things. With the passing away of the old problems, new problems confront us. Modern inven-

tion has smashed the clock and pitched the geography
into the sea. The map of the world, so completely
altered that it really begins to look like the Fourth of
July, lends itself as a telescope to the point of view.
Concentration is becoming the universal demand, the
survival of the fittest the prevailing law. The idiosyncrasy of the Nineteenth Century was liberty. The
idiosyncrasy of the Twentieth Century is markets. Be
it ours to look to it that we steer between the two
extremes of commercialism and anarchism, for, if we
have not come to the heritage, which God and Nature
and the providence of our fathers stored up for us, to
employ it in good works, we had better not come to
it at all.

Thoughtful Americans, true to the instincts of their
manhood and their racehood, answering the prompt-
ings of an ever-watchful patriotism; carrying in their
hearts the principles of that inspired Declaration to
which their country owes its being as one among the
Nations of the Earth; carrying in their minds the
limitations of that matchless Constitution to which
their Government owes its. stability and its power;
conscientious, earnest Americans, whether they dwell
in Massachusetts or in Kentucky, cannot look without
concern upon the peculiar dangers that assail us as we
plow through the treacherous waters which, for all our
boasted deep-sea soundings, threaten to engulf our
Ship of State, and, along with it, the old-fashioned lessons of economy, the simple preachments of freedom
and virtue, in which those fathers thought they laid
the keel and raised the bulwarks of our great Republic.

That which we call Expansion—coveted by some,

'deplored and dreaded by others—is a fact. The newly acquired territories are with us, and they are with us to stay; a century hence the flag will be floating where it now floats unless some power stronger than we are ourselves turns up to drive us out. The very thought of the vista thus opened to us should give us pause, should chasten and make us humble in the sight of Heaven, should appall us with the magnitude and multitude of its responsibilities. If we are to turn the opportunities they embody only to the account of our avarice and pride; if we are to see in them only the advancement of our private fortunes, at the expense of the public duty and honor; if we are to tickle away our consciousness of wrongdoing with insincere platitudes about Religion and Civilization and to soothe our conscience whilst we rob and slay the helpless, with the conceits of a self-deluding National vanity, then it had been well for us, and for our children, and our children's children that Dewey had sailed away, though he had sailed without compass, or rudder or objective point, into the night of everlasting mystery and oblivion. But I believe nothing of the kind. I believe we shall prove a contradiction to all the bad examples of history, to all the warning voices of philosophy, to all the homely precepts of that conservatism which, founded in the truest love of country, yet takes no account of the revolution wrought by modern contrivance upon the character and movements of mankind. I believe that the American Union came among the Nations even as the Christ came among the sons of men. I believe that Constitutional Freedom according to the charter of American liberty is to Government what Christianity is to religion; and, so believing, I would apply the principles and precedents of that Charter to the administration of the Affairs of the outlying regions and peoples come to us as a consequence of the War with Spain, precisely as they were applied to the territories purchased of France and acquired of Mexico; not merely guaranteeing to them the same uniformity of laws which the Constitution ordains in the States of the Union, but rearing among them kindred institutions, essential not less to our safety and dignity than to their prosperity and happiness. Entertaining no doubt that this view will prevail in the final disposition, my optimism is as unquenchable as my Republicanism; and both forecast in my mind's eye centuries of greatness and glory for us as a Nation and as a people.

We are upon the ascending, not the descending scale of National and popular development. We are to re-create out of the racial agglomerations which have found lodgment here a new species and a better species of men and women. We are to revitalize the primitive religion, with its often misleading theologies, into a new and practical system of life and thought, of Universal Religion, to which the Declaration of Independence, the Constitution of the United States and the Sermon on the Mount of Olives shall furnish the inspiration and the keynote, to the end that all lands and all tribes shall teem with the love of man and the glory of the Lord. We are passing, it may be, through an era of acquisition and mediocrity, a formative era, but we have made and are making progress; and, in spite of the threats of Mammon, the perils that environ the excess of luxury and wealth, in spite of the viciousness and the greed, we shall reach a point at last where money will be so plentiful, its uses so limited and defined, that it will have no longer any power to corrupt.

Although this is an Association of Merchants, and Boston Merchants at that—professedly committed to the principle that " business is business "—sometimes though wrongfully accused of " gainefulle pillage "— I am sure that there is no one amongst us who does not feel that the unscrupulous application of money on every hand has been and still is the darkest cloud upon our moral horizon, the lion across our highway, standing just at the fork of the roads, one of which leads up patriotic steeps of fame and glory, the other down into the abysses of Plutocracy, opening his ferocious jaws and licking his bloody lips to swallow up all that is great and noble in the National life.

The Hercules who strangles that lion shall be called blessed in the land, and this leads me to take note of the presence with us here to-night of a Hercules, who is said to know more about that lion than any other Hercules, living or dead. I mean, of course, the Chairman of the National Committee of one of the two great parties contending for the sovereignty of the people, the distinguished, the eminent Senator, the honored neighbor and friend who sits near me. Though not a Kentuckian himself, he has a brother who came to Kentucky to bear away upon the wings of love one of our fairest daughters. According to the law of the vicinage down our way the circumstance makes us " kind o' kin," as the saying is, and by that token, I have a proposition to submit to him. If he accepts it, I will go bail that my party associates ratify my act.

He knows and I know how hard it is to raise money even for the legitimate purposes of a National Campaign. Yet many people imagine that more or less it is merely to give the skillet an extra shake or two. Those who have least actual familiarity with money are pronest to thinking of millions as millionaires think of pennies. Thousands of good people believe that for everybody except themselves money grows on bushes, and that all elections are knocked down to the highest bidder. The bare fact is lowering both to our political standards and our standards of morality. The mere statement is in a sense degrading. Nevertheless, it is undoubtedly true that money is as essential to political battles as powder and ball to actual battles, and the proposition I have to submit to my friend, the Senator from Ohio, is that he and I come to an agreement about what sum of money the two organizations will require honestly to tide them through to the next Presidential election; that we raise this sum on a joint note and divide the proceeds equally; and that, when the election is over, the party carrying the country shall pay the note! If it be an inducement, I will further agree that the money to be raised shall be of standard weight and value, expressed in gold and silver and paper convertible into either at the will of the holder!

But, whether this or some other plan be reached to abridge the use of money in elections, I do not doubt that we shall in the end weather the breakers of Plutocracy.

It is true that, possessed of no great aristocratic titles, or patents of nobility, money becomes, and will probably remain, the simplest and readiest of all our standards of measurement. Yet, even now, it is grown such a drug in the market, that some far-seeing men, finding it so plentiful and easy to get, are giving it away in sacks and baskets. Time will show that its value is relative, and that after the actual needs of life, it will buy nothing that wise men will think worth having at the cost either of their conscience or their credit. Give me the Right—not in the character of an abstraction, so often misleading to theorists and doctrinaires—not as a flash of fancy, so often irradiating the dreams of the visionary with its illusory hopes —but the plain, simple Right in plain and simple things, obvious to the reasonable and the fair-minded, arising out of the common-sense and common honesty of the common people, relating to the actualities of Government and life, and driving home to the business and bosoms of men—and I care not for the golden contents of all the "bar'ls" that were ever tapped by sordid ambition, or consecrated themselves as rich libations on the altars of opulent partyism.

The people, as a people, can never be corrupted. The whole history of a hundred years of Constitutional Government in America, the moral lesson and the experience of all our parties, may be told in a single sentence, that, when any political organism, grown over-confident by its successes and faithless to its duty, thinks it has the world in a sling, public opinion just rears back on its hind legs and kicks it out. In that faith I rest my hope of the future of the country; sure that in the long run, wrong cannot prosper, and that an enlightened public opinion is a certain cure for every ill.

Gentlemen, Kentucky salutes Massachusetts! Come and see us! You shall find the latch-string always hanging outside the door!

BROWN.

Brown, Benjamin Gratz, an American politician and orator, born at Lexington, Ky., May 28, 1826; died in St. Louis, Mo., December 13, 1885. He was admitted to the bar in Louisville in his native State, but soon removed to St. Louis, and entering the Missouri Legislature in 1852 remained a member of that body for fourteen years. He was a determined opponent of slavery, and in 1857 delivered a famous anti-slavery speech. He edited the Missouri Democrat, an extremely radical Republican newspaper, and as the spokesman of the State Free Soil movement was defeated as its candidate for Governor in 1857 by a small majority only. On the opening of the Civil War he raised a regiment for the Union cause and led a brigade against the Confederate forces. He sat in the United States Senate 1863–67, and in 1871 was elected Governor of Missouri. The following year he was the unsuccessful candidate for the Vice Presidency, on the ticket with Horace Greeley. After his defeat on this occasion, he resumed the practice of his profession at St. Louis. Brown was a man of great ability and an eloquent, earnest public speaker. A speech delivered by him at St. Louis in September, 1862, furnishes an adequate example of his powers.

ON SLAVERY IN ITS NATIONAL ASPECTS AS RELATED TO PEACE AND WAR.

FROM ADDRESS DELIVERED AT ST. LOUIS, SEPTEMBER 17, 1862.

THE lover of his country is not apt to be discouraged as to the eventual triumph of its arms. The lost battle, the miasmatic campaign, abandoned lines and blown-up magazines are regarded as incidents of war. They are deplored, but not held as conclusive or even significant of the ending. There are "signs of the times," however, in our horizon that have a gloomier look than lost battles. And darkest and strangest of all the discouragements that have of late befallen must be considered the spectacle presented by the government in its dealings with this terrible crisis—reposing itself altogether upon the mere barbarism of force.

One would think when reading the call for six hundred thousand men to recruit our armies, and seeing there no appeal to or recognition of the ideas that rule this century, not less than this hour, that as a government ours was intent on suicide—as a nation we had abandoned our progression. Can it be that those who have been advanced for their wisdom and worth to such high places of rulership do not understand that since this world began, the victories of mere brute force have been as inconsequent as the ravages of pestilence and as evanescent

as the generations of men.   Or can it be that, understanding, they care only for tiding over the present
contest to bequeath revolt and internecine war as
the inheritance of those who are to come after them.
That would be virtual disintegration—national
death.

If the government undertakes to abandon the
revolution in its very birth-pains—if it intends to
have no reference to the ideas of which it is the
representative—if it contemplates a disregard of
the progressing thought that not only installed it,
but has carried it so far forward since installation—
if it is determined to found its dominion over subjugated States, not in the name of a principle that
shall assimilate its conquest and assure their liberties,
but of simple power—then will it place itself by its
own action in the attitude of other and equally
gigantic powers that have attempted the same
work and have failed.   It may have its day of seeming successes, but even that will entail an age of
complications.

Does not Poland, as fully alive to-day, after ninety
years of forcible suppression, as on that morning of
the first partition, convince us that this thing of the
dominion of power without the assimilation of
nations can only continue upon condition of an ever-
recurring application of those forces that achieved
the first reduction?   Does not the uprising and the
cry for a united Italy, after five hundred years of
fitful effort, continuous conflict, and successive disintegration under the tramp of a multitudinous
soldiery, tell how fixed are social laws, how faithful

to freedom are peoples, and how certain the retribution following upon those policies of government that sacrifice the future to the present, the moral to the mere material, the consolidating the foundations of a great commonwealth to the hollow conquest, the mock settlement, the outward uniformity? History is full of such illustrations, because history repeats itself.

But I need not go with you further in citing its judgments in condemnation of that reliance upon physical force which deems itself able to dispense with any appeal to principle. We cannot, if we would, cast behind us the experience of eighteen centuries of Christian amelioration, in which mankind have been learning to rely upon moral and intellectual forces rather than simple violence in their dealings with each other as nations. Not that civilization has surrendered its rights of war, but that it insists that ideas shall march at the head of armies. Napoleon III., when he announced that the French nation alone in Europe made war for an idea, intended to represent it as leading, not relapsing from the civilization of the age. And therein he both uttered a philosophic truth and penetrated the secret of success.

Strip the choicest legions of the inspiration they derive from a controlling, elevating cause—especially that cause whose magic watchword cheers to victory in every land—and in vain will you expect the heroic in action or the miracle in conquest. It is a coward thought that God is on the side of the strongest battalions. The battles that live in memory

—that have seemed to turn the world's equanimity upside down—have been won by the few fighting for a principle as against the multitude enrolled in the name of power. When, therefore, it is conceded that the mere announcement of a policy of freedom as the policy of this war would paralyze the hostility of all the sovereigns of Europe and wed to us the encouragement of their peoples, why is it that so little faith obtains among our rulers that it would equally strengthen the government here amid the millions of our own land? Have the populations of our States fallen so low—become so irresponsive to the watchwords of liberty—that it is not fit to make such an appeal to them? Is there no significance in the fact that amid the five thousand stanzas that have vainly attempted to exalt the unities of the past into a nation's anthem—a song of war kindling the uncontrollable ardors of the soul—one alone, proscribed like the "Marseillaise," has been adopted at the camp fire—

> "John Brown's body lies a moldering in the grave,
>   His soul is marching on."

Six hundred thousand soldiers summoned to the field, and for what? The nation asks of the President, for what? Is it that the government may wring a submission from the possible exhaustion on the part of the seceding States, that shall be a postponement, not a settlement, of this great crisis, and that shall be unrelated to the causes that have produced it, or the progression on our part that has put on the armor of revolution? If so, the government will find when perhaps it is too late, that in addition to the rebellion it will have to confront a public opinion that has no sympathies with reaction, and that will withdraw, as unitedly as it has hitherto given, all its trust from those in power. Or is it that grounding this great struggle upon its true basis, upholding the national honor whilst battling for the national thought, our armies are to be marshalled under the flag of freedom, and the peace achieved is to be one that shall assure personal and political liberty to every dweller in the land? If that be so, let the fact be proclaimed, not hidden from the people, and there will need no call from President, no conscription from Congress, to recruit the ranks of the soldiers of the republic.

The two great revolutions of modern times which mark the most signal advance in political freedom, that of England during the Commonwealth and that of France in 1789, have this among many other striking features of similarity—that in each case a large part of the empire resisting the advent of free principles, took up arms again the government to contest the issue. In the *Vendée*, as in Ireland, it became necessary to establish by force the supremacy of the new order. It was antagonism by the population of whole sections, and in both instances, courses of conciliation having proved worthless, a stern and vigorous policy of subjugation was required. That even the success which crowned such measures was only partial and transient, demanding a supplemental work of assimilation, is also well worthy of attention. But in subduing the resistance now presented, this nation has that to contend with,

not less than that to assist it, which was not present
in either of the parallels cited.   I allude to slavery,
the strength and the weakness of the South.

Look steadily at the prospect.   Nine millions of
people in all—five millions and a half of whites ad-
dressing themselves exclusively to warfare, sustained
by three millions and a half of blacks drilled as slaves
to the work of agriculture.   Such are the official
statistics of the seceding States.

With the whites the conscription for military
purposes reaches to every man capable of bearing
arms;   with the blacks the conscription for labor
recognizes neither weakness, nor age, nor sex.   Solitary drivers ply the lash over the whole manual
force to transform plantations into granaries.   This
allotment necessarily gives to war the largest possible number of soldiers and extracts from labor the
greatest possible production of food.   Combined,
protected, undisturbed, the relation so developed
presents a front that may well shake our faith in any
speedy subjugation.

Of these five and a half millions white population,
the ratio over the age of twenty-one which, according to statistical averages, is one in six, will give a
fraction over 900,000 men, from which deduct as
exempts or incapables twenty per cent., leaving
720,000, and add on the score of minor enlistments
one-half of those between the ages of sixteen and
twenty-one, or 55,000, and there existed 775,000,
as the total possible Confederate force in the outset.
If from this number 100,000 be stricken off as the
aggregate of the killed, disabled, imprisoned and

paroled since the outbreak of the war, and 70,000 be added as the probable number of recruits from Kentucky, Missouri and Maryland, there will result 745,000 as the effective force. From these are to be taken the men needed for the civil service, for provost and police duties, and for regulating the transmission or exchange of productions—certainly not less than 90,000, and there remains an aggregate of 655,000 as the fruit of thorough conscription.

Perhaps, however, it is right to make from such rigid possible military array a deduction in favor of the population which abandoned the seceding States since the war began and that which, intrinsically loyal, has evaded enrollment. In default of any certain information, this may be placed at 55,000 men, thus leaving 600,000 soldiers fit for service and ready to be concentrated and marched as the skill of their commanders may determine.

Such is the strength of the array that now contests and resists the cause of advancing freedom in the nation. That the strength is not overestimated; that the conscription has been remorseless, is proven by every critical battle-field where our armies have been outnumbered, and is to-day doubly attested by our beleaguered capital and widely menaced frontiers. There, then, is the rebellion stripped to the skin. Look at is squarely. Those 600,000 soldiers stand between us and any future of honor, liberty or peace. How are they to be disposed of, defeated, suppressed?

It is an imposing column of attack, but it has also its element of weakness and dispersion. Remember that in making such an estimate it has been predicted upon the fact that the whole available white population was devoted to the formation of armies. No part was assigned to the labor of the field or workshop, to production or manufacture; but all this vast organization reposes for sustenance—not to speak of efficiency—on the hard-wrung toil of slaves.

Reflect, furthermore, that this whole foundation is mined, eruptive, ready to shift the burden now resting on it so heavily. The three and a half millions of black population engaged in supplying the very necessaries of life and movement to the Confederate armies, are all loyal in their hearts to our cause and require only the electric shock of proclaimed freedom to disrupt the relation that gives such erectness and impulsion to our adversaries and such peril to ourselves. Years of bondage have only sharpened their sensibilities toward liberty, and the word spoken that causes such a hope will penetrate every quarter of the South most speedily and most surely.

Emancipate the industry that upholds the war power of the South; destroy the repose of that system which has made possible a levy *"en masse"* of every white male able to bear arms; recall to the tillage of the field; to the care of the plantation; to the home supports of the community a corresponding number of the five and a half millions whites, and there will be put another face to this war.

Compel the rebels to do their own work, hand for hand, planting, harvesting, victualling, transporting ——to the full substitution of the three and a half millions blacks, now held for that purpose, and where now they advance with armies they will fall back with detachments; where abundance now reigns in their camps, hunger will hurry them to other avocations. It needs only that the word be spoken.

A national declaration of freedom can no more be hidden from the remotest sections of the slave States than the uprisen sun in a cloudless sky. The falsehoods, the doubts, the repulsions that have heretofore driven them from us, will give place to the kindling, mesmeric realization of protection and deliverance. In the very outset their forces, which now march to the attack, will be compelled to fall back upon the interior to maintain authority and prevent escapades *"en masse."* Insurrection will not so much be apprehended, for where armies are marshalled and surveillance withdrawn, the slave is wise enough to know that a plot with a centre— an uprising—would be sure to meet with annihilation, whilst desertion from the plantations is only checked by the repressive rules of our own lines.

The right to do these things needs not to be argued; it is of the muniments of freedom, of the resorts of self-preservation, of the investure that charges the government with the defence of the national life. And in this hour can be effected that which hereafter may not be practicable. Occupancy of the entire coast, with many lodgments made by our navy, a penetration of the valley of the lower Mississippi, giving access to all its tributary streams, and the exposed front of Virginia, Tennessee and Arkansas, give ample basis for extending such a proclamation. Resuming the advance ourselves, with augmented forces, we shall find the 600,000 Confederates compelled to detach one-half their force for garrisoning the cotton States, whilst of the remaining 300,000 large numbers will necessarily fall out to replace the industrial support of their families along the border. State by State, as it is occupied and liberated, will recall for substitution those spared to offensive war in reliance upon slave production. The 300,000 will speedily become 100,000, and instead of concentrating back upon their reserves, massed in imposing column, as has heretofore been their policy when temporarily checked, the very condition of the South will require a wide dispersion of their forces. Conquest and suppression will thus be rendered matters of absolute certainty. The double result of immensely diminished numbers in the Confederate armies and of its separation into broken columns for local surveillance over all threatened slave territory, is thus seen to flow from emancipation as a war measure.

In the grave contest on which we have entered for life and for death, no appreciative judgment can be formed of the absolute necessity of writing freedom on the flag that leaves out of view the organization of the labor and the valor for military purposes of the population thereby liberated. The substitution of freed blacks, whenever they can relieve for other duties the enlisted soldier, has already so far commended itself in defiance of slave codes and equality fears, as to have been adopted in some divisions of our armies. The wisdom that should have foreseen in such a policy extended as far as practicable the addition to-day of 50,000 soldiers to the effective fighting force of the government, perhaps changing the fate of critical campaigns, has been unfortunately wanting. And yet the army regulations, as applied to the muster-rolls of our forces, will show that nearly twice that number of disciplined troops could have been relieved of ditching, teaming, serving or other occupation, and sent to the front. Moreover, any policy which looks distinctly to the subjugating and occupying, militarily, until the national authority shall be sufficiently respected to work through civil processes, the States now in rebellion, must embrace within its scope the employment of acclimated troops for garrison and other duties during those seasons fatal to the health of our present levies.

The diseases of a warm climate have already been far more destructive to the lives of our soldiers, as shown by aggregated hospital reports at Washington, than all other battlefields, and hereafter in the prevalence of those epidemics so common in the Gulf States, our battalions, if subjected to Southern service, would melt away disastrously. It is not possible, therefore, to separate the holding of the rebel States from the employ of acclimated troops. And for that purpose but one resource exists—the liberated blacks, whose veins course with the blood of the tropics. Arm them, drill them, discipline them, and of one fact we may be sure—they will not surrender.

I take it that a race liberated by the operation of hostilities is entitled by every usage of warfare to be armed in defence of those who liberated them, and, furthermore, I take it that a people made free in accordance with the humanities of this century, is entitled by every right, human and divine, to be armed as an assurance of its own recovered freedom.

This step will be at once the guarantee against future attempt at re-enslavement and the bond that no further revolt on the part of the States occupied shall be meditated. Above all else, it will be assurance unmistakable that no disgraceful peace, no dismembered country, no foresworn liberties, will end this war. What, shall we stand halting before a sentimentality, blinking at shades of color, tracing genealogies up to sons of Noah, when our brothers in arms are being weighed in the scales of life and death! Go, ye men of little faith; resign your high charges, if it be you cannot face a coward clamor in the throes of a nation's great deliverance.

Go and look yonder upon the pale mother in the far northland, weary with watching by her lonely hearth for the bright-faced boy's return. Her hope had nerved itself to trust his life to the chances of the battlefield; but the trundling wheels bear back to her door a stricken form, in coarse pine box, with the dear name chalked straggling across, indorsed "fever." Listen then to the wail of crushing woe sobbed out by a broken heart, and say to her if you can, general, statesman or President, that you refused the aid that would have saved that double life of mother and son. Verily, the graves of the northmen have their equities equally with those of the rebellion.

There are those, strange to say, who, in addition to the war now waged by us against five and a half millions of whites, would add to the task of reduction thus imposed upon our government the further work of taking possession of and deporting to other lands the three millions and a half of blacks. Disregarding the assistance that might be derived from the co-operation and enfranchisement of the slave labor of the seceding States, they would not only strip the slaves of the present uncertain hope of personal freedom which may be found within our lines, but, still viewing them as "chattels," to be dealt with as fancy may dictate, would serve a notice on the world that the best usage they can hope for from risking life to render us aid, will be transportation to climes and countries beyond the reach of their knowledge, and that only inspire ignorance with terror. According to such, the practical solution of the present crisis consists:

FIRST. In conquering the rebellion by making its cause a common cause, as against us, by both master and slave.

SECOND. In holding the conquered territory and superinducing a state of peace, plenty and obedience by the deportation of all who are loyal and of all who labor.

With such the magnitude, not to say impracticability, of migrations that would require—even if all were favoring—transport fleets larger and costlier than those employed for the war, is not less scouted

at as an obstacle, than the resistance to be foreseen
from the unwilling and the depopulation that may
be objected by the interested is treated as a fanaticism. Without challenging the sincerity of those
who advocate such views, it will be sufficient to say
that I differ from them altogether. I do not believe
the government has "chattel rights" in the slave
emancipated by act of war any more than the rebellion had; and I do believe that the doctrine of
personal liberty, if it be worth anything—if it be not
a sham and a delusion—if it is to have any application in this conflict—must be applied to them.

It is not in behalf of the noble and the refined, the
generous and the cultivated, that the evangels of
freedom have been heretofore borne by enthused
army in the deliverances history so much loves to
delineate and extoll, but to the down-trodden—to
the ignorant from servitude—to the enfeebled in
spirit from long years of oppression. Why, then,
shall those liberated in this country be bereft of the
rights of domicile and employ? Because they are
black, forsooth!

That answer will scarcely stand scrutiny by the
God who made us all. It would, moreover, justify
slavery as fully as extradition. Deportation, if
forcible, is in principle but a change of masters, and
in practice will never solve the problem of the negro
question as growing out of this war. If voluntary, it
needs not to be discussed in advance of emancipation. The lot of the freed race will be to labor—in
the future as in the past—but to labor for the wage
and not for the lash. That there must be coloniza-

tion as a resultant of the complete triumph of the national arms, and the complete restoration of the national authority, no one can reasonably doubt.

But it will be a colonization of loyal men into and not out of the rebel States. The great forces of immigration, fostered and directed, will work out the new destiny that awaits the seceded States— the assimilation that must precede a perfect union. What it has done for the Lake Shore, for the Pacific coast, for the Centre and the West, that will it do for the South also, when no blight of slavery lingers there to repel its coming or divert its industrial armies. And if in the development caused by its vast agencies, those natural affinities, so much insisted on by many, shall lead the African race toward the tropics, to plant there a new Carthage, it will be one of these dispensations of Providence that will meet with support and co-operation, not hindrance and antagonism from the friends of freedom on this continent.

The half-way house where halt the timid, the doubtful, the reactionary in this conflict, hangs out a sign: "The Union as it was." Within its inclosure will be found jostling side by side, the good man who is afraid to think, the politician who has a record to preserve, the spy who needs a cloak to conceal him, and behind all these the fluctuating camp followers of the army of freedom. Not that there are no wise and brave men who phrase their speech by the attachments of the past; but that such have another and purer significance in their language than the received meaning on "the Union as it was." All

13—6

who look at events which have come upon us, see
that "the Union as it was" contained the seeds of
death—elements of aggression against liberty and
reaction through civil war. Its very life-scenes, as
time progressed, were ever and anon startled by the
bodeful note of coming catastrophe, to be lulled
again into false security by pæan songs to its excellence—like some old Greek tragedy with its inexorable fate and its recurring chorus. And tragic
enough, it would seem, has been its outcome to dis-
sipate any illusion.

Is it believed that the same causes would not produce the same results to the very ending of time?
Is it wished to repeat the miserable years of truck-
ling and subserviency on the part of the natural
guardians of free institutions to the exaction, arro-
gance and dominion of the slave power through
fear of breaking the thin ice of a hollow tranquillity?
Is it longed to undergo new experiences of Sumner
assaults, Kansas outrages, Pierce administrations,
Buchanan profligacies, knaveries and treasons, with
spirited interludes of negro-catching at the North,
and abolition hanging at the South? Is it desired
to recall the time when the man of Massachusetts
dared not name his residence to the people of Carolina; when free speech was a half-forgotten legend
in the slave States, when the breeding of human
beings to sell into distant bondage was the occupation of many of the élite of the borderland; and when
demoralization, that came from sacrificing so much
self-respect to mere dread of any crisis or mere hope
of political advancement, had dwarfed our states-

men, corrupted our journalism, and made office-holding disreputable as a vocation?

For one, I take witness here before you all, that I want no such Union, and do not want it, because it contained that which made those things not only possible, but probable. I trust that I value as much as another the purities of a Union, the excellencies of a constitution, the veracities and accomplishments of a former generation, but who would be the blind worshipper of form rather than substance—of a name, rather than a reality—of a bond that did not bind, and a federation that has resulted only in disjunction? There are those I know who regard "the Union as it was" as a sentiment significant of material prosperity—unrelated to rights or wrongs, and as such they worship it, just as they would a State bank corporation with large dividends, or any named machine that would enable them to buy cotton, sell goods, or trade negroes. But such should be content to pass their ignoble lives on the accumulation of other days, and not dare to dictate to others a return to such debasing thraldom.

Of one thing they may be sure—that the great Democracy of this nation will insist that the Union of the future shall be predicated upon a principle uniting the social, moral and political life of a progressive people—and purged of the poison of the past. When asked, therefore, as the charlatans of the hour often do ask, would you not wish the "Union as it was" restored, even if slavery were to remain intact and protected—say emphatically, No! say No! for such an admission would be a self-contradiction—a yielding of all the longings of the spirit to an empty husk whose only possible outcome we see to-day in the shape of civil war.

It is, perhaps, the fate of all revolutions involving social changes, to be officered at the outset by the inherited reputations, great and small, of the fore- going time, and so far as this fate has fallen on oui nation, it is less to be wondered at than deplored. But soon there comes the time for change, when the Fairfaxes, the Dumouriers, the Arnolds, must give place to soldiers of the faith. And, hopeful to say, it has ever happened that conjointly with the public assumption of the principle of the Revolution, medi- ocrity, routine, half-heartedness have passed from command, and victory has replaced disaster. So much is historic. We may take comfort then; for the uses of adversity are ours.

Pro-slavery generals at the head of our armies are the result of pro-slavery influence in our national councils, and the hesitancy of the government to pro- claim officially any distinct policy of freedom has kept them there. By no possibility, however, can such, even if the chance victors of to-day, remain possessed of the future.

I do not underrate the prestige of military suc- cess—but military prestige is as naught before the march of revolution; and it is only when revolutions are accomplished, that the reputations of great captains become great dangers. Pro-slavery gen- erals, therefore, are only dangerous now from the disasters that accompany their administration. Their appreciation of the present being at fault, their methods, their reliances, their results will be inconsequent, and without force. Witness the miserable months of projected conciliations, of harmless captures, of violated oath taking, of border State imbecilities, of Order No. Threes, of paroling guerrillas, of halting advances and wasted opportunities. Could these things have been possible to commanders comprehending either the magnitude, the characteristics or the consequences of the war that slavery has inaugurated, and that must end in slavery extinction or the abandonment of our development as a free people? Or can it be possible that the same series of incompetencies and sham energies shall be prolonged indefinitely? No! It needs not that I should insist how surely all such must give way before the force of a public sentiment which, when once on the march, speedily refuses to trust any with responsibility who are not born of the age.

It was just such a common thought of the Long Parliament that gave a "new model" to their army and a "self-denying ordinance" to themselves, extirpating insincerity from the former and imposing stoicism and self-sacrifice on each other. It was a similar growth of public opinion in France that set the guillotine at work to keep account of lost battles with unsympathizing generals. The pregnant question, then, of this crisis is, how long, my countrymen, shall we wait for the "new model" and the "self-denying ordinance" and the swift punishment in this day of calamitous command and disgraceful surrenders.

No one has ever read of a more touching spectacle

in the life of nations, than that now presented by this people. Beyond any parallel it has made sacrifice of those things dear to its affection—I might almost say traditionally sacred from violation. All its rights of person and of property have been placed unmurmuringly at the disposal of the government, asking only in return a speedy, vigorous, uncompromising conduct of the war upon a true principle to an honorable ending. The habeas corpus has been suspended, not only in the revolted territory, but likewise in many of the loyal States. A passport system, limiting and embarrassing both travel and traffic, has been enforced with rigor. The censorship of the press not only controls the transmission of news, but curtails even the expression of opinion within restrictions heretofore unimaginable.

Arbitrary imprisonment by premiers of the cabinet, banishments summarily notified, exactions levied at discretion, fines assessed by military commissions, trials postponed indefinitely—in short, all the panoply of the most rigid European absolutism has been imported into our midst. It is not to complain, that these things are recited; for, so far as necessary, they will be, as they have been, cheerfully borne with; but to show how tragic is the attitude of this nation and yet how brave.

The President of the United States, to-day, holds a civil and military power more untrammelled than ever did Cromwell; and, in addition thereto, has enrolled by the volunteer agencies of the people themselves, a million of armed men, obedient to his command. Nay, did I say the President was absolute as Cromwell? In truth, I might add that of his officials intrusted with administering military instead of civil law—every deputy provost marshal seems to be feeling his face to see if he, too, has not the warts of the Great Protector.

If this were the occasion for stale flatteries of the constitution and the Union, it might well be asked just here, where, in that much-lauded parchment and league is the warrant for these things specifically? But I carp not at such technicalities. Give him, rather, more power if necessary—give him any trust and every appliance, only let it be not without avail.

And yet with all this sacrifice, with all this effort, with quick response to every demand for men and money, what do we see? A beleaguered capital, only saved by abandoning a year of conquest and long lines of occupation; the confidence of the whole nation shaken to its very foundations by accumulated disasters and halting policies; and the grave inquiry, mooted in no whispered voice, by men who have never known fear in any peril, can this country survive its rulers? I do not say the doubt is justified; but I do say that it exists in many minds that have been prone heretofore to confidence. We have seen fifty thousand soldiers, the élite of the nation, sacrificed, and six hundred millions of treasure, the coin wealth of the people expended. We have reached the stage of assignats and conscriptions, and are now summoning the militia of the loyal States to repel invasion. And can any one cognizant of our actual condition, and not misled by false bulletins, or varnished glories, stand forth and say with truth and honor, we are any nearer a solution in this hour of the great crisis in which we are involved than we were a year ago? I challenge a response. Or will any delude you long with the belief that a great victory will accomplish the ending? I do not believe it.

In the presence, therefore, of such thick-coming danger, and having borne itself so continently and so well, has not this nation now the right to demand of President and of cabinet, and generals, that there shall be an end of policies that have only multiplied disasters and disrupted armies, and a substitution of civil policies that shall recognize liberty as the corner-stone of our Republic, and write "Freedom" on the flag.

In conclusion, let me say that the time has passed when such a demand could be denounced, even by the most servile follower of administrations, as a fanaticism, for the chief of the Republic has himself recognized his right to do so, if the occasion shall require, in virtue of being charged with the preservation of the government. He has, furthermore, become so far impressed with the urgency that manifests itself, that he has ordered immediate execution to be given to the act of the last Congress, prescribing a measure of confiscation and emancipation.

This day, too, is the anniversary of its enforcement, as it is the anniversary of the adoption of the original constitution of the United States. Let us, then, in parting, take hope from the cheering coincidence. The act of Congress, it is true, is but an initial measure, embarrassed by many clauses, and may be much limited by hostile interpretation. Still, it can be made an avatar of liberty to thousands who shall invoke its protection, and the instrument of condign punishment to those who have sought the destruction of all free government. And more than all else, its rigid enforcement and true interpretation will give earnest to the nation of that which must speedily ensue—direct and immediate emancipation by the military arm, as a measure of safety, a measure of justice and a measure of peace.

Brown, John, a celebrated American abolitionist, born at Torrington, May 19, 1800; died at Charleston, W. Va., Dec. 2, 1859. He emigrated to Ohio in early youth, and in 1855 removed to Kansas and with his large family of sons took an active and aggressive part in the struggles with the pro-slavery advocates there. In 1859 he planned an invasion of Virginia in order to liberate the slaves, and on Oct. 16, with twenty-two associates, he surprised the small town of Harper's Ferry, and captured the arsenal and armory. He and the survivors of his small force were taken prisoners the next day by the national troops, and delivered over to the Virginia authorities. After a trial Brown was hanged on the second of the following December.

WORDS TO GOVERNOR WISE AT HARPER'S FERRY.

GOVERNOR,—I have from all appearances not more than fifteen or twenty years the start of you in the journey to that eternity of which you kindly warn me; and, whether my time here shall be fifteen months or fifteen days or fifteen hours, I am equally prepared to go. There is an eternity behind and an eternity before; and this little speck in the centre, however long, is but comparatively a minute. The difference between your tenure and mine is trifling, and I therefore tell you to be prepared. I am prepared. You all have a heavy responsibility, and it behooves you to prepare more than it does me.

LAST SPEECH TO THE COURT.

NOVEMBER 2, 1859.

I HAVE, may it please the Court, a few words to say. In the first place, I deny everything but what I have all along admitted,—the design on my part to free the slaves. I intended certainly to have made a clean thing of that matter, as I did last winter, when I went into Missouri and there took slaves without the snapping of a gun on either side, moved them through the country, and finally left them in Canada. I designed to have done the same thing again on a larger scale. That was all I intended. I never did intend murder, or treason, or the destruction of property, or to excite or incite slaves to rebellion, or to make insurrection.

I have another objection; and that is, it is unjust that I should suffer such a penalty. Had I interfered in the manner which I admit, and which I admit has been fairly proved (for I admire the truthfulness and candor of the greater portion of the witnesses who have testified in this case),—had I so interfered in behalf of the rich, the powerful, the intelligent, the so-called great, or in behalf of any of their friends,—either father, mother, brother, sister, wife, or children, or any of that class,—and suffered and sacrificed what I have in this interference, it would have been all right; and every man in this court would have deemed it an act worthy of reward rather than punishment.

This court acknowledges, as I suppose, the validity of the law of God. I see a book kissed here which I suppose to be the Bible, or at least the New Testament.

That teaches me that all things whatsoever I would
that men should do to me I should do even so to
them. It teaches me, further, to " remember them
that are in bonds, as bound with them." I endeavored
to act up to that instruction. I say I am yet too
young to understand that God is any respecter of persons. I believe that to have interfered as I have
done—as I have always freely admitted I have done—
in behalf of his despised poor was not wrong, but
right. Now, if it is deemed necessary that I should
forfeit my life for the furtherance of the ends of justice, and mingle my blood further with the blood of
my children and with the blood of millions in this
slave country whose rights are disregarded by wicked,
cruel, and unjust enactments,—I submit; so let it be
done!

Let me say one word further.

I feel entirely satisfied with the treatment I have
received on my trial. Considering all the circumstances,
it has been more generous than I expected. But I
feel no consciousness of guilt. I have stated from
the first what was my intention and what was not. I
never had any design against the life of any person,
nor any disposition to commit treason, or excite slaves
to rebel, or make any general insurrection. I never
encouraged any man to do so, but always discouraged
any idea of that kind.

Let me say also a word in regard to the statements
made by some of those connected with me. I hear it
has been stated by some of them that I have induced
them to join me. But the contrary is true. I do not
say this to injure them, but as regretting their weak-

ness. There is not one of them but joined me of his own accord, and the greater part of them at their own expense. A number of them I never saw, and never had a word of conversation with till the day they came to me; and that was for the purpose I have stated.

Now I have done.

DATE DUE

 1909